Y0-CAY-471

SIZZLE
&
SUBSTANCE

SIZZLE & SUBSTANCE:
Presenting With the Brain in Mind

Design/Layout by Tracy Linares
Editing by Karen Markowitz

Dedicated to my wife Diane
for her incalculable love and support

Printed in the United States of America
Published by The Brain Store, Inc.
San Diego, CA, USA
ISBN #0-9637832-9-7

For additional copies, or bulk discounts, contact:
The Brain Store, Inc.
4202 Sorrento Valley Blvd. #B
San Diego, CA 92121 USA
(858) 546-7555 phone • (858) 546-7560 fax
Email: info@thebrainstore.com
www.thebrainstore.com

Sizzle & Substance:

Presenting With the Brain in Mind

Eric Jensen

PREFACE

Presenters and trainers who don't understand how the brain naturally learns best are sailing in rough seas without a chart.

You are about to discover a dynamic system of principles that ensures optimal learning and guarantees satisfied audiences. This system, known as brain-compatible training, has been distilled from the current multi-disciplinary research on the brain and learning that is informing top presenters and educators worldwide. *Sizzle & Substance* is not about this research however; it is rather a handbook of strategies that operates on the premise that when information is presented in brain-friendly ways, learners feel good, excel in learning, remember more, and are fired-up to take the next step. In short, brain-compatible principles are revolutionizing the training and development field. *Sizzle* offers both you and your future audiences the opportunity to excel as you explore presenting with the brain in mind.

Most of us just don't have time to read all the current literature that informs our work—from the subject of our expertise, to psychology, communication studies, biology, neurology, and education. I know this because you've been telling me for years. Well, here it is finally—the result of your requests—a book that brings it all together for you in a practical and efficient package. You can start using it right away. As you read through *Sizzle*, you will be presented with planning tools to engage your thinking about using brain-friendly principles in your next presentation. Apply the plan to your next training, then judge for yourself its effectiveness. I'm sure you'll be pleased with the results.

Presenters and trainers who don't understand how the brain naturally learns best are sailing in rough seas without a chart. You, however, will soon be zipping along in fair weather with a brisk wind at your back. In some cases, you'll discover new presentation strategies to try out; and in other cases, you will receive confirmation that what you've been doing all along is, indeed, brain-compatible. In either case, understanding the principles of brain-compatible training and development will put you on the playing field with the "stars." And one of the pleasant side-effects of brain-compatible training is that the entire process is joyful. Imagine such a concept: a painless approach to achieving high-level success! Happy presenting... smooth sailing!

The audiences of yesteryear were satisfied with a good show and a few useful tips. Today's audiences are demanding and sophisticated. They want cutting-edge information, customized to their needs, plus time for discussion and implementation. They expect to learn practical and useful things presented in a compelling and memorable way. Oh, and one more thing, they still want a good show.

Eric Jensen

TABLE OF CONTENTS

SECTION ONE
Preparing to Sizzle

Chapter:

SECTION TWO
Openings That Ignite a Room

Chapter:

SECTION THREE
Essential Sparks

Chapter:

SECTION FOUR
Fires That Inspire the Mind

Chapter:

SECTION FIVE
Captivating Closings, Carrying the Torch

Chapter:

APPENDIX

SECTION ONE: *Preparing to Sizzle*

Chapter

CHAPTER 1

Planning Brain-Compatible Presentations

In the last two decades, dramatic research on the brain has led to a paradigm shift that is revolutionizing the way we approach training and development. Whether you're a corporate trainer, staff developer, department manager, motivational speaker, classroom teacher, or college professor—with ten months or ten years of experience—brain-compatible principles will benefit you and your audiences. The brain is an amazing organ, but until recently, we really didn't know that much about it. Though, we don't know everything yet about how we absorb and processes information, what we do know provides us with a dynamic system for training in brain-friendly ways.

Before scientists discovered the value of vitamins, we survived on those extracted naturally from the foods at our disposal. However, once we realized that we could ensure the best possible chance for health with nutritional supplements and exercise, most of us incorporated them into our lives. Now that we know how the brain naturally learns best, incorporating these principles into our presentations ensures a healthy learning diet. When we train with brain-friendly methods, audience resistance vanishes, attention and recall improves, and motivation increases naturally. The days of "talking to brick walls" or wondering if there are "any lights on in there" are over. How does this happen—all with less effort and more joy? When you train with the brain in mind, you are working with the brain rather than against it. When an individual's brain is engaged, their resistance to learning is disengaged.

This book is designed to be a practical and engaging resource itself; therefore, we have included a series of planning exercises to inspire your thinking and to provide opportunities for personal meaning-making. As you apply what you've read to the interactive activities, you will be engaging your brain and planning your next presentation at the same time.

Key Topics

- *The Brain Prefers Multi-Modality Input*
- *The Brain Requires Down Time*
- *The Brain Is Meaning-Driven*
- *Project Designs With the Brain in Mind*
- *Benefits of Mind-Mapping*
- *Seven Common Presenter Mistakes*
- *Seven Step Training Model*
- *Honoring the Learning Phases*
- *Notes and Prompts Are Good*
- *Timing Tips and Techniques*

Brain Connection

The Brain Prefers Multi-Modality Input

It is difficult to over-stimulate the brain. The brain thrives on rich, multi-sensory input. It is designed to process information on many paths, in different modalities, and on multiple levels of consciousness. The slower, more linear pace of traditional instruction, actually reduces understanding. Though a feeling of being flooded with stimulation may *temporarily* overwhelm learners, the data will be processed and sorted by the brain amazingly well.

As trainers, we do not need to ration stimulation or assemble information in neat little packages for fear of overwhelming our audience. Consider the intensity of stimulation a child experiences on a trip to the zoo: all of their senses are impacted at once. And it is such a trip that is usually remembered for a long time. In a typical training or presentation, however, we expect learners to sit and listen as we "stand and deliver." In short, many trainers have actually learned to present in a way that inhibits learning. A brain-friendly presentation reflects an orchestration of stimulation on multiple levels involving multiple senses and learning styles where individual choice and preference is provided for. The process is not always neat. Since a great deal of learning happens on a nonconscious or subconscious level, what may appear to be messy may, nevertheless, be quite effective for pattern detection, meaning-making, memory imprinting, and learning.

Remember back to the days when you first learned to ride a bike. Did your "trainer" sit down with you and review the history of bicycles, the mechanics involved, safety procedures, and the principles of balance before giving you the opportunity to try it? Probably not. Rather, your teacher likely ran along beside you as you attempted to steer, pedal, balance, and listen to instructions all at the same time. You probably experienced a temporary feeling of sensory overload which you were amazingly able to synthesize into a new skill learned rather quickly. Had you been required, however, to listen to a lecture on bike riding before attempting it, you would have likely found something else more compelling to do.

Brain Connection

The Brain Requires Down Time

While planning for rich, multi-sensory stimulation in your next presentation, consider that the brain also needs processing or down time. We are not designed to maintain continuous focus. Attempting to maintain an audience's attention 100 percent of the time is, in fact, counter-productive. In order to really learn something, the brain has to make meaning out of the input by going internal. Individuals will take in information better when it is not forced on them and when it is allowed to be processed in a way that makes sense for them. This imprinting process or neural fixing only happens when there is no major competing stimuli.

To account for our need for reflection, plan for breaks, low-energy activities, and free-time. A menu of activities can be offered to choose from (i.e., reviewing your notes, going for a short walk with a learning partner, drawing a mind-map, closing your eyes, refilling your water bottle, stretching, listening to music, etc.) Choice is a very important element here as it allows the learner to feel free to reflect on the training in a way that makes sense for him/her.

The Brain Is Meaning-Driven

Perhaps of most importance in the initial planning stage of your presentation is the question, is your message meaningful? The brain is meaning-driven. Meaning is more important to the brain than information. Your message must, therefore, be meaningful to you to convince others of its relevance. If it's not, the audience will pick up on your disinterest immediately. If you don't feel strongly about the message you're carrying, you're wasting your time. In our search for meaning, we seek patterns, associations, and connections between the data presented and that which we've already stored. Each pattern that is identified adds to the learner's perceptual map and provides a sense of relief from the state of confusion, anxiety, or stress that accompanies raw data. If meaning cannot be made from your presentation, the audience will quickly show signs of boredom and frustration.

The brain is meaning-driven. Meaning is more important to the brain than information.

Beyond being meaningful, your message must be clear and distinguishable. If you have three or four messages that seem disassociated, the audience will feel lost. A brain-friendly strategy for eliminating audience mind wandering or non-verbalized questions (like where is she going with this? Or, how does he think this relates?) is to provide a big-picture outline or map of your presentation from the outset. This will help the brain identify patterns, relevance, and meaning. This also assures your audience that you have a plan–which you will because this book ensures you do. By the time you complete all of the "Engage Your Brain" sections throughout *Sizzle & Substance,* you will not only have a solid plan, but it will be a brain-friendly one that promises to sizzle with substance and make you a leading force in the industry.

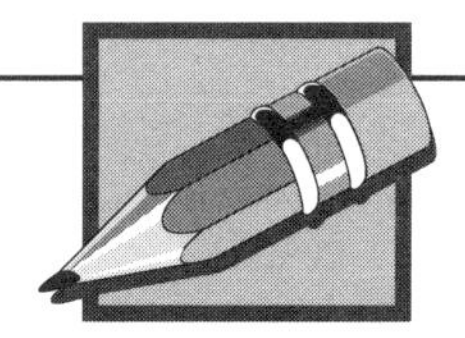

Engage Your Brain:

Planning With the Brain In Mind

What is the primary purpose of your next training or presentation? What do you want the audience to receive?

What is your primary message? What relevance and meaning will your audience derive from it?

How does your presentation stimulate your audience visually? How does it meet the needs of auditory learners? How does it meet the needs of kinesthetic learners?

In what ways will you provide down time? What choices will you offer your audience?

Planning Saves Time

Though good planning is, of course, an investment of time, I find that it always pays off. I actually walk through the whole presentation in my mind as I'm planning it; and my confidence gets a boost. When I'm planning a new presentation, I find that it usually requires about a two-to-one planning to "real-time" commitment. This means that if you're planning a one hour training, it will probably require about two hours of planning. For a one-day seminar, plan on one or two days of planning. Naturally this time requirement is lessened the more you've done the training or presentation. And, of course, the time requirement may be greater if the material is very complex or if other presenters are involved.

The best way to ensure your presentation will meet the needs of the audience is to find out about your audience in advance. Who are you presenting to? What does this audience have in common with other audiences you've had? What's different about them? Your customers or clients are your market. Doing market research is a little like playing detective. Some of the questions will be simple to answer while others may require more research. The following questions will give you a framework for this important aspect of your presentation:

Engage Your Brain:
Who Is Your Audience?

What will be the likely mindset of your audience?

What is their level of expertise in the topic?

Are your ideas likely supported by the audience? Are they controversial?

Is attendance mandatory or voluntary?

Continued...

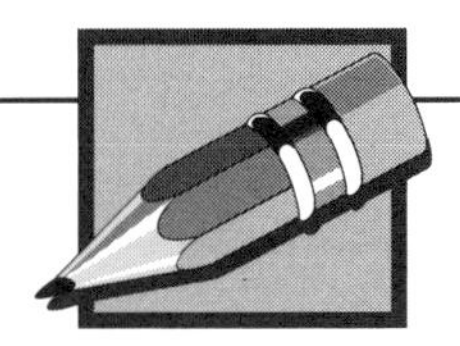

Engage Your Brain:
Who Is Your Audience

Continued...

What do members of your audience bring to the table?

What is the primary reason they are attending?

What do members of the audience have in common?

What will likely be the age and gender breakdown of the audience?

What are the expectations of the audience in terms of quality?

Who are your "inside" contacts?

What are the likely biases and beliefs of your audience?

How much time is allotted for your presentation? Can you go a few minutes over the allotted time if necessary?

What slang words or loaded vocabulary ought to be avoided with this audience?

Is anyone else speaking before you? Who? and What is their topic?

Note: The more questions you ask and the better you answer them, the better you'll be able to prepare a custom fit for a particular audience.

Benefits of Mind-Mapping

If you are predominantly a visual learner you may already be familiar with the value of using a graphic organizing system, such as mind-mapping, to further plan your presentation. Thinking through a training on paper helps us see the big picture, the connected ideas and patterns, and provides a creative outlet for preparing an overview for the audience. Mind-mapping is simply putting your ideas down on paper using headings, symbolism, color, drawings, and connecting elements to identify relationships between ideas. The end result is a sort of road map or a blueprint. Other graphic organizing techniques such as clustering are effective, as well, though some important differences do exist between techniques.

Mind-mapping is simply putting your ideas down on paper using headings, symbolism, color, drawings, and connecting elements to identify relationships between ideas. The end result is a sort of road map or blueprint.

While any visual or graphic system can sort material, the unique value of mind-maps is that you'll understand and remember your material better. Why? When done properly, mind-maps appeal powerfully to the right side of the brain which processes color, pictures, symbols, and relationships. When used in conjunction with the traditional appeal of words which is primarily a left-hemisphere activity, mind-maps can be a fantastic learning tool. When done with a partner, mind-maps can also appeal to auditory and kinesthetic learners. You can use mind-mapping techniques for note-taking, reviewing material, problem- solving, studying, decision-making, or planning nearly anything. In this case, we'll use it to plan our next presentation. The following example illustrates a hypothetical presentation on brain-compatible learning.

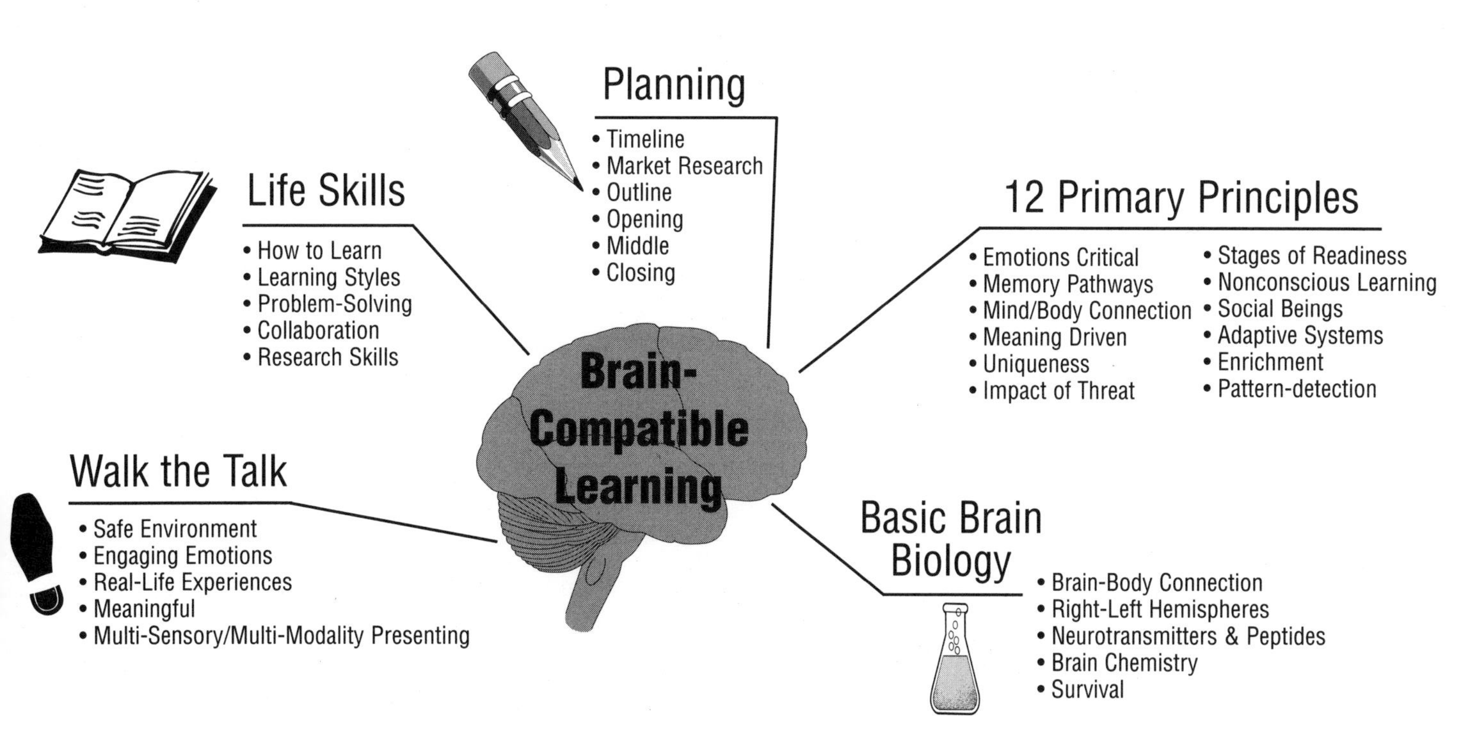

Engage Your Brain:
Mind-Mapping Your Next Presentation

Here's how:

1. *Using colored markers or pencils, represent the main topic of your presentation in the center of the page.*
2. *Using whatever techniques feel most natural for you (drawing, labeling, symbols, multiple colors, etc.) add branches to represent your primary sub-topics.*
3. *Add details to the branches and connecting elements to personalize your map for the right brain.*

Mind-maps have countless organizing possibilities. They can be used to plan, organize, and process virtually any kind of information. Used with non-fiction material, the branches might be labeled by chapter subheadings, or common and likely categories such as who, what, when, where, and why, or by segments such as history, geography, and sociology. In organizing material of a fictional nature, branches might be labeled with characters, setting, plot, conflicts, and resolution.

Personalize your mind-map to achieve optimal effectiveness. To really appeal to the right brain, use at least three colors, and use pictures and symbols for each key idea. Print words boldly using medium thick colored, pens. Vary the size of your printing to signify degree of importance. Use a different color for each branch and use arrows and lines to show relationships. Be creative. The more zest, action, and personality you put into your mind-map, the more impact it will have on you. You can expect immediate results: learning will be more fun, and your understanding and recall will increase. Mind-mapping is not only a great way for you to learn new material, it is a wonderful technique to teach participants. Incorporate it into your next presentation as a down time activity; then, have fun watching brains sizzle. Now, let's review the most common mistakes presenters make.

Be a Brain-Friendly Presenter:
Avoid These Seven Common Mistakes

Limit content

1 Many presenters try to cover too much information and end up over-presenting. It is far better to limit the quantity of information learned and concentrate on the quality of learning. The mind-map process above was intended to help you clarify the key points of your next presentation and to help you identify how main aspects of your training relate to each other. In general, a one hour talk is long enough to cover about three to five key points: Any more than this, and you start losing quality. Once you're at a place in the planning process where your mind-map closely reflects your refined plan, turn it into an overhead transparency. This is a great way to give your audience an overview of the session.

Humanize your content

2 Presenters who talk about content rather than people, are missing the boat. In order for the information you're covering to be relevant, learners must make meaning out of it. Even in a technical training, the audience enjoys hearing about the human side of a story. Thus, balance coverage of content with talk about your passions, frustrations, hopes, dreams, and setbacks. This is how top presenters develop rapport with their audience; they become real to them. Introduce your colleagues or spouse to the audience if they're there. Bring the human element into

your work. Always balance the cognitive elements with the emotional elements. The body and brain are not separate entities. Nor are our bodies and brains separate from our emotions. We learn best when our brains are engaged and our bodies are emotionally charged.

Customize your presentation

3 It is not uncommon (even for veteran trainers) to underestimate the uniqueness of each audience. Whether you've done the presentation two times or twenty, always treat each audience and each training as unique. Research the make-up of this particular audience in advance to gain insights about their relevant needs and interests. Customize your presentation to the demographics of each audience. Personalize your examples. Refer to their particular profession(s). Make them feel like you're speaking directly to them as individuals.

Over-prepare

4 Lack of preparation is always obvious. Prepare, prepare, prepare. Before each training review all of your material and ask yourself if it is still current, if they it reflects the interests of this audience, and if it is of the highest quality. If your materials don't meet your highest standard, it's time for an update.

Strong opening

5 Failing to get your audience's attention in the first 30 seconds of your presentation is presenter's suicide. Your audience makes up their mind very quickly whether you're worth listening to or not. Make sure you have a plan for an attention-getting opening. Be clear, crisp, enthusiastic, and approachable.

Avoid jargon

6 Using jargon-full language or being unnecessarily technical will usually turn off an audience. Instead, use metaphors, analogies, and examples to make even the most complex subjects more accessible. As an example, one neuroscientist calls the cellular bonding between peptide messengers and receptor sites "molecular sex." This gets the audience's attention, inspires a chuckle, and says it all.

Develop rapport

7 Presenters who don't understand the value of developing rapport with their audience will limit their own success. Some audience members won't even be interested in what you have to say until you have proven that you are interested in them. Make eye contact with individuals. Be enthusiastic. Vary the pace when you talk. Get out from behind the lectern. Use gestures, humor, and personal examples. Involve the audience by asking them for their opinion, do a quick survey with them, or incorporate audience questions into your presentation. If you get them involved, not only will you be developing good audience rapport, you'll be enhancing their memory. Provide pertinent information right away (i.e., when you expect to field questions, where the bathroom is, if it's okay for them to move around while you're presenting, etc.). This way, the audience doesn't have to be preoccupied with matters unrelated to the training.

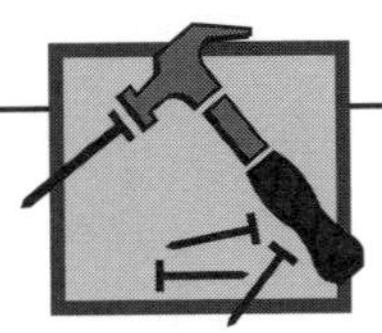

Tips & Tools for Presentations That Sizzle

- Get excited over your material; role-model joy!
- Bring something special that is relevant to your presentation: book, article, music, or prop.
- Pre-expose your audience to the material. Display an overview on a flip chart, bulletin board, or overhead transparency outlining your presentation.
- Do something slightly different than what your audience might expect: new seating, music, posters on the walls, etc.
- Open your presentation with a positive greeting, excitement in your voice, and a word of appreciation for your audience.
- Gain your audience's initial attention with a special quote, mystery question, object of interest, a music lead off, or with an unusual story, case history, or overhead transparency.
- Answer the question that every participant asks themselves: "What's in this for me?"
- Read the state of the audience and stay in touch with it throughout the training.
- Provide general objectives for the presentation.
- Provide pre- and post-view attractions and declare your talk's uniqueness factor.
- Never read your presentation word-for-word. Rather use an outline with key phrases, words, and topics highlighted to jog your memory.
- Use visual aids to prompt thinking: flip charts, white boards, overhead transparencies, or computer-based projection systems.
- Be excited about what you do; implore learners to write down something every few minutes as you talk.
- Make your presentation relevant to your audience!
- Lecture a maximum of 12 to 20 consecutive minutes, then stop to avoid saturation! Have learners stretch, stand, reflect, and discuss things to break up the lecture format.
- If you lose your place or have a mental block, give everyone a quick stretch break long enough to get you back on track.
- Activate your audience's curiosity by doing an experiment with them.
- Ask questions of your audience like, "Has anyone ever had this happen before...?"
- Conduct quick audience surveys by asking for a show of hands.
- Review key points on an overhead transparency.
- Have learners share or review what they have learned with a partner.
- Always end on a "high note"— a memorable story, interesting statistic, or catchy slogan.

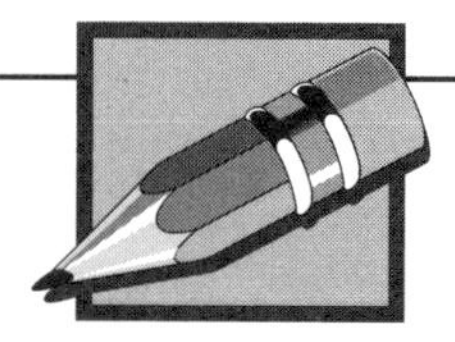

Engage Your Brain:
Framing the Training

Outcomes/Objectives
What do you want to accomplish? What will the participants want to accomplish?

Vehicle for Learning
What multi-modality approaches will you incorporate? (i.e., case study, role play, simulation, experimentation, game format, etc.)

Time Factors
What is the total training time? How can you most effectively use it?

Topic
Have you designed a "menu" for learning that ensures participant involvement in the process and provides for some personal choice?

Issues
What is your slant or angle on the topic(s)? What message(s) do you wish to convey?

Audience/Market Demographics
Have you determined the demographics of your audience? What is the primary profession represented? What do they have in common with each other? What differences exist?

Resources
What resources will you need to accomplish the objectives? What resources will participants need to accomplish the objectives? Are these resources available?

Action
What else needs to be done to set your plan in motion?

Brain-Friendly Training Sequences

Determine outcomes in measurable terms and be sure that they are of value to your audience. Consider their ethical and moral implications and be sure they are emotionally comfortable for participants. Secure participant agreement in the objectives early on in the training. In some cases, you may only need to secure a commitment to work towards the outcomes, while in other cases, it may be beneficial to have the participants co-create the objectives.

Start with the end in mind. Once in a while you might use the "as if" frame. To do this, act as if participants have already mastered the material. Describe a "future" party and have participants walk around and talk to each other. Have them congratulate each other (with congruency and emotion) about the success they've just experienced in your class. Role playing helps embed the newly introduced material into the learner's evolving self-image.

Role playing helps embed the newly introduced material into the learner's evolving self-image.

The following two training formats provide simple and effective approaches for planning brain-friendly presentations. They can be used as a check list after your planning is complete, or they can be followed more directly as you go along.

INDUCTIVE - Specific to General

◆ ***Pre-expose Participants to Learning***
Tell the group what they'll be doing and why as you progress through the training; pre-expose them to the content you'll be covering days, hours, and minutes before actually presenting it.

◆ ***Facilitate Hands-On, Real-life Experiences***
Facilitate learning activities that are meaningful and relevant: field trips, guest speakers, games, role plays, theatrical performances, participant presentations, etc.

◆ ***Debrief Participants With Partner Learning Exercises***
To provide an opportunity for discussion and engagement of learning, ask participants to take 10 steps in one direction; then, to reach out and touch the person nearest them. This is their partner for the exercise. Give them instructions about what they'll be doing next.

◆ ***Conduct Whole Group Discussions***
Facilitate a large group discussion following partner interactions. Ask partners to share what they talked about, elicit ideas, tie in the relevant research.

◆ ***Encourage Participants to Apply Learning and Set Goals***
Have participants decide which strategies they want to commit to using.

DEDUCTIVE - General to Specific

◆ ***Pre-expose Participants to the Learning***
Tell the group what they'll be doing and why as you progress through the training; pre-expose them to the content you'll be covering days, hours, and minutes before actually presenting it.

◆ ***Establish Relevancy***
Use personal experiences first, professional experiences second. Ask audience questions (i.e., "How many of you have had this happen to you?").

Participant readiness and the presenter's experience level are also critical factors to consider in the planning stage.

◆ ***Point Out Links to Related Subjects or Research***
Present the science side. Give names, locations, history, references, results, etc.

◆ ***Encourage Participants to Generate Applications for the Research***
This is usually best facilitated within the context of a team or temporary group.

◆ ***Facilitate Participant Sharing***
With partners or in small groups, have learners discuss their views, feelings, and applications for the material. Whatever groupings you use, change them regularly to generate fresh ideas.

◆ ***Give Participants an Opportunity to Make Personal Decisions***
Participants choose how they wish to apply what they've learned.

Brain-Friendly Training Format

The following seven-step training model serves as a brain-compatible guideline for planning your next session. It is not a road map; rather, it reflects the general path learning takes. Each step is important to the brain, so whether you have 45 minutes or 45 hours, honor all seven steps. Participant readiness and the presenter's experience level are also critical factors to consider in the planning stage.

Seven-Step Training Model

Step One: Neural History - What do participants already know?
Key words: discovery, assessment, malleable, acceptance
- Customize your training for each particular audience; determine audience demographics.
- Pre-expose your audience to the content; provide an overview of the session.

Step Two: Learning Environment **-** How does the learning environment feel to participants?
Key words: safety, comfort, inviting
- Set up systems for success; create an expectation for the learning.
- Consider participant's physical comfort.
- Ensure a feeling of emotional safety and openness.

Step Three: Context for Success - Are participants feeling connected, involved, and capable?
Key words: expression, connection, activation
- Give your audience a way to express how they feel: surveys, discussions, paired sharings, etc.
- Build rapport with the audience; make sure they feel comfortable with other participants.
- Activate prior learning; make connections with new learning.

Step Four: Acquisition - Are you providing participants with multi-modality input?
Key words: direct, indirect, states managed
- Create an immersion environment; provide hands-on action-oriented learning activities.
- Tap into as many of the senses as possible - especially sight, sound, and touch; elicit emotions.
- Keep participants in a receptive, engaged learning state.

Step Five: Elaboration - Are participants making meaning out of the content?
Key words: feedback, ownership, meaning
- Deepen understanding of the topic.
- Use research, dialogue, and projects.
- Take time for discussion and making action steps..
- Demonstrations can be role playing, hands-on activities, assessment, mind-mapping, debates, performances, etc.

Step Six: Memory Encoding - Have you provided down time to process content?
Key words: rest, incubation, emotions, associations
- Encourage reflection; provide breaks, a day off, and/or mind-mapping time.
- Use mnemonic devices, post review, and memorize key ideas.
- Participate in rituals associated with success; highlight the results of the learning.
- Share ideas and acknowledgments with each other.

Step Seven: Functional Integration **-** Are participants integrating the learning?
Key words: personal, academic, support
- Give participants the opportunity to demonstrate their learning.
- Ask learners to answer the question, "what if...?"
- Apply the learning to the participants' employment and/or profession.

Honoring the Learning Phases

At the start of any successful training, the presenter must take responsibility for putting their participants into an excited, positive, and productive physiological learning state before anything else. Partially, this can be accomplished by emulating flexibility, enthusiasm, empathy, and love. Establish rapport with the participants. This can be done on a conscious level by discovering the ways in which you are alike. Or, it can be done unconsciously with the use of artful matching and mirroring of your participant's body language, gestures, and voice quality. In addition, the presenter must create a favorable relationship in the participant's mind with the subject. In order for the participant to want to learn it, they need to be curious and understand the relevancy and global nature of the content.

At the start of any successful training, the presenter must take responsibility for putting their participants into an excited, positive, and productive physiological learning state before anything else.

Other important aspects of the starting stage include choosing relevant materials, clearing audience expectations, giving positive learning suggestions, embedding commands, using opening rituals and relaxation exercises, implementing early learning restimulation, and selling the benefits of the learning to participants. Also determine at this stage how you'll form teams, how you'll convey interest in and caring for participants, how you'll incorporate physical activity, how you'll build trust, and establish credibility, ground rules, etc. This is a good time for an "as if" frame where the participants go into the future and congratulate themselves on their successful learning.

Once participants have been pre-exposed to the content and prepared for success, it is productive to present an initial overload of ideas, details, themes, and connections. Allow a feeling of temporary overwhelm in learners which will be followed by anticipation, curiosity, and a determination to discover meaning out of the chaos. Over time it all gets sorted out brilliantly—just like the real world of learning. Offer enough choice to engage many learning styles. The acquisition phase should never be introduced by the teacher directing learners to, "go home and read chapters four and five." Rather, the acquisition phase should be experiential and immediate putting all participants on equal ground. Learning is best when it's based on discovery, needs, and common themes.

As participants begin to process the learning in the elaboration phase, genuine thinking is required. Whether you facilitate an open-ended debriefing of the learning activity or incorporate partner sharing or some other device that encourages dialogue and thinking, make time for discussion. If you don't, participants may not ever make intellectual sense out of the learning.

Following a period of meaning-making, provide a time for memory encoding which can be either active or passive. Active review might include oral group recall, use of lap boards for visual recall, or hand signals for kinesthetic recall. Passive review might include an eyes-closed process with soft music in the background while the presenter recounts the key ideas. This could also be a relaxed re-delivery of the same material using music as a background. The purpose is to "carry" the material in a relaxed way, while you add the content as a secondary backstage addition. In other words, focus the attention on the relaxation so the material is received subconsciously. Other down time activities might include a break, an outdoor activity, a recess, silent time, journal writing time, a relaxation or stretching exercise, or simply a change of subjects.

The elaboration and functional integration phases provide participants with the opportunity to demonstrate what they know. If the learning is not made personally relevant, it probably won't hold. Learning is optimized when the learner fashions a model or metaphor for the new learning. An excellent strategy for encouraging this to happen is to incorporate group work, teams, and learning partners. Group work also helps participants integrate content into the affective domain, the right-brain hemisphere, and the unconscious mind. For example, when original material is learned visually, but gets reinforced in group discussion on an auditory or kinesthetic level, it will have a greater impact on us. Role play, simulations, and skits are also especially good strategies for facilitating this integration. Other suggestions include: providing question and answer time, a panel discussion, having participants design test questions, a project, working model, mind-map, video, or designing a newsletter. This is also an excellent time for review, wrap-up, and to help participants feel confident and competent with the material presented, to preview the next class, offer congratulations, additional resources, and future pace them to utilize the learning. The all-important love of learning is reinforced at this stage. Never miss it!

Your closing might include group acknowledgments, participant sharing, or a time to demonstrate learning. Make it fun, light and joyful. Music, streamers, horns, and compliments all add to a joyful celebration of learning.

Your closing might include group acknowledgments, participant sharing, and a time to demonstrate learning. Make it fun, light, and joyful. Music, streamers, horns, and compliments all add to a joyful celebration of learning. Your celebration can be as simple as giving a class cheer or high-five, or as elaborate as a class-designed and produced potluck. The following planning worksheet will guide you through each stage of the seven-step training model.

Engaging Your Brain:

Planning for the Seven-Steps of a Brain-Friendly Training

Step One: Neural History

How will you discover participant's interests and backgrounds?

How is this audience unique?

What are the primary characteristics of this group?

What does the average participant in this training already know?

How will you assess participants' prior learning?

How will you pre-expose participants to the topic and provide the classic big picture for them to connect with prior learning?

Step Two: Learning Environment

How will you ensure participants' success?

What ground rules will help ensure a safe learning environment?

What is the physical environment of the training like? Are there things you can do to enhance participants' comfort?

Step Three: Context for Success

How do you expect to build rapport with your audience?

Since learners need to feel connected to the topic before you begin, how do you plan to elicit value and relevance with the content?

How will you facilitate participant goal setting?

Will you be incorporating any learning-to-learn skills in your training? How will you present these?

How will participants know what your strong positive expectations are for learning? Will participants get an opportunity to state their expectations, as well? How?

How will you provide for participant choice in the learning experience?

What learning activities will you include to enhance personal relationships among participants?

Step Four: Acquisition

The optimum "hook" is a novel experience that meets strong personal learner needs and taps into curiosity and real-life themes; how do you plan to hook your audience?

Have you planned for a strong immersion learning environment? Is the learning interesting? Does your training incorporate multi-modalities? How?

How will you incorporate body movement into your presentation?

Since the brain learns particularly well with exposure to concrete experiences first, what will you provide that is real, physical, or concrete?

What peripherals for nonconscious learning will you incorporate?

How will you elicit emotions?

Step Five: Elaboration

How will you ensure participants receive sufficient feedback?

How will you tie current content into participants' prior learning?

Will participants receive additional information in the form of suggested resources if they wish to follow up on a topic? Are there videos or books you can bring with you to share?

Have you provided the audience with an opportunity to discuss their learning with each other? Have you incorporated teamwork, small group discussion, or a forum/debate activity?

Have you planned a question and answer time? How will you handle audience questions during the training?

Will participants have the opportunity to act in a presenter role?

Is your training planned like a big jigsaw puzzle making more and more sense to participants as the pieces fit together?

Step Six: Memory Encoding

What down time activities will you be incorporating? Do learners have a choice in the process?

What activities will you incorporate to help participants process emotions elicited from the learning?

Have you provided participants with an opportunity to sort, analyze, or make mind-maps of the material presented?

If your training format is multiple days, have you provided participants with the ideal incubation strategy: to have, at least, several hours or, ultimately, days away from the topic before reviewing it again?

Step Seven: Functional Integration

Have you planned some verification or evaluation activities that allow participants to exhibit their new skills or learning? How will this be done?

Have you incorporated both a written assessment and a verbal assessment process into your training?

Have you related the learning to participants' workplace?

Have you incorporated a closing celebration? What will it include?

How will the ritual and celebration engage participants' emotions? Do participants have a say in the process?

Of course all of the preceding questions may not relate to your particular situation. Don't worry about fitting your training into a set mold. Rather, design your plan with the thoughts presented in this chapter in mind. Be flexible. The type of training, time constraints, audience make-up, competing needs, and complexity of each situation varies a great deal. Ask yourself, "Does this fit? Could this fit? How else can I meet these needs?" The best presenters combine two critical planning qualities: they structure in the things they know work well, and they remain flexible enough to try out new things, too.

Notes and Prompts Are Good

Many of the very best trainers in the world use notes. The key is to use them effectively.

How can you present new material without notes and prompts? Why try? Most presenters need support especially when presenting new content and you don't need to be embarrassed about it. Many of the very best trainers in the world use notes. The key is to use them effectively. The following strategy has proven simple and effective.

First create a generalized outline of your training or use the mind-map you designed in this chapter. Include only the key parts of your presentation in it. This outline will be kept near you at the front of the room when you are presenting. If you prefer, posters, props, or overhead transparencies can also act in this capacity. Some presenters like to put their outline on a large sheet of paper and post it on the back wall. Whichever method you choose, be sure that your key ideas are highly visible to you so that you don't have to lose eye contact with your audience.

Next include on index cards whatever additional notes you need for each of your key points in the outline. Color code them to the corresponding key points in your main outline. Now you are ready to do a mental rehearsal of the material. As you rehearse, fill in vague areas with additional index cards where necessary. If you want to take this step a bit further, you can write out your entire presentation on notebook paper which will then be put aside. When you rehearse your presentation, visualize and feel yourself doing all of the steps in your notes. This is a crucial stage in the planning process.

Timing Tips and Techniques

Here are a few key considerations to be aware of when planning your allotted presentation time:

◆ *Start on Time*

If there is a speaker after you, they'll appreciate starting on time so avoid going over.

◆ *Emphasize the Opening and Closing*

Plan your presentation for a strong opening and closing. Set up timing reminders along the way so that, if necessary, you can cut something out and still keep your closing totally intact.

◆ *Overview and Review*

At the start, provide your audience with an overview of how their time will be spent. Summarize the most critical information you'll be presenting. This way if you run out of time, the audience will still receive the full value of the seminar.

At the start, provide your audience with an overview of how their time will be spent. Summarize the most critical information you'll be presenting.

◆ *Present the Positive*

Avoid making the audience think they got ripped off. Don't tell them all the things you *don't* have time to do. Simply tell them what you *do* have time to do. In general, avoid telling the "behind the scenes" stuff. Don't tell them about the guest speaker that didn't show up, or the microphone problem you didn't anticipate. I once had a Nobel laureate planned as a guest speaker who, at the last minute, canceled. Fortunately, I had a back-up speaker lined up who pitch hit for me. The audience never knew the difference.

◆ *Breaks*

Let the audience know when a break is coming up so that they know you are aware of the time. You might say, "In about 10 minutes we'll be taking a break, so this is a good time to ask questions if you have any."

◆ *Evolutions* Evaluations?

Consider when the best time is to have participants complete evaluations or feedback forms. If you want them to leave the room as soon as the training is over, set time aside during the training for doing evaluations. If you want them to complete them on their own time and speed up the exit process, let them know that it's fine to hang around afterwards to do this. I've found it most effective to do the "official" closing, then let participants linger and do evaluations while the music is still playing and people are mingling.

The method of the enterprising is to plan with audacity and to execute with vigor.

–Christian Bovee

CHAPTER 2

Bringing Logistics to Light

When you or I experience a great presentation, we usually say something like, "It was very moving." Or, "The speaker was very charismatic." Or, "They really knew their stuff." These are typical reactions but they are a small part of the whole. The truth is, great presentations are more than a dynamic speaker; they are an orchestration of many little things. They are the sum of the parts. This chapter sheds light on how we, as trainers, can benefit from paying attention to the myriad of factors that impact learning on the conscious and nonconscious levels.

- *Environmental Factors Impact Learning*
- *Equipment and Technical Support*
- *Room Arrangements and Seating Plan*
- *Supply Plan*
- *Support Staff Plan*
- *Planning Your Introduction*
- *The Dress Plan*
- *Prepare Your Audience With Advance Communications*

You don't need to be a rocket scientist to be a top presenter. You do, however, have to be willing to master the planning elements known as logistics. This encompasses arranging the set-up and usage of supplies and support materials including equipment, displays, music, overheads, and handouts. When it comes to planning the logistics do the very best you can every single time. Most presenters have heard the old adage "The one time you give only 80 percent will be the one time it will matter the most." So, don't compromise in this area. If you know the right thing to do, do it! If you believe in a multi-sensory presentation, do it. If you believe in audience participation, include it. If you believe in posters and peripherals, use them every time. If you believe in the power and value of music, play it. If you think people learn better in groups than from lectures, facilitate groups. In short, make your motto "If you believe in something, do it!"

Brain Connection

Environmental Factors Impact Learning

Emanuel Donchin of the University of Illinois says that we assimilate most information non-consciously. This means that our brain is constantly processing data even when we don't know or feel like it is. Physicist Walter Freeman says that our brain is operating at 97 percent of its energy capacity even when we are at rest. What this tells us is that even the details in the training environment—like lighting, temperature, peripherals, and sound—all powerfully impact the brain. If we are aware of this, we can influence these and other factors to the learner's advantage. Consider the potential for learning in an environment rich in auditory, visual, and kinesthetic cues. When environmental factors are taken as seriously as what's presented verbally, nonconscious learning is optimized.

You and I know that there have always been and will be circumstances that make this motto tough to live by. You might get only enough time for a 1-hour presentation when you need four hours. Or, you might get a location that is less than ideal for your training. The reality is that you do the best you can with what you have. In your mind, you must be able to answer the question, "Did I sell out?" with a resounding "No!" every time. So, while the end result of your presentation may not be worthy of an Academy Award, at least you'll be able to sleep at night.

Equipment and Technical Support Plan

Using and planning for the use of technical equipment is an aspect of training and development that cannot be avoided by the successful presenter in today's world.

Using and planning for the use of technical equipment is an aspect of training and development that cannot be avoided by the successful presenter in today's world. That is unless you are so successful that you can afford to keep a technician on staff. If, however, you are in charge of organizing the technical aspects of your presentation yourself, I can't over-emphasize the importance of doing it well. In addition to planning the logistics such as, what will be the most effective way to present visuals, what equipment and training will be required, and how cost-efficient is it, you must also plan for contingencies such as, what to do if the equipment breaks or malfunctions. Some of the technical equipment options widely used by today's speakers are presented below.

Computers

With current computer technology, it is easy to project data directly from your laptop computer monitor to a large screen (even up to a large size). This highly professional format has, in fact, become the industry standard; and the software for it is improving quickly. The font, color and graphics capabilities of this option make it exceptional. In addition, this technology allows you to make quick changes to your training materials, print notes, cue cards, or handouts.

Software

There are many choices now available in presentation software. Some of the most popular software programs used by trainers and speakers are PowerPoint, Freelance Graphics, and Harvard Graphics.

Ionizers

A growing number of businesses are using ionizers to increase alertness and optimize learning in the workplace. Ionizers—small electrical units that charge the air with negative ions—have been shown to improve air quality and productivity. Studies suggest that between 57 and 85 percent of the population is strongly affected by poor air quality and respond positively when air contains more negative ions. How much of a difference do ionizers make? Fresh air is still best, but if your situation doesn't allow for it, ionizers are second best. They cost from $100 to $400 and can be purchased at most housewares or hardware stores.

Projection Systems

Many presenters now use huge-screen projection systems rather than the traditional TV screen for showing videos. They usually work with a high-intensity overhead projector to deliver a huge picture. Good ones are made by In-Focus, Canon, Kodak, and Hewlett-Packard to name a few. If you're presenting at a convention center or hotel, they may have a big screen TV you can use; however, sometimes they charge for it. At one location, the daily rental rates were so high, it was cheaper for me to buy a 35" TV than to rent the big screen TV for six days. Remember to compare the daily rate with the weekly rate if you're going to use it for more than three days.

The best thing about transparencies is their low cost and flexibility. Whereas your voice or video is fleeting, the static transparency can make a powerful impression.

Sound Systems

If the facility you are using does not have a professional quality sound system, either bring your own or rent one from a local audio-visual company. Today, you can purchase a system that will allow you to custom-record your own tunes or sound effects on a CD.

Video

There are many uses for video in the training environment today. You can video tape your entire seminar for your own improvement purposes. You can produce videos to sell as follow up or review. You can show pieces of inspirational or instructional videos to help illustrate the topic. However, I never show more than 10 to 15 minutes of video at a time. After this, the audience goes into a "trance-state" and is less likely to really learn from it. Show only what you're willing to debrief later on.

Podium

Use an amplified podium if you want to convey position, authority, or pomp and circumstance (i.e. a special event). Otherwise, for a standard training or informal talk if you can avoid using a podium, do so. If you do use one, however, set it back from the group a bit so you can walk in front of it if you feel like it.

Overhead Transparencies

Traditional transparencies are being used less as trainers rely on computers more. The best thing about transparencies, however, is their low cost and flexibility. The down side is that as audiences become more sophisticated, their expectations of quality and professionalism increase. Color printers can now produce clean, eye-catching messages, so if you're going to use transparencies, make them first class. Try to avoid making them in a hurry. However, if you're in a pinch and you can't print in color, print in black and white and then use a permanent color marker (not water color) on the back of the transparency to dress it up, fill in spaces, add a colorful touch, etc. Whereas your voice or video is fleeting, the static transparency can make a powerful impression. Consider the following important points in planning for their use.

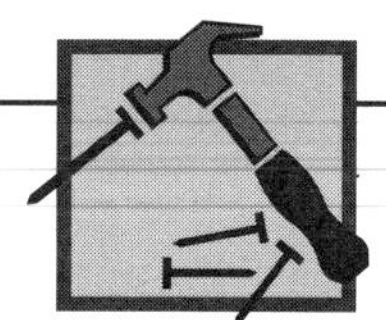

Transparency Tips & Tools

- Big and Simple: Make the letters large and easy to read.
- Color: Nearly everyone today expects colorful visuals.
- Graphics: A picture conveys a thousand words. Avoid complicated pictures or drawings.
- Use only the top 70 percent of a transparency to avoid cut off.
- Build up complex ideas with multiple transparencies—start general and get more specific.
- Use a small pointer (laser pointers are now affordable) or pen rather than your finger or hand.
- Label each transparency in number sequence with a Post-It Note.
- Turn off the projector when it's not in use for 15 seconds or longer.
- Store your transparencies in plastic sheet protectors that fit into a 3-ring binder. Leave them in the plastic when using them so that they are protected.
- Always pre-test the projector. Use a strong bulb and be sure your projected image fills the screen. Sit far back in the room to make sure the transparency is readable.
- Use just one key idea per transparency unless you're displaying a list or summary.
- Never use a page out of a book as is; always re-do it to make it more readable.
- During break time leave a cartoon or affirmation on the screen.
- During down time put up a nature scene or other soothing image.
- Lighting in the room ought to be bright enough for participants to take notes, but dark enough to have a bright image on the screen.
- Face your audience; avoid talking to the screen. If necessary, make a paper copy of the transparency to use as your cue card.

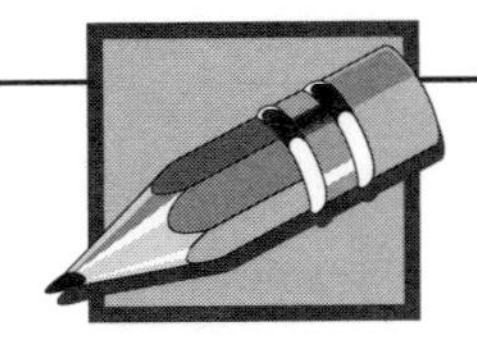

Engage Your Brain:
Initial Logistical Planning

Today's date: __________ Name of Sponsor/Host: ______________________________

Title of presentation:__________________________Date of presentation: ____________

Fee agreed upon: ________Work #/name of main contact: (_____)___________________

Mailing address: _______________________Alternative phone #'s:_________________

Description of audience (expected size, demographics, training mandatory or not, experience level, etc.):

____

____

____

Based on the make up of this audience, what approach and content will best serve them?

____

____

Description of room (size, lighting, equipment, and supplies available/needed):

____

____

Budget: ____

Notes to myself:

____

____

Room Arrangements and Seating Plan

When planning your room arrangements, keep in mind that a comfortable physical environment enhances learning, attention, and satisfaction of participants. Seating, lighting, temperature, staging, visual stimuli, auditory stimuli, and kinesthetic stimuli all contribute to the environment. The way you prepare for these factors will, of course, vary depending on the type of presentation you are conducting. Customize your room arrangement plan for each presentation you do. As seating is a major consideration at this stage, anticipate which of the following types of learning activities or formats you will be facilitating during your training. Then determine if the corresponding seating suggestions will work for the facility or venue you're planning to use.

When planning your room arrangements, keep in mind that a comfortable physical environment enhances learning, attention, and satisfaction of participants. Customize your room arrangement plan for each presentation you do.

Decision-making

Set up chairs for maximum eye contact. For groups smaller than 40, participants seated at tables is the norm.

Lecture

Set up chairs in theater style–no tables, chairs facing the front of the room in a fanned out format with outside wings angled more towards the front . See example on next page.

Teamwork

Start with flexible seating—chairs only. Once teams have been formed, add tables. If teams have already been formed, use 6 foot tables or round tables. The 8 foot length tables are too long for teamwork unless you double them up, two across.

If your training involves a combination of lecture, audience participation, role playing, and group activities, you'll need a large area that is flexible or multiple spaces to break out into.

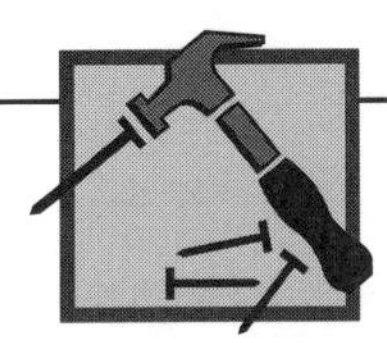

Seating Tips & Tools

- Use a podium if you want to convey position, authority or pomp and circumstance (i.e. a special event). If you're going to use a podium, set it back from the group, so you can walk in front of it if you'd like. Otherwise, for a standard training or informal talk, if you can avoid using a podium, do so.

- For group decision-making processes, arrange chairs so that group members have maximum eye contact with others involved in the process. A large circle or several smaller tables work best.

- For a mood of formality or for decision-making processes facilitated by the presenter, arrange chairs in a large "U" shape. This arrangement is best for groups with 6 to 25 members.

- For an informational talk, lecture, or demonstration, a theater style arrangement of chairs is effective. Chairs are arranged facing the front of the room in a fanned out pattern so that the wings of the audience are angled more towards the front center.

- For encouraging teamwork, when teams have yet to be formed, start with flexible seating–chairs only. Once the teams are formed, bring in tables.

- For teamwork in which teams have already been formed, use 6-foot long tables or round tables. Tables that are 8 feet in length or longer are too long for effective teamwork unless they are doubled up two across.

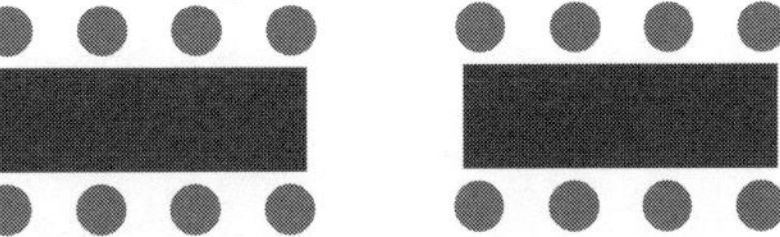

- For trainings that involve a mixture of lecture, audience participation, role plays, and activities, use large areas. You can have teams work at tables and have break out areas for other activities.

Supply Plan

First break your supply needs down into two areas. The first area includes supplies you can generally expect the host facility to provide. In general, the less you have to rely on them, however, the safer it is. On the other hand, the better the on-site supplier is, the less you have to carry. The venue ought to, at least, provide the following:

- Flip-chart easel and pad
- Flowers—a vase or bouquet for the front table or podium
- Wireless microphone
- Pitcher of water for you
- An electronic pointer
- Box of facial tissue
- Packages of colored dots—give to participants to mark items in their workbook that are especially important

Every presenter or trainer carries a supply bag or "tool box." The contents vary dramatically depending on the type of training, general time frames, and audience make up. The items that most all presenters need in their tool box, however, are included in the following list.

Essential Trainer Supplies

__ Tape, Scissors, Tacks
__ Extra batteries
__ Blank transparencies (if using overhead projector)
__ Blu-tak (reusable adhesive)
__ Boxcutter or penknife
__ Brochures of related events or products
__ Client file
__ Computer (laptop)
__ Course notes, travel itinerary, outline, transparencies, and handout masters
__ Electronic laser pointer
__ Energy bars
__ Extension cord
__ Flip chart paper
__ Hammer, screwdriver, and pliers
__ Handouts (copies + masters)
__ Introduction (prepared by you)
__ Legal pad for notes
__ Microphone system
__ Multiple outlets/Surge control unit
__ Music system (CD/cassette player)
__ Name tags
__ Order forms if you have product to sell
__ Pens: ball-point, colored felt pens, and overhead-transparency markers
__ Post-It notes
__ Products or books for reference, demonstration, or to sell
__ Projection system
__ Props and manipulatives
__ Recorded music you may be using
__ Support materials: articles, research, books
__ Videos you may be using
__ Water (bottle or pitcher)
__ Whistle, noisemaker, or other attention-getting device

Support Staff Plan

If it works for you financially, work with a partner or assistant. You'll appreciate having someone who can put out fires for you. This allows you to stay focused on the audience and the content and still have things run relatively smoothly. If you are unable to bring an assistant with you, identify someone (usually it's your sponsor) who can act in this role instead.

If you are relying on an on-site person, arrive early or better yet, check in by phone before arrival. Go through a checklist to ensure expectations are reasonable and that everyone has a "Plan B" if something breaks down.

The most important support you need is from the supervisor of the participants. If you're working in-house with a company, make sure you've met with the supervisor ahead of time. You'll want to go over the agenda, expectations, and most importantly, the plan for follow-up support. Without good follow-up, even your best training is likely to stop short of having maximum value.

Sponsor Check List

A list of sponsor responsibilities similar to the following will ensure communication between you and them. Put your expectations of the sponsoring party in writing and get their signature on it if not spelled out in your contract.

1. Have all participants been contacted and their registration confirmed? Has starting time and location been confirmed?

2. Who will have access to the room and at what time can the presenter begin set up? Has somebody been identified to assist with the set up? Their name and phone number is:

3. In an emergency, who else can be notified? How?

4. Who will be copying the course workbooks?
(Please see that only one side of the paper is copied so that participants can use the other side for notes. Please copy 10 to 20 percent more than expected number of registrants.)

Continued...

Continued...

Sponsor Check List

5. My introduction will be sent to you under separate cover on this date:

6. Please provide for the following music/sound system requirements:

7. Please have the sound system pre-tested and set for operation by:

8. Please provide a sturdy flip-chart stand with a full pad of paper.

9. Please provide a full set of fresh colored markers containing at least three dark colors (black, blue, brown).

10. Please provide an overhead projector that has been pre-tested and is set for operation by: (Please ensure the bulb is bright and that the projector is positioned to fill the screen)

11. Please provide a spare bulb for the overhead projector should it be needed. Is the projector lens and glass clean?

12. Please provide a projector screen that is at least 10 feet by 10 feet in size.

13. Please provide one pre-tested stationary microphone (have this set up for use if the group size exceeds 60 people). Hand-held microphones are not recommended unless it's a very formal presentation.

14. Please provide for the following additional audio-visual equipment: (film projector, slide projector, computer stand, VCR/monitor, TV, extension cord, etc.)

15. Please monitor the room temperature so that it remains between 65 and 70 degrees, unless otherwise notified.

16. Should the temperature need adjusting, who is responsible?

17. Please arrange for coffee, tea, ice water, and juice service in the morning and soft drinks, water, or juice for the mid-afternoon break.

18. Please prepare the room and audience seating as indicated in the enclosed diagram. Arrange set up to be completed by:

Sponsor's Signature:______________________________________ Date:_____________________

If you have any questions, please call me at: __________. Please complete this checklist by: ___________, sign, and fax it back to me at the following FAX number:______________________. Thank you for your important contribution to our success!

Planning Your Introduction

If someone else will be introducing you, it is best to prepare your own introduction. Unless you know the speaker well and trust that they can do an excellent job, write out a script and send it to the person in advance. The following is an example of a short, sweet, and effective introduction:

We're very excited about our presenter today. For 15 years, she has worked successfully with dozens of fortune 500 companies and consistently gets rave reviews. Articles on her work have been in all the top training magazines. She's got a real passion for learning, personal growth, and fun. You're in for a real treat today, so give a warm welcome to....

The Dress Plan

Generally, dressing somewhat more formally than your audience, but not so formal that their focus shifts to what you're wearing is a good rule of thumb.

Choosing appropriate attire is mostly common sense. Generally, dressing somewhat more formally than your audience, but not so formal that their focus shifts to what you're wearing is a good rule of thumb. If you over-dress, it is easy to remove a jacket for a more casual look; however, it's more difficult to go the other way. If your audience is all upper-level executives, an expensive suit is not overkill, as long as it's tasteful. But if you're addressing, for example, the cottage industry, blue-collar workers, or teachers, you might want to tone down your look. Times are changing and many presenters are going more casual.

Generally, men wear suits for formal presentations and sport coats and slacks for more informal presentations. A white shirt and dark tie is still the protocol for formal wear, while colored shirts are more accepted for casual wear. Region is definitely a factor in dress, as well as the culture in which you're presenting. In New England and the South and upper Midwest, for instance, you'll find more white shirts and suits than in the Southwest. Make sure your belt and shoes match and are of first class quality. For both genders, darker colors are still considered more credible, but they are also more conservative. Find the middle ground between credibility and interest. If you know that you already have high credibility with your audience, you can wear lighter, more casual clothing. If you're trying to convey credibility to a doubting audience, you're safer to dress more formally and in darker colors.

Generally, women still wear dresses or skirt suits for formal wear. However, pant-suits that maintain a high level of professionalism are also acceptable. Accessories should add to and not distract from your professional image. Carry a briefcase or discreet handbag. Women tend to be judged quickly by their appearance–especially hair style, make-up, and the "loudness" of clothing. Therefore, avoid wearing distracting colors or noisy jewelry. Sensible shoes and attire that is comfortable and allows for ease of movement are of paramount importance.

For both genders, if you're wearing something unusual that is bound to draw attention, simply mention it early on in your presentation so that curiosity about it is decreased. As an example, when I was in South Africa, I purchased some "safari" animal ties. I thought they were very beautiful, and wore them to a presentation. The audience, however, did not have the same experience that I did, and thus, could not relate. When I noticed this, I simply mentioned, "You can tell I'm a sucker for tourist stuff; when I was in Africa, I just *had* to buy a wildlife tie."

There are many ways of communicating in advance with your audience to help ensure a successful presentation. Your goal is to learn participants' needs and wants ahead of time so you can better customize the course.

Prepare Your Audience With Advance Communications

There are many ways of communicating in advance with your audience to help ensure a successful presentation. Consider the suggestions on the following page to determine what might be appropriate for your next training.

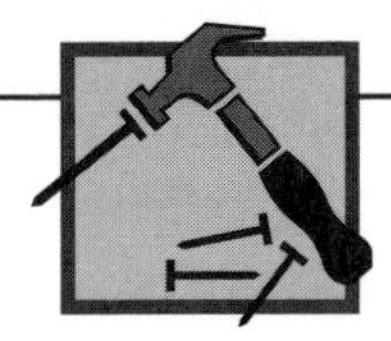

Preparation Tips & Tools

- Send registrants a party-like invitation. Incorporate a theme, make it colorful and fun, and include directions, goals, dress expectations, etc.
- Send registrants a brief article that would give them highlights or background information on the topic.
- Create a short video that piques their interest or gives them an overview of the field. For my brain courses, I send a 15-minute preview video.
- Send a brain teaser to stimulate interest. It could be a jigsaw puzzle piece that needs the rest of the pieces to make sense or even a part of a story or article torn out of a larger article. This works great as a first day icebreaker—participants look for others holding pieces to the puzzle. This activity can also be the basis for forming teams.
- Send participants a pre-course survey to determine their background and level of experience.
- Prepare a top-10 list of FAQS (frequently asked questions) for your participants. Include the answers to questions like, Do we get a workbook? Will refreshments be provided? When's lunch? Will it be fun? Will I be embarrassed? What if I have to miss a day?
- Create a "Course Survival Guide" or even a "Fun Kit" for attending the program. You can include silly items like a stress-reducing toy, a multi-colored pen, Post-Its, a pair of Groucho glasses, or an energy bar.
- Send an audiotape or CD with a greeting on it and, perhaps, a theme song for the program. Choose music that fits the course, like for a customer service training, send "I Can't Get No Satisfaction" or "Simply the Best."
- Send a book if it fits the course you're offering. When I do presentation courses, I send this book. If it's a brain course, I send a book called *Brain Facts*.
- Send the course logistics, rules, and agenda in advance so that you can save precious training time. Avoid the dull stuff and leave more time for the substance of the training.
- Ask participants to fill out a list of goals. Learn their needs and desires ahead of time so that you can better customize the course.

In all human affairs there are efforts, and there are results, and the strength of the effort is the measure of the result.

–James Lane Allen

CHAPTER 3

Red-Hot Handouts and Fiery Graphics

Gone are the days when the standard for visual presentations was boring typewritten overheads. Today's sophisticated audience expects highly professional displays. Investing in such is worthwhile for sure: not only does it serve to better embed your message, but it also reinforces your credibility and commitment to your profession. Whatever graphics you choose, be sure that they are congruent with your words. Make them interesting, colorful, dramatic, and engaging. Since my own presentations are on the human brain, it's easy for me to choose a graphic. I've collected hundreds of non-copyrighted brain icons, symbols, photographs, and illustrations that can be used for various purposes. This provides me with a lot of flexibility. If I'm talking about the biology of the brain, for instance, I'm going to choose a more detailed and scientific brain graphic than if my purpose is establish a logo for a particular workshop.

- *The Role of Repetition*
- *Presentation Software Basics*
- *How to Fly With Flip-Charts*
- *How to Design Red-Hot Handouts*
- *How to Maximize Graphic Impact*

What's in it for me? Title

Certainly it is a good idea to highlight the title and main points of your presentation with a graphic or other visual enhancement. It is also beneficial to include an audience benefit in your title. For example, consider the difference between these two titles: "Applications of Recent Brain Research" or "Brain-Smart Trainings that Boost learning by 50%." There's no doubt, that the second title is much more dynamic and compelling. The graphic and title should appear together as a unit each time it is used. All successful companies know the importance of name recognition. Consider the brand name that comes to your mind when you think of a handsome cowboy on a horse; or how about a simple graphic of an apple displayed in layers of rainbow colors. This is what you want to develop. Whether it is name recognition for your company, your own name, or an individual workshop title, you want the consumer to connect your name with an image or vice-versa.

Brain Connection

Repetition of Input Improves Memory

Studies suggest that repetition of input, thus increased usage of a neural pathways, increases myelination–the fatty sheath that coats axons–and improves memory. This sheath can increase the speed of transmissions up to tenfold in neural communications. In a typical training, much of our learning is filed in short-term declarative memory which is the weakest of memory systems. Therefore, reinforcement through multiple pathways (including eye-catching handouts), is worthwhile. This chapter presents tips for taking full advantage of this important memory principle.

In general, today's audiences also expect color. Indeed, it's a colorful world out there. Once *USA Today* set the standard of using color in newspapers, nearly every newspaper in America, from big city to small town, followed suit. When using color, there are some tips to keep in mind. Be sure to use it appropriately. If your audience is multicultural, for instance, use colors that represent diversity. Use graphics that include representation of both boys and girls; and don't just rely on the stereotypical colors—blue for boys, pink for girls. Color choices can make subtle, and sometimes not so subtle, statements about your mindset and patterns of thinking, so be conscious of this. Also, avoid overdoing color. Splashes of color can draw attention to the important areas you really want your audience to remember. Lastly, be aware of the underlying meaning of colors. For example, green, as in traffic signals, means "go" and depicts action. Black can infer credibility, the past, or something unchangeable. Blue is a soothing color and can imply take it easy or relax. Navy blue is considered a conservative color. Red emphasizes stop and take notice or danger. It also stirs emotions. Pastels are generally very calming but not as attention-grabbing. Intense color will bring your presentation to light.

Color choices can make subtle, and sometimes not so subtle, statements about your mindset and patterns of thinking. Splashes of color can draw attention to the important areas you really want your audience to remember.

Somewhere near the beginning of your presentation you will want to display a mind-map or other organizing strategy that represents an overview of the training. This step also provides a good opportunity to incorporate graphics that appeal to the right-brain. When covering highly technical information, use bar graphs and/or charts to present visual comparisons. Graphs and charts are most effective when they are color coded for maximum contrast. Use an area chart to show volume. This provides the audience with a visual sense of how much of something you're referring to. Flowcharts are great for illustrating complex processes broken down into simple, understandable steps.

Be conservative with your font choices. Be sure that the font you choose, for instance, is easy to read. Also, use just one or two font styles per document or page. For greater contrast, use the bold or italics functions, or alter the font size of the same font. Use a large font size or heavier font choice for titles, headings and most important points. Generally speaking, three different font sizes per page are enough. More than this is probably an indication that you are trying to present too much information on a page. Also, don't overemphasize points (even important ones) by using all of the possible treatments available (i.e., large size, bold, italics, and underline). Rather, pick one or two treatments for emphasis.

Make overheads and/or posters highly readable. To do this, use the largest font size possible and keep lines of type down to about five or fewer. Phrases or bullets are an effective way to get your information across without writing lengthy sentences. Also, it is easier to read words that are written in upper- and lower-case letters, rather than all caps.

End your presentation with a catchy graphic. I often use an overhead that reads "Thank You" in conjunction with a key graphic that is intended to leave a positive final impression. The closing overhead can also include a message about a follow-up seminar or instructions for evaluating the session.

Always have somebody else, besides yourself, proofread your training materials. Sometimes the simplest mistakes can slip by the author because you've looked at the piece too long. It is always better to seek a fresh pair of eyes in the proofing stage.

Always have somebody else, besides yourself, proofread your training materials. Sometimes the simplest mistakes can slip by the author because you've looked at the piece too long. It is always better to seek a fresh pair of eyes.

Presentation Software

The advent of presentation software has increased the accessibility and convenience of using high quality, eye-catching visuals and handouts. Not only does the wide range of software choices allow you to produce your own professional-looking handouts, they reduce the time and expense involved each time you want to make a change. The most commonly used software packages for visual presentations are PowerPoint, Freelance Graphics, and Harvard Graphics. PageMaker and Quark are popular for page layout. Macromedia Freehand, Corel Draw, and Adobe Illustrator allow for maximum flexibility in creating illustrations and drawings. Your drawings can then be imported into other programs you're using for the final presentation. If you do not have access to the necessary computer equipment or if your time is limited, large copy centers can usually produce your handouts for a nominal fee.

Flying Through Flip-Charts With the Greatest of Ease

Flip-charts are a valuable presenter's tool that, if used productively, can really save time and make a presentation more visually appealing. During a presentation I conducted a few years back, I clocked how much time I actually spent writing out flip-charts while the audience passively watched. When I discovered it absorbed about 10 percent of the total training session, I decided this wasn't the most productive use of limited time. Though there are times when it is appropriate to write while the audience watches—for instance, when you are recording the group's brainstorming ideas—most of the time, the following tips will optimize the process:

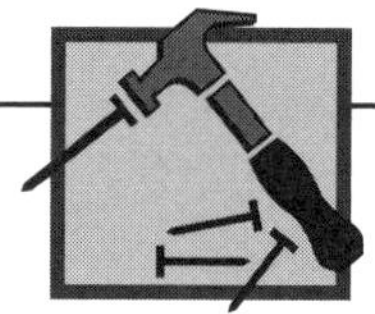

Flip-Chart Tips & Tools

- As much as possible, write out the information you wish to present ahead of time.
- Stand to the side while you talk to ensure the audience has maximum view.
- Prepare your presentation with flip-charts on every other page. This way, you have a sequence prompter, and room for spontaneity with the blank pages inbetween. Plus, the extra page better covers the next flip-chart.
- Use thick bright marking pens that show up a good distance away.
- Usually only the top two-thirds of a flip-chart page is visible to the audience. To make the stand higher, put it on a pedestal or add leg extensions. Leg extensions can be easily made using the plastic piping (PVC) that plumbers use.
- Only use flip-charts with groups that can easily see and read them. Generally, this means groups under 40 to 90 people. However, this greatly depends on the type of room and chair set-up and how high you can elevate the visuals.
- Use as few words as possible to present key points.
- If you can draw at all, add your own creativity to the visuals. Even if they're not masterful works of art, they will help boost attention and memory.
- If you find yourself making out the very same flip-charts for each presentation, this tells you something. Turn this information into a permanent poster or overhead. Laminating posters is a great way to retain their freshness and improve their durability.
- Post a flip-chart page in the back of the room and label it "Parking Lot." Divide the page into four quadrants: 1) Questions, 2) Kudos, 3) Concerns/Requests, and 4) Networking. Encourage participants to add their comments to the page. Post-It Notes can be supplied for convenience. Check the Parking Lot for comments or requests frequently. Most importantly, respond to each comment. As you deal with them, you can peel off the Post-It Note freeing up the space for other comments.

Designing Red-Hot Handouts

Handouts are basic fare at most trainings and seminars these days. People value having something concrete to refer to and keep after the training is over. Your handouts can be as simple as an outline or review of what was covered or as formal or involved as a seminar workbook. In deciding how you will incorporate handouts, consider how much time you have, the context and content of the seminar, your budget, and the background, personality, and expectations of your audience. Once you have decided the approach you want to take, the following tips will help you prepare handouts that sizzle in your audience's hands.

In deciding how you will incorporate handouts, consider how much time you have, the context and content of the seminar, your budget, and the background, personality, and expectations of your audience.

Handout Essentials

- Use fewer, rather than more pages.
- Include references for your work.
- Provide handouts at the start of the session or as participants register or enter the room.
- Make them interactive—leave blanks for participants to fill with information covered in the presentation.
- Print on only one side of the page—leave the other side for notes.
- Include a one-page summary or outline of your presentation.
- Do not provide too much detail—include only key ideas.
- Don't overuse graphics; use enough to provide visual interest.
- Number the pages for easy reference.
- Tell the audience whether or not the pages are reproducible.
- Make sure that your name and phone number are on several pages.
- Give additional resources for follow-up.
- Have others proofread the handouts for you before printing.
- Print 10 to 30 percent more handouts than you think you'll need.

It's more important to have clear, simple, visually interesting pages in your handouts than to have gobs of "impressive" content pages that are never read because they're too dense or detailed. Ideally, your handouts will have a natural order to them that follows your presentation format. A comprehensive seminar should include the following components:

Cover Page

The cover page includes the title of the presentation, your name, a place for their name and an icon or graphic that highlights the topic of the presentation. Give your presentation a strong title. Instead of "Fundamentals of Customer Service," say "How to Turn Your Customers into Raving Fans in 7 Easy Steps." Then follow through on your promise. If possible, print your cover page, at least, in color.

Ground Rules Page

In my handouts, I title the ground rules page, "How To Make This Seminar a Terrific Success." This page is not necessary for short talks, but it is essential for seminars that are a day long or more. See the example below:

How to Make This Seminar a Terrific Success

1. ***Relax...*** This seminar will be active, enjoyable, and well worth your time.
2. ***Read the posters and signs around the room...*** and feel free to jot notes and incorporate the ideas into your own trainings. The pages in this notebook are for your personal use only. They are copyrighted. So if you want to use this information in your own trainings, be creative and do an even better version yourself. Not only will you increase your learning this way, but you will likely improve on the concept, as well.
3. ***Socialize...*** Sit next to someone whom you don't know very well or at all, but would like to. A wealth of knowledge and experience is represented in this room. Learn from each other. One of the benefits of this seminar is that individuals like yourself (with at least one like interest) have been brought together for a period of time. Take full advantage of it. It is a good idea to move to a different seat in the room after the break or lunch to maximize your contacts.
4. ***Take care of yourself...*** If you need to stand up, or move around, or go to the lobby, do it. If you need to leave early, please let someone around you know and don't forget to leave your evaluation on the back table.
5. ***This seminar could be one of the most valuable...*** difference-making things you do this year. Give it a chance; apply yourself. What you may gain is greater satisfaction, fun, knowledge, experience, and a lot of valuable life skills.
6. ***Write down good ideas...*** and things you want to remember from the training. Draw bright, eye-catching illustrations or symbols on your notes like you do in mind-mapping. This will reinforce your learning and help you recall the material later. The memory is rarely as faithful as the enthusiasm of the moment.
7. ***Do your very best to leave your domestic concerns at home...*** Turn cell phones off. Use the 500-mile rule: if this training were 500 miles from work, would you make that same phone call?
8. ***Follow directions please...*** If they're unclear, ask or look very confused.
9. ***Your presenter can only be responsible for your concerns...*** to the extent that you share them. If this program is not meeting your needs, talk to the presenter at the break or lunch. If you have questions, feel free to ask them anytime.
10. ***Enjoy yourself...*** Open up to the process... and now, let's get started!

Hook Page

The purpose of the hook page is to illustrate the relevance of your topic. It is most appropriate for audiences that are mandated to be there. With an audience that is required to be at the training, you will need to win them over. In my presentations, I call this page something like "Top-10 Reasons to Learn About Brain Research." See sample below.

Top-10 Reasons to Care About Recent Brain Research

10. You've already made the effort to be here today, you might as well take advantage of it.

9. You could learn some important stuff about how the brain impacts your health and sense of well being.

8. Now is the new renaissance of brain research. You could meet the next da Vinci, Einstein, or Curie.

7. It can help you get ahead in life. You could become smarter and have a much better memory.

6. The brain is three amazing pounds of goo, fat, and mush. It eats up 20 to 25 percent of your body's energy. It's good to find out where all that energy is going.

5. Amazingly, every audience is full of brains. You can tap into that brain power.

4. You could learn some really interesting things like how to lower your stress at work, how to boost learning, and how to engage all of your learners.

3. It's one of my top personal hobbies (actually it's in third place). The other two are closely guarded secrets.

2. We will all get old someday and then, you'll really, REALLY care about it! And... (drum roll please...) The number one reason to learn about the brain is:

1. You are losing brain cells at the rate of about 10,000 per day. This is the last day of your life with this many cells. Live it up!

Goals Page

For workshops of a day or longer, it makes sense for participants to set goals. Your goal page should not only facilitate the discovery of participant's goals, but also why they want to reach them. The "why" is often a great motivator.

Summary Page

There ought to be a single page that summarizes your entire presentation. This review must be clear, accurate, and interesting. If you provide this for your audience, their understanding and enjoyment will increase dramatically.

Content Pages

It's particularly valuable to ask participants what obstacles they might encounter and how they would deal with them. This takes them out of your presentation and puts them into the real world. It also plants a seed for them to apply what they have learned.

This section may be 5 or 50 pages depending on the length of your workshop and the complexity of the information involved. Typically, a presenter can effectively cover about 10 to 20 pages per day, depending on the nature of the training.

Note Pages

I rarely allow separate pages for notes. I simply encourage participants to use the backside of the handouts as a measure to save trees.This also makes notetaking possible where the notes relate to the handouts.

Additional Resources Page

Many participants enjoy knowing where they can get more information on your topic. Be sure to list the following:

- Recommended books
- Technical books
- Videos available
- Graduates testimonials
- Related workshops and seminars
- Key people in your field
- Movies or videos to rent
- Products to purchase
- Best conferences to attend
- E-mail or Internet contacts and Web sites

Action Plan Page

When your workshop is over, is the learning done? Hopefully not. Ask participants what they want to do with what they've learned. Ask them to be specific. It's particularly valuable to ask them what obstacles they might encounter and how they would deal with them. This takes them out of your presentation and puts them into the real world. It also plants a seed for them to apply what they have learned. Complete the following example for your own real-world learning.

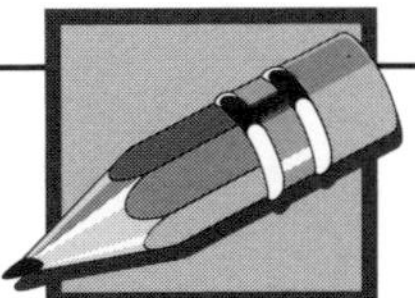

Personal Action Plan

Given what I now know about presenting with the brain in mind, what ideas and strategies will I begin to use next:

1.____

2.____

3.____

4.____

5.____

I'll start implementing these by (date) : ______________________

We are often motivated by feelings. In the long-run, how will I feel about implementing these ideas? How will this make a positive difference, help others learn, lower my stress or raise my satisfaction level? In other words, what is my primary motivation for following through?

____

____

____

____

____

____

____

Great job! You DO make a difference!

Evaluation/Feedback Survey

This is certainly one of the most important aspects of the handout packet. Plan on experimenting until you get the quality and quantity of feedback that's useful for you right. See example below:

Super-Quick Seminar Feedback Questionnaire

Seminar Title:______________________________Date: _________Location:________________

1. What I enjoyed the most or got the most value from was: ______________________________

____

2. What I disliked the most or got the least value from was:

____

3. What I plan to use and implement right away is:

____

4. The obstacles I am most likely to face in implementing what I learned are:

____

5. The best way for me to overcome these obstacles is:

____

6. What would you say to another person who is considering taking this training?

____

7. Comments or suggestions you would like to share with the presenter:

____

____

My overall evaluation of this program is: (circle a number below):

1	2	3	4	5	6	7	8	9	10
poor	fair	so-so		OK	good		excellent		Wow!

Please print your full name and address on the back ***ONLY*** if you'd like to be notified about future trainings or to receive our new catalog.

Engage Your Brain:
Planning Your Handouts

Do you have a catchy title for your next presentation? Does it state a benefit? What other titles might be good?

What graphic element(s) do you think would add interest and meaning to the title of your seminar?

What will your handout packet or workbook include? What are the considerations that are influencing your decision about what to include? How much will it cost to do what you really want?

What bright ideas came to your mind as you were reading this chapter? How will you implement them?

Flaming enthusiasm, backed by horse sense and persistence, is the quality that most frequently makes for success.

–Dale Carnegie

CHAPTER 4

Taming the Flaming Butterflies

We say that we have "the butterflies" when we feel nervous, stressed, anxious, or afraid. This mind-body state is caused *not* by a frightening circumstance itself, but rather by our reaction to the circumstance. Another person in the exact same situation, may respond in a completely different way. Nervousness can come on suddenly; it might be a reaction to an unanticipated event, or something as simple as a larger than expected audience. Or it might be something that disappears as soon as you are actually on stage. Your comfort level with nervousness increases the more you push through whatever scares you. Even the most experienced trainers may experience nervousness at times. A presenter who works with unruly teenagers all year long may be terrified at the thought of presenting to his peers at a staff development workshop, or, a high-level corporate trainer may experience anxiety at the thought of presenting to her daughter's class. It is pretty safe to say that most of us still get nervous. The following five steps, however, are guaranteed to help you tame those flaming butterflies, or, at least, get them to fly in formation.

Key Topics

- *Master Your Material*
- *Internal Chemicals Influence Mind States*
- *Get Acquainted With Your Audience*
- *Master the Details*
- *Master the Room*
- *Master Yourself*

Step 1: Master Your Material

When you know your material inside and out, you can relax and concentrate on the group rather than your next point. Your sense of humor or other positive personality traits are more likely to find expression when your energy is not completely absorbed in the content. When you are confident with your material, your memory will be better and you'll feel more spontaneous. And of course, the audience picks up on your relaxed state which then relaxes them. Presenting old material is rarely a problem, but most presenters experience some stress when presenting new material. Top-level presenters use the strategies on the next page to help them master the new content; you can too!

Brain Connection

Internal Chemicals Influence Your Mind States

Moods and states are created and circulated throughout the body by neurotransmitters and peptides. Peptides, in fact, carry over 98 percent of all internal information. A state of nervousness, therefore, is not just psychological, it's physical. The body reacts with a variance in blood pressure, blood chemistry, breathing rate, and/or heart rate. All of us know how uncomfortable this can be! Did you know, however, that you can tame your butterflies by learning to manage the things that impact your states? This chapter explains how.

◆ ***Practice your presentation in front of another person...*** or a small group. Put together a volunteer audience, if necessary. Break up your presentation into smaller chunks and practice just one at a time if this is more manageable. The important thing at this stage is to stay open to feedback from others. Discover the pros and cons of your performance.

◆ ***Try out questionable or controversial statements...*** jokes, comments, opinions and content with others before incorporating it into your presentation. In doing so, comments or jokes that prove unpopular can be dropped before it really counts.

◆ ***Talk through your presentation on a tape recorder or videotape...*** Go back and review the tape as if you were in the audience. Be objective. Would you be interested in listening to yourself? Do you have any distracting habits? If so, *now's* the time to make the changes, before you are actually in front of a live audience. Remember to rehearse the material under various conditions. The brain recalls best under matching states and contexts. For example, if you think you're going to feel a bit stressed when you present, then rehearse it under a bit of stress. Matching states in the practice stage will ensure your recall of information when the time calls for it.

When you know your materials inside and out, you can relax and concentrate on the group rather than your next point. Your sense of humor or other positive personality traits are more likely to find expression when your energy is not completely absorbed in the content.

◆ ***Study the styles of other successful speakers...*** Ask yourself what they are doing that you like. Ask yourself how you can incorporate their techniques. When you have a clear concept of what you want to say and how you want to say it, then begin visualizing yourself successfully doing it. Keep your visualization positive. Any time fear creeps in and your visualizations get negative, stop them immediately. Relax and build that positive image again. Make it a multisensory image to strengthen its power. Do it over and over. *Visualizing* success repeatedly is like *doing* multiple successful trainings. Soon, you will be an expert.

◆ ***Test and quiz yourself...*** In the days preceding your session, practice presenting the key points again. Mind-map it! Then, when you have a few moments, write out the opening one minute of your presentation. These simple acts of preparation can powerfully reinforce your confidence.

◆ ***Remember your memory strategies...*** All memory is state and context dependent. This means that what you learn in one state of mind (or body), you'll best recall in that same state. If you rehearse your talk under relaxed, calm conditions, the content will likely disappear under conditions of stress. You must commit to rehearsing your material under deadlines, under pressure, when you have no notes. and when you have to get it right because something is at stake. If you're not familiar with the facility you'll be presenting in, visit it in advance and get a feel for the room while you walk through the key parts of your talk. Sit where the audience will. Get a feel for potential distractions, distances, and the acoustics.

◆ ***Utilize various memory tools...*** that will help you remember information even when you're stressed. Some good examples follow:

> ***Posters:*** Put up posters around the room that serve to prompt you and serve as peripherals for the audience.
>
> ***Memory Peg System:*** Link each part of your talk up to a fixed item for better recall. If, for instance, your presentation is on the brain and you have seven key areas to cover, you can associate each of these seven areas to a number, or body part, or planet, or state, or car model. The possibilities are endless. The association you choose will depend on what you know best and how you like to learn.
>
> ***Transparencies:*** Use transparencies to organize the order of your key points. Transparencies, like posters, will serve you and serve as visual reinforcement for your audience.
>
> ***Mnemonics:*** This long-used memory system associates the first letter of a word you want to remember to a sentence. Two well-known examples are, "Every Good Boy Does Fine" for remembering the notes of the music scale—EGBDF; and "My Very Educated Mother Just Sliced Up Nine Pickles" for remembering the order and names of the planets.

All audiences have certain commonalties. Once you understand them, your fear of the unexpected will be diluted, eventually to the point of evaporation.

Step 2: Get Acquainted With Your Audience

As you gain experience with different sizes and make-up of audiences, your butterflies will naturally begin to take flight and leave you to bask in the glow of achievement. All audiences have certain commonalties. Once you understand them, your fear of the unexpected will be diluted, eventually to the point of evaporation. See "Commonalities Between All Audiences" on the following page.

◆ ***Discover as much as you can about your audience...*** in advance. What is the average age and experience of the participants? What are their specific job titles? Are they attending voluntarily or are they required to attend? What has happened in the past year, week, or 24-hours that might change their mindset about being at your training? Once you have learned about your group, tailor your talk to ensure it meets their needs.

◆ ***Consider arriving the night before your presentation...*** if it is at a conference center or hotel so that you can meet participants in the dining room, lobby, bar, or around the pool before your actual presentation. Find out how far they have traveled, how they like their job, and what they are happy or unhappy about. Learn names and specific examples to use in your talk. This key strategy may give you a much appreciated boost of confidence right when you need it—when you're breaking the ice. Then, be sure that there are no last minute loose ends left so that you will be free to greet audience members as they enter the room.

◆ ***Make eye-contact with one person at a time...*** as you begin to talk. The alternative—looking out over a huge group—can be intimidating. Instead, when you begin speaking, pick someone on the left side deep, then the right side close up, then move to the left side close-up, then the right side deep. Keep this rotation going as long as it works for you.

Commonalties Between All Audiences

- People like to be recognized as individuals, not just as a group.
- Some people need to know that you care about them, before they care about what you know or have to say.
- People like to know what they can expect in advance.
- People will mirror back to you your own perception of inadequacy or adequacy.
- People like to laugh: It relaxes them.
- People learn best when all (or most) of their senses are involved.
- Most of what we learn is learned nonconsciously.
- People are likely to be more attentive if you involve them.
- We are social beings. People generally want to know who they're sitting next to, who you are, and why you're doing what you are.
- People process information based on how it fits into their own unique schematic of life-experience, and how it serves their personal needs.
- People who feel safe open up and their resistance vanishes.
- As you role-model risk-taking, people open up to taking risks themselves.

Step 3: Master the Details

If you do presentations long enough and often enough, almost anything can and will happen. It's Murphy's Law for presenters. The good news is that you can reduce the number and intensity of disasters by some simple smart moves. Plan ahead. Have a "plan B" for nearly everything. What if your flight is delayed? Do you know the alternative flights? What about a rental car? What if your overhead projector bulb goes out? What if the room is changed from the original plan? What if you have a sore throat the morning of your presentation? What if the number of participants is more than you anticipated?

◆ ***Ask, ask, ask...*** The single best skill most experienced presenters have learned is to get good at asking questions. Here are some questions that usually run through my "logistics brain." Which room will the presentation be in? How many will be there? Who is in charge? Where will they be? What about lunch? What about breaks? Where are the bathrooms? How many are there compared to the group size? Are there alternative bathrooms?

If you do presentations long enough and often enough, almost anything can and will happen. It's Murphy's Law for presenters. The good news is that you can reduce the number and intensity of disasters by some simple smart moves.

◆ ***Prepare your handouts well in advance...*** Consider what you'll do if they get lost. What is your "plan B" if you mailed them and they don't show up? What if the electronic equipment (computer, overhead, video, or music player) breaks down? To keep your stress down, plan, problem-solve, and plan some more.

◆ ***Arrive early...*** Arrive the night before if you're traveling from out of town. Check the room ahead of time. Build relationships with the staff who might be responsible for the room.

◆ ***Keep your planning notes handy...*** Your checklists will likely come in very handy at this stage.

Step 4: Master the Room

Tame those butterflies flying out of formation by getting physically comfortable with the specific room you'll be using.

◆ ***Gather information...***

a. by telephone interviews
b. by an advance visit to the facility
c. by arriving a couple of hours early

◆ ***Stay calm...*** If you arrive to look at your room and it's a disaster, keep your cool. Ask yourself, "What's the first thing that participants will notice when they arrive? What absolutely has to get done and what's just an option? Where can I find some help to get the job done?" One of the first things to start up when you get to a room is the music.

◆ ***Take nothing for granted...*** Never assume something is handled by someone else. Personally check out the microphone system, the music system, the lighting, the projection system, and all the other technical devices you'll be using. Take nobody's word for it. Sorry—you can't afford to be lax! Learn how to work things yourself in case there's no local representative available when you need them.

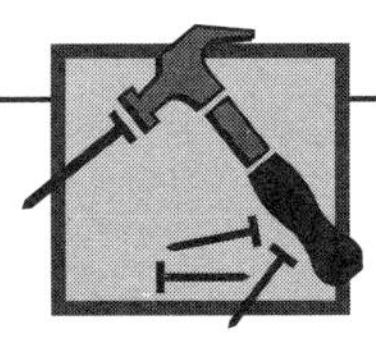

Tips & Tools: Know the Facts

- Location of rest rooms
- Location of drinking fountain
- Location of telephones
- The person responsible for technology
- Best spots for lunch
- Controls for lighting
- Location of electrical outlets
- Where to find staff support

Step 5: Master Yourself

This butterfly-tamer strategy is simple but not easy: Work on your insecurities from within. After all, there's only so much that you can do to know your material, your audience, all the logistics, and the working environment. Though simple in concept, looking within can be the most difficult step of all. Here's some ways to get started:

◆ ***Pay attention to your nutrition...*** What you eat can make the difference between a poor or great presentation. Keep plenty of water nearby. Drink five to eight glasses of water per day. Many have found healthy snack bars (i.e., Cliff Bars, PowerBars, etc.) to be a terrific solution for mid-morning and mid-afternoon energy slumps. If you are presenting new material and want to be at your sharpest, increase your protein intake and reduce your carbohydrate intake, and eat the proteins first. For breakfast, you might have juice, fruit, eggs, ham, or cottage cheese. For lunch, have a tuna salad or chicken Caesar salad. Have only one cup of coffee for each three hour time span; more caffeine than this, promotes nervousness rather than reducing it.

◆ ***Learn to manage your feelings...*** If you are having a bad gut feeling about an upcoming workshop, perhaps, your fear has gotten the best of you. Use your feelings to your advantage, however, by reviewing your efforts to date. Are all the loose ends tied up? If something is lingering, or if your plan B still needs some work, let your gut feelings be the necessary incentive to complete your planning.

◆ ***Visualize success...*** Instead of worrying about how you'll do or worrying about failing, do the opposite. Worry about how well you'll do. Worry about how excited your audience will get. Did you ever stop to think that visualizing is simply a form of goal-setting? You can either visualize something positive or something negative. Every thought you think, every time you think it, strengthens the neural pathways. This means that whatever you think or visualize is what is likely to happen. Remember, worrying doesn't make something negative happen, but it can increase the likelihood of it happening.

Work on your insecurities from within. After-all, there's only so much that you can do to know your material, your audience, all the logistics, and the working environment.

◆ ***Redirect your self-talk...*** Self-talk is what you say to yourself either before, during, or after your presentation. Our self-talk can get very negative without us even realizing it. Perhaps you start thinking something like, I'm nervous; I feel like I'm going to blow this presentation, or this is a difficult group to work with; why did I agree to do this one, anyway?" This cruel inner voice can be unrelenting until you take control of it. Every time you hear this non-productive voice make a point to stop it immediately. To do this take a deep breath and say to yourself, "I can control how I respond. I will be relaxed and confident. I will be creative and in control of myself. Things will turn out great."

◆ ***Do warm-up activities to wake up all the areas of your body...*** Start by relaxing your eyes. Put your palms over them and press gently. Then stretch your face by making as many different faces as you can. Scrunch it up and make it as small as you can. Then, open it up as wide as you can. Shake out your hands to get your circulation moving. Give yourself a neck rub. Do neck circles. Allow your butterflies to be metamorphosed into positive energy.

◆ ***Just before you go on stage, pause and take a deep breath...*** Do something physical to get your energy back in your body. Do some cross-laterals–touch opposite knees, elbows, shoulder blades. Take a slow, deep breath again. Stretch your shoulders or back slowly. Stretch your face muscles again. Shake out your hands. Now move to the front and greet your audience feeling alert and poised.

◆ ***Stand erect with shoulders back...*** Feel your confidence flow through you as you stand before the audience and continue to breathe deeply. Next, put yourself in the middle of your presentation. Imagine what it feels like to be succeeding at the task at hand, to say what you want to say, and to get the response you were hoping for. Let your self-confidence take over. Now, act as if you have just finished your presentation and you feel good. People come up to you and thank you for it. A warm glow comes over your body; all went well. You relax and smile.

Start now. Don't just read a book on how to be a top presenter, use what you are learning and apply it to your very next talk.

◆ ***Relax...*** As you are being introduced, tighten your muscles for a few seconds by tensing or clenching your fists or other body areas. Then, let the tension go. As you do this repeatedly for a few minutes, your butterflies will flit away.

You Can Do It

Yes, it happens everyday. No matter where you are in the world, presenters are working miracles with diverse audiences. They plan ahead, do their homework, master their self-talk, visualize success, and learn to better manage their feelings. You, too, can do this. Start now. Don't just read a book on how to be a top presenter, use what you are learning and apply it to your very next talk. The following worksheet will assist you in this process.

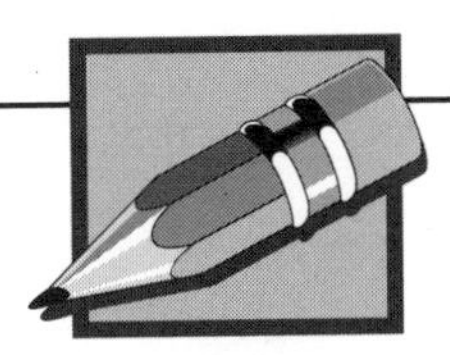

Engage Your Brain:
Taming the Butterflies

What content are you concerned about mastering before your next presentation? If it is very technical, what memory strategies do you think might help in the process?

Do you have various people lined up to act as your test audience(s)? How do you expect to match states between practice sessions and the real thing?

What kinds of things do you do to calm yourself just before going on stage? Are there other strategies you want to incorporate in your next presentation?

What are some areas you feel you could improve in? Do you fall into the negative self-talk trap sometimes? Do you have a plan for moving through these challenge areas?

What are three goals and objectives you can focus on for your own development in your next presentation?

SECTION TWO:
Openings That Ignite a Room

Chapter

CHAPTER 5

What Presenters and Hot Cakes Have In Common

Chemicals in the brain known as neurotransmitters cause a stronger "imprinting" on the brain upon initial exposure to new environments, information, or people. This helps explain the critical impact of first impressions; and thus, underscores the importance of the first 30 to 60 seconds of your opening. This is the best opportunity you will have to create magic. During this distinct first-time mind state, make every effort to gain the attention of your audience. Make them laugh or smile. Provide their brain with some intense stimulation. Bring in something novel to share with them. Or start with a dramatic and inspiring musical score. It is critical to take full advantage of this opening state.

At this point you may be wondering what presenters and hot cakes, do in fact, have in common? So, rather than telling you straight out, I think a little suspense would prove more fun. Your challenge, therefore, is to see if you can figure it out by the time you reach the end of this chapter. Do you accept the challenge? If so, keep reading. If not, I hope you'll keep reading, anyway.

The opening of a presentation has many purposes, but most importantly, it is to orient the audience, provide a preview of the material you'll be covering, and to motivate, inspire, and establish some rapport with them. The first priority, however, is to start off on the right foot—to fire up the room in those critical magic minutes. A carefully orchestrated preparation can make possible a significantly better training experience. The introduction or "set induction," as it is often called, will ultimately maximize the effectiveness of your entire presentation, so plan it well and practice it more than any other part of your presentation.

- *The Biology of First Impressions*
- *The Three Ps: Professional, Personal, and Positive*
- *The Environment and First Impressions*
- *Emotions Drive Attention, Meaning, and Memory*
- *Eliciting a Positive State*
- *Avoiding Dead-End Openers*
- *Relationships Before Content*
- *Starting on Time*
- *Establishing Relevancy*
- *Creating a Safe Climate*

Brain Connection

The Biology of First Impressions

Studies suggest our brain has a high attentional bias that's especially strong in the first few seconds of exposure to something new or novel. It may be a result of what neurobiologists call the "imprinting" effect. First impressions are imprinted or embedded more deeply in the brain due to a special chemical balance at this time. These chemicals or neurotransmitters include adrenaline, noradrenaline, epinephrine, ACTH, and vasopressin. Once the initial moments of a new activity have passed, the brain and body return to the more "normal" chemistry, and the fixative stage is gone.

From the moment they walk into the room, participants begin to form first impressions which will lead to the lasting impressions they leave with. Beyond forming impressions about how you look and feel, they will be judging how the environment looks and feels. Some of the influences that will impact their perceptions are room temperature, sound quality, peripherals on the walls, seating comfort, seating formation, lighting, music, availability of water and refreshments; and perhaps most importantly, how welcomed they feel.

It is not unusual for participants to immediately notice the temperature of the room. Therefore, make sure that it is well within the general comfort zone of 68 to 72 degrees Fahrenheit. Make sure that your music system is working correctly—that you have a pre-recorded CD or tape playing with an appropriate song selection for the particular group. See that the refreshment table is set with fresh ingredients and all the necessary accouterments. And see that your staff is relaxed and ready to graciously greet all the arrivees as they enter the room.

First impressions are being formed fast. The audience may not know that you are a person of moral character, that you're an expert in your field, and that you have substantial success under your belt. All they have to go by is what their senses perceive in that moment.

Professional Materials

Arrange for participants to be given their workbooks or other training materials as they enter. In so doing, they will have time to preview it before you start and will have a common ground for initiating conversation with each other. Forget the notion that if participants have handouts in front of them, they'll be distracted from the presentation. If Broadway subscribed to this philosophy, you would receive your playbill after a performance was over; and most likely, it would go unread. Most people benefit from pre-exposure to material and many people learn the material better with more personal time for review. Make sure your materials are clean, colorful, up-to-date, error-free, and professional looking.

Personal Presentation

First impressions are being formed fast. The audience may not know that you are a person of moral character, that you're an expert in your field, and that you have substantial success under your belt. All they have to go by is what their senses perceive in that moment: your remarks, posture, grooming, dress, voice, attitude, and movements. Thus, your dress ought to be professional if that is the impression you want to create. Whether it's accurate or not, people judge your level of success by your dress, grooming, style, poise, and confidence level. Most importantly, smile and be personable. Personally greet as many participants as possible.

Making a Grand Entrance

As you approach the stage or podium upon being introduced, enter on the audience's left side and move towards their right side to speak. The reason for this is that, in general, people have a right ear hearing and attention preference for understanding new information. When you are oriented in this way, your audience will be using more of their right-brain hemisphere which has been shown to result in more positive first impressions.

Before you begin to speak, the audience generally gives you a few seconds of eye contact and ear contact. This is the magic moment. A 3 to 5 second pause at this moment may seem like an eternity, but it is a dramatic attention grabber. It adds emphasis and puts weight behind your opening statement before you even open your mouth.

Before you begin to speak, the audience generally gives you a few seconds of eye contact and ear contact. This is the magic moment.

Whatever your greeting, put energy into it! It could be "good morning," or "Hi and welcome to...." Congruence is critical at this time. Make sure your verbal message is also conveyed by your body language and gestures. Project your voice and think about speaking directly to each and every person.

The Affect of Positive Wording

Use words in their positive form! Make sure that what you are saying is exactly what you want to occur. Words have a powerful impact on your audience so, for the sake of clarity and overall effectiveness, use the positive form. Which of the following openings do you think is more effective?

1 "Good morning! My name's Eric Jensen and I'm pleased to be here. Today our session is on the brain, and we'll be discovering fun, relaxed, and effective ways to learn with total comfort and ease. And although you may not yet be thrilled, you may soon be as excited as the past participants who have done well in this course. Expect to succeed and have a great time today."

2 "Hi, I'm Eric Jensen. Whew! It's going to be a hot one today. Hopefully we won't suffer too much inside here. A couple of reminders before we get started: Even if you dislike being at trainings, just bear with me. For me, training isn't work—it's what I enjoy doing. So I'll try to make it bearable for you, too. This isn't like other groups. Here there'll be no boredom, and nothing forced. Also, we'll move past old limitations and totally destroy our negative attitudes about training."

Obviously, the first introduction is much better. With each word we hear or read, our brain does a search to find the meaning from our past experiences. Consider the statement, "Don't think of the color red; think of any color, but red." What color must you think of to understand the sentence? Red, of course! In the case of "no struggle" the mind must first think of struggle in order to consider "no struggle." Obviously, we don't want participants to think they'll struggle in our group! In your presentation, and especially in your openings, avoid the use of negatively-referenced words. Use the positive! Now, go back to the two introductions and compare the kinds of words that were used and their impact on you.

Words From Introduction 1:

Pleased, unusual, new, discover, fun, relax, efficiency, total comfort, ease, thrilled, join, success, easily, learned, and great.

Words From Introduction 2:

Hot, suffer, dislike, bear, forced, boredom, old, limitations, destroy, and negative.

Is there any doubt in your mind which introduction is likely to produce a more favorable outcome? Both attempt to say the same thing. One of them is stated in the positive (with the purposeful exception of "not thrilled") and the other is stated in the negative. The difference is hopefully obvious.

Clear and Focused

Know exactly what you want to achieve in the opening seconds of your presentation. A sense of vagueness is equivalent to sudden death, and the opportunity for creating a positive first impression will be lost forever. To test how clear your focus is, write down your opening objectives as succinctly as possible. For example, "I want positive engagement in the first 30 seconds." If you aren't able to be this specific, keep tweaking your opening until you reach complete clarity of purpose.

To test how clear your focus is, write down your opening objectives as succinctly as possible. For example, "I want positive engagement in the first 30 seconds." If you aren't able to be this specific, keep tweaking your opening until you reach complete clarity of purpose.

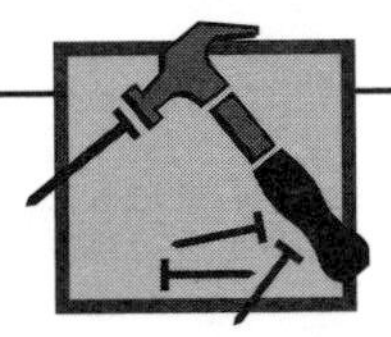

Tips & Tools for Openings That Sizzle

- Play inspiring music.
- Greet the audience with positive affirmations and tell them that you are excited to be with them: "Good morning—I'm Eric Jensen. It's a pleasure to be here today."
- Provide the name or title of your presentation: "The title of our brief session today is "Training with the Brain in Mind."
- Present a "hook." Sell them on the value of the talk; plant a suggestion about how enjoyable and valuable the session will be; or guarantee that they'll leave with specific benefits, such as, "Today you'll discover the three most important things you can do to boost motivation, understanding, and on the job transfer. If that is of interest to you, raise your hand and say, 'Yes'!"
- Give something away—even if it is silly; freebies get attention.
- Tell a brief story of something true that happened to you recently.
- Give an amazing bit of factual trivia: "Did you know...?"
- Share a particularly appropriate quotation.
- Ask an outrageous question of the audience.
- Humor can be good if it's tried and true (and good)!

Note: Once you have elicited a positive first impression, an appropriate next step is to conduct an icebreaker that involves deeper audience participation. This will keep the momentum going and let participants know that it will be an active day. Some suggestions follow:

Icebreaker Tips & Tools

- "Before we get started, let's wake up the body with a quick stretch. Please stand up and..."
- "Please turn to the person next to you and introduce yourself."
- "Before we jump in, let's find out who our neighbors are. Please introduce your self to three other people and tell them what you do."
- "To get ourselves going, we'll each need a ballot to vote with. Rather than having everyone come up for them at once, decide among the people around you who will be the ballot runner for your immediate area."

Brain Connection

Emotions Drive Attention, Meaning, and Memory

For years emotions were treated as a separate entity to the brain and learning. While the old model addressed primarily the intellectual aspects of training and development, the prevailing model suggests that we learn with our mind, heart, and body together which are all chemically and electrically linked by neurotransmitters and peptides that float throughout the body. To ignore any aspect of the system is to close a door on an essential element of learning. When your audience's emotions are engaged, they will recall the learning better, it will be more meaningful to them, and their focus will be more sharply maintained for a longer period of time.

Eliciting a Positive State

Eliciting a positive state involves engaging positive emotions. Emotions and mind states operate hand-in-hand. Since our memory is so associative, the first feelings that the audience experiences will be linked to you, the presenter.

Eliciting a positive state involves engaging positive emotions. Emotions and mind states operate hand-in-hand. Since our memory is so associative, the initial feelings that the audience experiences will be linked to you, the presenter. If the audience feels bored, you are the "object" linked to that boredom. The solution is simple: Make sure that you do everything you can to engage an immediate positive feeling from participants. How? Some of the best ways include providing a warm greeting, priming their thinking with interesting questions, stimulating multiple senses, and eliciting laughter or smiles.

Make your introduction warm, friendly, and inviting. Be generous with your eye contact and smile. Enjoy "taking in" all of your participants for a moment, so that they know you have personally seen them and have acknowledged their presence. Let them know by your facial expressions and body language that you are happy to have them in the group and that you are excited about the upcoming session. Make sure that your posture says you are open and accessible to them. It is better to invite attention than to demand attention.

Certainly the use of humor can be a great opener, but be careful. Jokes must be simple, short, understandable to everyone, and offensive to no one. I often use quotes from the morning's local paper, or references to something everyone finds universally funny. If you have a tried and true line, use it. But never risk something new and untested with an important audience. For a safe and humorous opening, you can always display an innocuous single-frame cartoon or ridiculous photograph on the overhead projector screen.

Another simple and effective opening strategy is to ask a leading question that elicits a positive state in the group: "How many of you would like today's session to be short, relevant, and to-the-point?" Or, "Who among you would like to learn something that can make you wealthy and bring less stress to your life?" Or, "How many of you here today are expecting an easy-to-understand, but very practical talk?" Whatever question you ask, make sure that it fits your presentation and that you can deliver on your promise. Your credibility depends on the fulfillment of their expectations.

Avoiding Dead-End Openers

Generally, most audiences can be fairly forgiving *after* they know and like you. But you don't have that luxury in the first few minutes of your opening. So, be sure that you don't make the following common mistakes:

- Starting too slowly; always start with enthusiasm and energy!
- Having a technology failure; always double-check all equipment!
- Starting late; If an emergency prevents you from starting on time, tell the audience when you will be starting and what has happened. For example, you might say, "Thank you for being here on time. There's been an emergency on the freeway near our hotel. Only half our group is here. We'll be starting 10 minutes from now. Until that time, please review your course materials; you can look forward to a great day."
- Starting with an apology; start with offering value, not an excuse. If you're late or your equipment took extra time and it is your fault, greet first, apologize quickly, and then get off to a good start.

One of your opening objectives ought to be to develop a connection with your audience as soon as possible. There is an art to building rapport with your audience; and once you have mastered it, you can lead participants almost anywhere.

Relationships Before Content

One of your opening objectives ought to be to develop a connection with your audience as soon as possible. The audience wants to know who you are. They know they will get some content from you, but before that happens, they need to determine if you care about them and why you care. There is an art to building rapport with your audience; and once you have mastered it, you can lead participants almost anywhere. The rapport-building strategies on the following page can bring you into the fold.

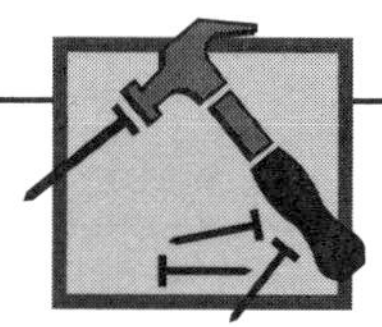

Rapport-Building Tips & Tools

- Talk about what you have in common: the weather, parking problems, an election, other people, etc.
- Empathize with their situation: travel challenges, slow elevator, curiosity, excitement, or anything common to a large part of the group.
- Share something personal or close to your heart.
- Treat them with respect so they know you care.
- Tell them a human interest story that relates.
- Provide relevant personal examples.
- Refer to particular things you've learned about trainees in your audience.

Note: Establish immediate relevancy. You can do this or you can encourage participants to do this, but it is a step not to be missed. Every trainee will, no doubt, be wondering, "What's in this for me?" Provide essential information from the start so that they can find the answer to this question quickly. Tell them what they can expect, what you expect, and how you anticipate the day going. The following tips will help establish essential relevancy:

Tips & Tools for Establishing Relevancy

- Let the learners tell you what they want to learn and hook into that.
- Do your market research to determine where their skills and interests lie.
- Share a story about how a past participant used what he or she learned.
- Start off with linking the training content or goals to a recent current event.
- Tap into the values common to the age group of your learners (i.e., security for ages 4-6 and over 60, autonomy for ages 7-11, affiliation for ages 12-16, independence for ages 16-25, etc.).

Starting on Time

Introduce yourself on time, even if you don't actually start. Do this whether everyone is there or not (unless there is an obvious major delay that has held up 25 percent or more of the group). Your time, as well as the participants', is valuable and deserves to be respected. Starting on time is one of the ways that you can begin to build trust and respect. Honor those who are on time and create a context where the audience feels they are worth being on time for.

◆ In the remote instance that you are late, never give excuses, regardless of the sincerity of your rationale. A better approach is to say something like, "I apologize for being late. My flat tire's the reason, but it's never an excuse to keep you waiting. Your time is important to me. I'll make it up to you, so let's get started right away and make the best use of your time."

◆ In a situation where it's the first meeting, some participants are missing but it's time to start, a good opening would be, "Good morning and thank you for being here. I appreciate you being on time, and in the next couple of minutes, the remaining participants who are looking for this room should arrive. We'll give them until five after, then start. Right now, let's take a brief moment to learn a couple of things about our neighbor."

◆ In a situation where it's not the first meeting of the group, many participants are missing, and it's time to start, an effective opening might be, "Good morning and thank you for being on time. Obviously some participants are not here, but it's time to start. Today we'll..."

◆ In the situation where it's time to start and everyone is on time, a positive opening might be, "Good morning and thanks for being on time! Give yourselves a hand! Today we'll be..."

The brain reacts to high stress and threat with the preemptive action of replacing higher-order thinking with survival thinking. Consequently, for optimal learning, you must work diligently to eliminate stress, threat, anxiety, and learner helplessness the your training environment.

Creating a Safe Climate

The brain reacts to high stress and threat with the preemptive action of replacing higher-order thinking with survival thinking. Consequently, for optimal learning, you must work diligently to eliminate stress, threat, anxiety, and learner helplessness from the training environment. One way to do this is to seek group responses to your questions rather than calling on individuals or relying on volunteers.

Strategies for Climate Control

- Ask open-ended questions to reduce participant's fear of being wrong.
- State your expectations clearly from the start. For example, say how you would like to field questions? Let them know if they should raise their hand, shout out, or wait until you ask if there are any questions.
- Assure the audience that they have a say in the process. Give them specific vehicles for input (i.e., your accessibility at breaks, a place to put written questions, or a time to address other concerns they may have).
- Don't be afraid to make a mistake; this is a good way to role-model your comfort level with risk taking and your trust in the group.

The introduction is essential for eliciting the mental state or mindset that will make the remaining minutes maximally productive. Whatever you do, don't skip this stage.

The 10-Percent Rule

In deciding how long your introduction ought to be, keep the 10 percent rule in mind. This guideline asserts that an introduction ought to consist of about 10 percent of the total presentation time. However, when a presentation is less than an hour in length, should you still use valuable time for this purpose? In all cases, the answer is an emphatic "Yes!" The introduction is essential for eliciting the mental state or mindset that will make the remaining minutes maximally productive. Whatever you do, don't skip this stage. Keep in mind that lifelong impressions have been made many times before in less than 30 seconds.

Well, you've made it to the end of this chapter; and I would bet you can imagine a few analogous characteristics between presenters and hot cakes by now. Here's my list to add to yours:

- Both require the right mix of ingredients to achieve perfect substance and form.
- When they're really good, you can't get enough of them.
- A variety of toppings keep people coming back for more.
- Both sizzle from the start and get better as they cook.
- Timing is everything.

Engage Your Brain:

Planning to Sizzle

What are your primary objectives for the opening of your next presentation?

How will you achieve these objectives?

Is your introduction clear, concise, interactive, interesting, funny and multi-sensory?

How will you ensure that participants' emotions are engaged? How will you establish relevancy with the audience? What relationship-building strategies will you implement?

What is your plan for practicing your introduction?

Courage and perseverance have a magical talisman, before which difficulties disappear and obstacles vanish into air.

–John Quincy Adams

CHAPTER 6

Strategies That Melt Resistant Audiences

The expression "buy-in" has become popular in training environments to describe an audience's approval of a presenter's ideas or approach. To achieve buy-in, a facilitator must earn the audience's attention and avoid intimidating them. The concept originated in business/sales where tremendous pressure is often applied to get the customer to buy. Some audiences, like some customers, are ready and eager to buy into what's offered, while others may want to, but don't, due to perceived threat, peer pressure, ignorance about the product or service, timing, or other situation that keeps them in a non-buy-in state. Forcing yourself on an audience won't inspire buy-in. They have to want to "follow" you on their own volition. This chapter will present time-tested strategies that are useful in changing the attitude of your audience from "no way, Jose" to "I'll give it a try." Not all of the strategies will work every time because each audience is unique, but if you listen carefully to your audience's verbal and non-verbal communication cues, remain open, and willing to shift gears appropriately, you will inspire their confidence in you.

This is a good time to remember what you learned about your audience from the market research you did in Chapter One. To successfully facilitate the buy-in process, you must show your audience that you have their best interest at heart. When initiating this process, it's helpful to know about the particular group's issues, concerns, biases, fears, and expectations. Who do they respect? What current situation are they collectively most concerned about? Are they resentful about being at the training or excited? The answers to questions like these can give you the critical bits of data necessary to facilitate a receptive learning state.

Key Topics

- *A "Buy-In" State Increases Receptivity*
- *Involve Your Audience With Questions*
- *Provide Key Information*
- *Empower Your Audience*
- *Help the Audience Trust You*
- *Icebreakers That Melt Resistance*
- *Change Perceptions With Pre-Tests*
- *Watch the Gradient Level*
- *Address Participants' Fears*
- *Use Selective Wording*
- *Reaching Agreement States Through Oral Contracts*
- *Promote Benefits*
- *Sell the Risks*
- *Gain Commitments*
- *Engage Emotions Early*
- *Be Responsive to Your Audience*
- *Increase Accountability*

Brain Connection

A "Buy-In" State Increases Receptivity

"Buy-in" is a state of mind that reflects participant involvement and agreement with a decision resulting in greater audience receptivity to the content and process being facilitated. We know that this specific condition is initiated by the brain's arousal, curiosity, and attentional states, and that the neurotransmitter group known as amines is involved. However, we still don't understand all of the dynamics of amines—like how agreement is activated on a biological level. However, it is clear that the chemical state you induce, as a presenter, will determine to a large degree, the success you'll have with the group. When you are able to activate a state of buy-in, audience resistance melts.

Involve Your Audience With Questions

To set the stage for participation and audience involvement, ask questions that stimulate their thinking. The audience needs to know that this won't be a passive training. Wait for them to respond to your questions; and role-model how you expect them to do this. If you want them to raise their hand to answer, put your own hand up in the air as you ask the question. The following questions will elicit instant participation:

- "How many of you had to drive for over an hour to get here?"
- "If we could accomplish these three goals today, would it be worth the time you'll have invested?"
- "For how many of you was being here someone else's idea?"
- "How many of you have heard of?"
- "Who wants to have some real fun today?"

Everyone in your audience has questions whether they come to you with them or not. Answering these questions up front will eliminate the possibility of the participants being distracted by them.

Provide Key Information

Everyone in your audience has questions whether they come to you with them or not. Some examples of questions that are bound to surface are, "What's coming up?" "What do I do if this happens?" Or, the most common one, "What's in it for me?" Or, "Will there be a test or evaluation on this?" Or, "Will I be embarrassed, threatened or pressured today?" Answering these questions up front will eliminate the possibility of the participants being distracted by them. Also, share with the group your expectations about asking questions. For example, let them know if you expect them to wait until you're done and ask if there are any questions, or if you prefer them to ask questions immediately. Another simple way to handle participant concerns is with a handout that addresses commonly asked questions. Whatever method you choose, announce it early in the presentation.

I generally outline my training objectives in the first 15-minutes of my presentation. Then I check in with the audience to confirm that the objectives set match up with their expectations. Once this step in the buy-in process has been done, I assure the audience that the day will be valuable, interactive, and fun. I solicit any questions and pause for their reply. If you've done your introduction well, there will likely only be a few questions, if any. Welcome questions at this point as they provide you with a built-in meter reading of how complete your introduction was. Of course, there are always audience questions that don't get answered for various reasons. If you know, however, some of the reasons why these questions never get asked, you can reduce the affect. The following page highlights some typical reasons for this and presents strategies you can use to counteract them.

Typical Reasons for Unanswered Questions

- Participants fear embarrassment (reassure them there are no dumb questions).
- Some participants are more visual or kinesthetic and less verbal (make it okay to talk to you at the break or give you a written message).
- They don't fully understand what you're talking about, but they don't know what to ask in order to get clarification either.
- They're not sure if, or when, you want to answer questions.
- They don't want to draw attention to themselves.
- They aren't sure how best to get your attention.
- They get tired of holding their hand up and not being recognized.
- They think you've noticed that they have a question, but you don't ever recognize them.

Note: Always recognize someone who is holding their hand up as soon as you see it. Even if you don't want to interrupt your thought immediately, at least, acknowledge the person. Say something like, "Jake, I see you have a question and I'll come back to you in a minute." Or "Lucy, we'll address your thought, momentarily." Never look past someone who obviously has a question or concern without noticing. This is a sure way to breed resistance and leave questions unanswered.

Empower Your Audience

Let your participants help generate content suggestions. The more participants are involved in their own learning, the more likely they are to get something out of it. Some simple strategies to facilitate this follow:

- Ask participants for ideas in advance. They can mail, fax, or e-mail them to you; or if you prefer, give them a number where they can call you.
- Keep an ongoing list of ideas the group has generated and include as many of them as time allows.
- Post a bulletin board in the back of the room for participant notes and suggestions. Post-It Notes work great for recording messages. Why not give everyone their own Post-It Note pad at the start of the session to encourage their interaction and involvement.
- Allow participants to brainstorm ideas or problems. Then have them form groups and generate solutions for themselves.

Help Your Audience Trust You

Creating an atmosphere of mutual trust and respect ought to be your highest priority. When participants feel trusted and respected, they are more likely to respond to you as a group. My favorite way to show participants that I respect and honor their thoughts and ideas is to ask open-ended questions. I then respond to them in such a way that it becomes apparent that I am genuinely interested in their contributions. For example, "What are some ways to reduce threat in learning?" The way I ask the question makes it okay to give multiple answers. Or, "Sometimes, we accidentally induce learner helplessness. Let's brainstorm out loud about a half dozen ways this happens..." Brainstorming is a questioning technique that allows many different participants to answer in a safe, no wrong answers environment.

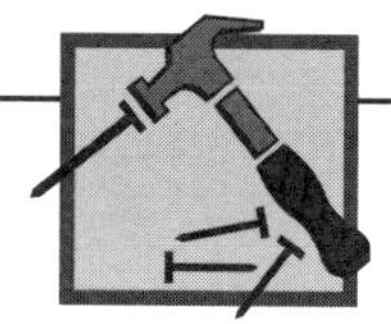

Icebreaker Tips & Tools

◆ ***Stretching To Music:*** Warm up the group with simple stretching exercises—variations include breaking into small groups and asking each group to choose their own leader.
◆ ***Baby Pictures:*** Ask everyone to send a baby photograph of themselves in advance. Number the back of each photo to identify whom they belong to. Display the pictures and let participants try to match them up.
◆ ***Name Tag Exchange:*** Have everyone write three to five descriptive qualifiers on their name tag like energetic, piano-playing, computer savvy, etc. Collect them and pass them out randomly with the instructions to locate the owner of their name tag.
◆ ***Hats:*** Make a silly hat (like a newspaper hat) on the first day and introduce yourself wearing it.
◆ ***Wanted Posters:*** Create a sample "Wanted" poster with information about yourself like hobbies, height, hair color, last seen in the vicinity of... etc., but do not include your name. Show yours to the group as an example, then ask participants to make their own wanted poster. When they're done, post the posters and give participants the opportunity to try and figure out who is who in the group.
◆ ***Shoe Sort:*** Form a circle with chairs and ask everyone to put their shoes in the center. Each person then gets a turn to pick up a shoe and try to guess the owner and tell why. This is best done with a group that knows each other.
◆ ***Fact Or Fib:*** Distribute an index card to each person and ask them to write their name plus three facts and three lies about themselves on it. Now have the group pair up, switch cards, and figure out which of the facts are true and which are fibs.
◆ ***Puppets:*** Everyone gets a cheap sock or paper puppet (if you're on a budget). Ask participants to create a character for the puppet that represents someone at work. Then, have them use their puppet to introduce themselves to the rest of the group.
◆ ***Stand And Go:*** You say, "All those who like classical music (or Chinese food or jazz or chocolate, etc.) please go to this corner. Then say, "All those who like rock-and-roll (or Italian food or waffles or Italian cars, etc.) go to a different corner." Once you have the audience in about 5 groups, let them meet each other and share what they have in common. Then you can remix them again.

Change Perceptions With Pre-Tests

A pre-test gives your audience the opportunity to realize what they don't know. Since arrogance is a potential block to buy-in and/or learning, the pre-test can be useful in encouraging humility. If your audience believes they already know everything about the topic on which you are presenting, there will be low buy-in. So, you're going to help them realize what they don't know and the benefits of knowing it.

I often do presentations on the implications of brain research in training and development. The buy-in always increases when I include a low-key questionnaire in the seminar handouts. Before starting, I ask participants to read the questions and check those which they do not know the answer to. Then I ask them to check the questions which they would like to know the answer to. I word the questions so they are as intriguing as possible. For example, "What are the three best foods to boost learning?" Or, "What five things should be done in the first 12 months of a child's life?" Or, "Why do we forget foreign languages that we learned in high school?" Or, I ask participants to do the quiz and tell them in advance that they will be able to answer all of the questions by the time the seminar is over. This strategy provides a link between your topic and the participant's interest. If the link is not obvious, help create one. Make sure your participants explore both their own relationship to the topic and the rest of the world's relationship to it. Bring in information regarding the external forces at play and the megatrends affecting the topic. The following are some strategies for making sure this happens:

- Use a video to introduce the topic.
- Bring in a recent magazine covering the subject.
- Share your own experience related to the topic.
- Talk to participants about related trends—global and local.
- Ask participants to share their insights about the topic.
- Have the audience pair up or work in small groups.

A pre-test gives your audience the opportunity to realize what they don't know. If your audience believes they already know everything about the topic on which you are presenting, there will be low buy-in. So, you're going to help them realize what they don't know and the benefits of knowing it.

Watch Gradient Level

The dictionary defines gradient as "a rate of regular ascent or descent." This means that there is a smooth and predictable transition from one point to the next. You are out of gradient when you do what's not appropriate for the moment in the timing of the group. How do you know what's appropriate? Use sensory acuity to check the responses of your audience. Be sensitive to language and subtle facial and body clues. Move to a new activity only when your audience is ready for it.

For example, when you first meet participants, a handshake or simple eye contact may be appropriate. After a strong bond of friendship has been established, it may be appropriate to hug them as part of a greeting ritual. But to hug someone the first time you meet them would be "out of gradient." In other words, the ascent to that point of intimacy has not been made, either gradually or predictably, yet.

Address Participants' Fears

The three biggest fears of participants are: 1) the session will be boring; 2) they won't learn anything (their time will be wasted); and 3) they won't be treated fairly (they might be embarrassed). Let's take a closer look at these fears and what to do about them:

Regardless of the value of the course, participants want to know right up front if you are compelling, fun, well-informed and able to make the time pass quickly. Show them early on that you plan on having a good time: Incorporate activities, games, music, laughter, joy, and plenty of opportunities for personal expression.

1 Are you interesting to hear and watch? Regardless of the value of the course, participants want to know right up front if you are compelling, fun, well-informed and able to make the time pass quickly. Everyone has had the misfortune of suffering through an uninteresting session; and the last thing participants want, is to get stuck in this situation again. Assure them, both verbally and non-verbally, that this training will be different. You can say to them, "I believe participants learn more when they enjoy what they are doing. We will definitely have fun today!" Then, show them early on that you plan on having a good time: Incorporate activities, games, music, laughter, joy, and plenty of opportunities for personal expression.

2 Are you competent? The second greatest fear of most participants is that they won't learn anything. It's important, therefore, to establish credibility and professionalism immediately so participants can relax and start to learn. The entire next chapter is devoted to establishing credibility. For the purposes of this chapter, the following brief introductions provide examples of how your introduction can inspire credibility—not necessarily by stating all of your qualifications, but by powerfully summarizing your experience:

New Presenter: "My name's Eric Jensen and I've been interested in science for over six years. I did successful graduate work in environmental science with an emphasis in systems thinking. You'll find I know my subject well. I like to present it in a fun and interesting way, so this should be a good one."

Veteran Presenter: "My name's Eric Jensen and I'm pleased to have you in this session. I've worked successfully with over 10,000 participants in the last 15 years, and I am confident you will also do well, learn a great deal, and have a good time. Because of the innovative way this course is organized, the learning will be fun and effortless."

3 Are you fair and trustworthy? This question is prompted by the thought of being evaluated and the fear of failure or, just as bad, not getting what is deserved. It's important for a presenter to give the participants some assurances and exhibit a sense of fairness. Assurance, quite simply, can be provided by saying something like this: "In the past, other participants have found me easy to talk to, and my evaluation methods fair. I believe you will too." Then do what you say you'll do. Always make sure your verbal and non-verbal messages match, and that you follow through with your promises.

Use Selective Wording

Studies show that tabloid headlines create immediate attention. You can use similar techniques to create interest in your content. Use words like *you* instead of *I*. For example, "Here's why you can remember names better after listening to music." People like to know who, what, how and why, so use these kinds of phrases. "Here's how we can understand history better." Use "now we are ready", not "nearly ready." Use immediacy and proximity to alert the senses.

Studies show that tabloid headlines create immediate attention. You can use similar techniques to create interest in your content. Use immediacy and proximity to alert the senses.

You can also get the attention of the whole group by addressing part of the group. Do you want your lower-performing participants to listen carefully? Simply say, "The next thing I'm going to talk about is only for those who consider themselves to be high achievers." Or say, "I only want those with green eyes to listen to what I'm going to say next." By creating exclusivity, you elicit the interest of everyone.

Reaching Agreement States Through Oral Contracts

In addition to having participants share expectations, share yours. They should know what you expect them to learn, the time frame, and in what form they will be required to demonstrate competency. Share your expectations and get agreement with your learners. An example is: "What I've heard from you is that you're interested in three main things today: 1) background on the brain; 2) practical applications; and 3) next steps. If that meets your expectations, raise your hand and say, "yes"!

In other words, give them your evidence procedure for determining if they have met your evaluation criteria. If it's appropriate, be sure to put the expectations in writing if they affect the evaluation process. Once in writing, the participants may refer to them later, providing greater certainty, peace of mind, and predictability.

Promote Benefits

What's more powerful, you explaining the relevancy of the course to participants and setting the goals or, the participants determining the relevancy of the session and setting their own goals? You know the answer. Learner-generated needs and goals are far more powerful than presenter-imposed ones.

The more a participant perceives the need for your material, the greater the buy-in. To "sell" the course, build on participant's needs. The following is a sample interaction of a presenter who is going to introduce learn-to-learn skills:

Learner-generated needs and goals are far more powerful than presenter-imposed ones. The more a participant perceives the need for your material, the greater the buy-in.

1. ***To help establish needs, ask:***
"How many of you think your studying takes too long?"
"How many of you fall asleep sometimes while doing your reading?"
"How many of you have had the experience of studying for a test, thinking that you know the material, then blowing it at test time?"

2. ***Suggest possible hooks:***
"Who would like to know three ways to cut study time in half?"
"Is there anyone here who'd like to be able to speed read?"
"Who in here would like to learn seven ways to have more free time?"

Now, ask them what they think they might get out of learning better study skills. This quick activity creates immediate recognition of participants' needs and offers benefits for taking your course. It can also create a feeling of commonality among participants. By hearing responses to these questions, participants get a sense of the needs of others. They know that others are in the same boat and this can lessen their fears of looking or feeling stupid.

Participants need to be clearly informed about the potential benefits of the course. Tell them what they can expect to learn or be able to do as a result of your training. If you can't think of benefits other than knowing the material well, you can be sure the participants won't see the benefits either! Spell out the benefits for them. For example:

Customer Service Benefit: You'll learn how to keep customers happy so that they buy again. This keeps sales up and makes you a valuable employee.

Quality Assurance Benefit: You'll learn how to elicit feelings of inter-departmental pride, teamwork, and achievement resulting in a more profitable company and happier employees.

Career Benefit: You'll learn strategies that will help you make more money, and have more independence, satisfaction, and security in your work environment.

Communication Benefit: You'll learn how to present your best self, gain personal confidence, speak comfortably in front of groups, and communicate clearly.

Sell the Risks

Some of us are motivated by positives, some of us by negatives. Ask your participants what their stake is in your group. Depending on the course, it might be appropriate for participants to know what possible consequences there are for not learning the material. Some potential consequences follow:

- Being behind or less competitive professionally
- Facing peer or family pressure
- Lacking information for important decisions
- Getting a poor grade
- Reducing opportunities or choices

Part of your strategy to evoke buy-in might be to make sure your participants perceive that the rewards of success are great and the price for failure is high.

Part of your strategy to evoke buy-in might be to make sure your participants perceive that the rewards of success are great, and the price for failure is high. Many participants don't relate workplace, classroom, or business training behavior directly to the real world. Help them understand that if they don't participate, they will learn less and that may translate to lower achievement and fewer chances for promotion, recognition, or success in life.

Gain Commitments

The main thing you need, as a presenter, is participant commitment to the "workability" of the group—meaning, participants' actions constructively add to group results, rather than detract or sabotage them. But before you ask for commitments from them, what is it you are committing to for them? Your list might be something like the following:

- To make the topic and learning relevant and interesting
- To allow for appropriate input
- To never embarrass anyone
- To be fair and truthful
- To negotiate any changes in scheduling or content with the group

Present this to your group before you ask them to commit to anything. The role-modeling is important. Then, you can say to your group, "Now you know what I'm committed to, let's play fair and do it both ways." Sometimes participants are afraid to make a commitment because of the consequences of failure. Make sure they know that they won't fail in your presentation. Once that's in place, you can facilitate participant commitment in numerous ways. The following methods are highly productive:

- Groups or teams brainstorm a list and post it.
- You offer a multiple choice list from which they pick.
- You take an informal poll by a show of hands.
- Individuals make their own list of commitments and pass them in.
- Seek group consensus.

The value of participant commitment is (1) they experience the process of making a promise and keeping it; (2) they experience the risk and success of commitments; and (3) they increase the chances of getting the desired outcome. The process of making and keeping a commitment helps a participant feel more powerful and in control.

Engage Emotions Early

We are driven by emotions. Therefore, the two best ways to get participation are to use physical or emotional experiences to hook the audience. Each has their place. The following seven strategies reflect some productive ways to engage positive emotions:

1. The presenter simply role-models the love of learning and enthusiasm about their job.

Example: Bring something to the group and share it with great excitement. Build suspense, smile, show off a new CD, book, object, clothing item, animal, etc.

2. Use celebration, acknowledgments, parties, high-five's, food, music, and fun! At the celebration, show off participants' work.

Example: When participants are done mind-mapping something, I'll often have them get up and present their work to five other people. I instruct them to locate at least two things they like about the other person's mind-map and share that with the person. I like to conduct this exercise in a celebratory atmosphere with music, refreshments, etc.

Continued...

Engage Emotions Early

3. Use theater, role play, and drama. The bigger the production, the higher the stakes, and the more the emotions are engaged.

Example: Your group volunteers to put on a skit. There's rehearsals, stress, fun, anxiety, anticipation, suspense, excitement, and finally—relief.

4. By setting up controversy. This could be in the form of a debate, dialogue, panel discussion, argument, etc. It can be real or artificial. Whenever you have two sides, a vested interest, and the means to express opinions, you'll get action!

Example: Ask participants to pair off, determine a subject, and argue a point whether they really believe it or not. Give participants 30 seconds each to present their most emotionally-compelling case in support of their viewpoint. Then switch. Ultimately, settle it physically; after the verbal controversy, facilitate a giant tug-of-war with partners on opposite sides.

5. Use rituals which instantly engage learners. They can include, arrival rituals, closing rituals, achievement rituals, and starting rituals.

Example: Start the session with an activity where everyone pairs up and are given three questions to answer. Instruct the groups to go for a short walk while answering the questions. The questions might be (1) What am I most grateful for in my life right now? (2) What am I most passionate about? And, (3) What goals do I want to set and reach for myself today?

6. Work in teams or partnerships which always engages emotions.

Example: Encourage teams to give a cheer each time they complete their tasks or reach a goal. Remind teams to continue doing their cheers throughout the day.

7. Conduct purposeful games, activities, and energizers throughout the session.

Other Strategies: Share a great story, human drama, or personal example to highlight relevance to participants. Music is great for evoking emotions, so use it and enjoy it! Incorporate team joke-telling contests. Each team gets three to four minutes to share their best joke with each other, then with the whole group. Use physical memory games where you help participants link up new learning with body parts ("Our first item was the importance of planning—let's liken that to our hands.")

Be Responsive to Your Audience

The audience will be more accepting if they feel you are genuinely concerned for their well-being. This comes across in dozens of ways. The following are a few examples:

- Provide stand and stretch breaks every 15 to 20 minutes.
- Make sure they know where necessary facilities are like bathrooms, food, phones, and convenient parking.
- Monitor and manage the room temperature for their comfort.
- Provide time for them to interact with each other.
- Make sure vehicles are in place for them to give you feedback—question time, written evaluations, and/or Post-It Note board.

The audience will be more accepting if they feel you are genuinely concerned for their well-being.

Increase Accountability

Even among the best and most willing participants, you'll want systems in place to keep accountability high. There are dozens of tools you can use to let each person know that they are expected to produce results. Sometimes the best way to accomplish this is to use peer interaction to generate high expectations and accountability within the group.

- You might say, "Turn to your neighbor and say 'Good morning!'"
- "Do this activity with a different partner than you had last time" (Changing partners often helps increase accountability.)
- "Change sides of the room; sit at least five seats away from where you were before."
- Ask participants to choose a team; teams then make verbal reports to the larger group.
- Ask participants to produce a mind-map with a partner instead of by themselves. Or, do a mind-map by themselves, then share it with a small group or partner.
- Teams create scorecards for self-assessment. This allows them to assess themselves on areas like productivity, cooperation, and fun.

Generally, it's a wise idea to increase accountability. Be careful though. If you use too many of the strategies too quickly, they can backfire. Use them gently, adding one at a time. Do it with a smile and you'll be able to generate a strong buy-in. Remember, participants don't always want to be in your presentation and they don't feel they need it. Put yourself in their shoes and respect their resentment. I didn't say give in or give up; just respect it. Once you remember what it's like for them, you'll be able to put into practice the appropriate strategies for achieving the optimal mindset for learning.

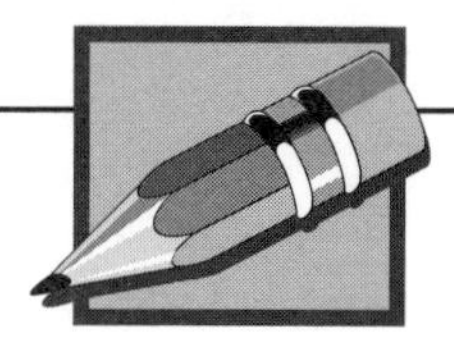

Engage Your Brain:

Planning for Maximum Buy-In

What strategies from this chapter will you incorporate in your next presentation?

How will you ensure buy-in from your audience?

What benefits will you promote in your presentation?

What strategies will you use to ensure high audience accountability?

What is the recipe for successful achievement? To my mind there are just four essential ingredients: choose a career you love; give it the best there is in you; seize your opportunities; and be a member of the team.

–Benjamin F. Fairless

CHAPTER 7

High-Caliber Credibility

Your credibility, as a presenter, contributes to the perceived value by the audience. Participants need to have a clear sense of your competency. Let them know who you are, and what you can do for them. Emphasize credibility, not authority. Excess authority may actually undermine the capacity of others to really hear you. When an inappropriate claim on authority is staked, a barrier inevitably results between audience and presenter. Master trainers have learned how to build bridges, not walls. Empowering others is far more effective than holding power over others. The more you provide participants with what they want—choice, a voice, confidence, security, and relationships, the more they will open up to your leadership. By reducing their apprehension or mistrust, the real business of learning can be accomplished simply and efficiently.

Many times authority figures demand respect based on their position. This is dangerous. If participants perceive you to be power-hungry, egotistical, incompetent, or if they believe you will misuse your power, they will likely try to shift the power scale—often at your expense. If your learners don't feel empowered, they will use whatever "currency" they have to gain some perception of control. Usually this currency is in the form of time, energy, and peer support—valuable trainer resources. However, at the same time, if they perceive you to be useful to them—if they believe you are competent—they will show respect towards you and learning will be optimized.

- *Bio-Chemical Response to Credibility*
- *Preparation Counts*
- *Body Language Speaks Volumes*
- *Increasing Your Voice Range*
- *The Power of Pausing*
- *Personalizing Your Presentation*
- *The Company You Keep*
- *Anchoring the Room*
- *Keeping Your Word*
- *Summarize Often*
- *Walking the Walk*
- *The Accuracy Imperative*
- *Earning Respect by Giving It*
- *Handling Audience Questions*

Brain Connection

The Brain Responds Bio-chemically to Its Perception of Credibility

Credibility may mean that the brain is releasing less adrenaline (threat is low) or more dopamine or epinephrine (if the "positive connection" is high). We know our brain is strongly affected by emotions; and emotions affected by neurotransmitters—the chemicals in the brain. Since emotions flavor our impressions of each other, we've come to label positive emotions as "the halo effect." Credibility is not something that you automatically have by virtue of your experience or education. It is something that is decided by your listener in each interaction. Making "brain-smart" presentations can enhance your credibility dramatically.

There are many ways to enhance your image. Consider that a thorough knowledge of your subject is just one element on the road to achieving credibility. The following elements also need to be considered as you work to build bridges with your participants and adopt a presentation style that exudes credibility.

Preparation Counts

Though thorough preparation does not automatically earn you credibility, it definitely helps. The more prepared you are, the more confident you'll be. Confidence cannot be easily faked. A savvy audience will identify false confidence quickly. There are no shortcuts here. You must prepare yourself well if you want to achieve high-caliber credibility. This does not mean, however, that you need to give a long dissertation about your qualifications. In fact, presenters with high credibility don't spend a lot of time highlighting their own qualifications. The second they open their mouth, it is obvious they know what they're talking about. Rather than providing your audience with a dry and self-serving laundry list of your credentials, consider *incorporating into* your presentation some of the following:

You must prepare yourself well if you want to achieve high-caliber credibility. The more prepared you are, the more confident you'll be.

- The number of years you've been in the profession or studied your area of specialty.
- The degrees you've attained or the schools you've attended.
- Your mentors, their standing in the field, and how they have influenced you.
- Innovative or important state-wide or national projects you've worked on.
- Articles or books you've published, or interviews you've granted.
- Memberships and offices you've held in professional clubs, organizations, or on committees.
- Personal experiences you've had while doing a related training.
- Conferences you've attended, or at which you've presented.

Once you feel you are ready to represent a body of knowledge or skill level in a field, stick with it. Become known as the "guru" in that specific industry. Very few people can be considered experts on many subjects. Focus your energy on your own specialized field. No one expects you to master everything. On the other hand, never pretend to be someone or something that you aren't. Never say you have a degree that you don't. Never say you've attended a school or have accreditation that you don't. It is better to surprise people by being *more* than they expected than to let them down when they find out you're less. Once an audience has been let down or mislead, it's particularly tough to regain credibility.

Body Language Speaks Volumes

Top presenters send powerful messages because their gestures are congruent with their content. When your non-verbal cues support your verbal message, your effectiveness is multiplied. While the content of your verbal message is usually weighted at about 10 percent of the total impact of your presentation, this leaves a 90-percent impact quotient that is influenced by non-content areas such as gestures, positioning, expressions, voice range, tempo, pitch, and volume.

The best ways for you to discover your full range of conscious and/or nonconscious communication patterns is to (1) tape record a real session and listen to the audio tape, (2) video-tape a real session and watch it, and (3) seek feedback from participants and other professionals.

The use of your body as a communication tool is probably one of the most under-represented areas of improvement possible for presenters.

The use of your body as a communication tool is probably one of the most under-represented areas of improvement possible for presenters. It's also an area which often takes significant coaching to reach mastery. The best way to improve the range and depth of non-verbal expression is to take acting lessons from a local junior college or university. In addition, voice training is excellent if you can find a good coach. A third option is to take a dance, mime, or movement workshop. Each of these skill areas has the capacity to help you achieve higher levels of success as a presenter. Skills such as clearer self-expression, voice projection and inflection, space utilization, and body language all enhance the professional trainer's repertoire and command.

Increasing Your Voice Range

As a presenter, you'll want to use several different types of "voices." If you consistently use the same tone, you're limiting your influence. Your range of voices ought to include the "approachable" voice, the "credible" voice, the "persuasive" voice, and the "emotive" voice.

The Approachable Voice is used when you are soliciting the opinion(s) or interaction of your audience. It is also used when the group is small (15 or less). This voice is higher, has more variance, and regardless of where the tonality starts out, it ends up higher at the end. More of a bobbing, up-and-down head movement is used. It's the voice that you use when you are asking questions or want the audience to interact more informally.

The Credible Voice is used when presenting factual information or something you want the group to recall. The credible voice has less variance, less inflection, and ends the sentence on a lower note with the chin down. The credibility comes from the fact that your statements end with finality, and an authority that says, "This is a fact." The pattern is like the famous four musical bars from Beethoven's Fifth: "Da-Da-Da-Dah!" Use this voice when you are telling it like it is, giving commands, calling for action, and/or presenting strongly-held opinions. With this voice, you're making your agenda obvious, you want to maintain position and influence. There are many legitimate times to use this voice; and the larger the group, the more you're likely to need it. It is the voice of control.

The credible voice is frequently used in traditionally male circles—sports, business, finance, and the military. In traditionally female circles, you'll hear the approachable voice used often. Both have important roles in the training and development environment. Learn the culture of your audience, and then use the voice that's appropriate in the moment.

If speaking well can build credibility, then it may come as a surprise to you that saying nothing can also build credibility.

The Persuasive Voice is generally used to give a command. For example, "Please sit down." This voice uses more volume and eye contact. To get the most value out of it, make sure you already have rapport with the group and avoid overdoing it.

The Emotive Voice is used to express feelings which keeps interest high. When you say, for example, "That was amazing," the audience can identify with you. When someone gives you a surprising or interesting bit of information and you respond by saying, "Really?", you are using your emotive voice.

The best presenters use a full-range of voices depending on what the situation calls for. Michael Grinder, author of *Envoy*, (1996) goes as far as saying, "The systematic use of nonverbals is the basis for all successful communication."

The Power of Pausing

If speaking well can build credibility, then it may come as a surprise to you that saying nothing, can also build credibility. Listen to the very best presenters—the ones that get you to think, that persuade, and really engage their audience. You'll find that one thing these presenters have in common is they have mastered the timing of their delivery. They know when to pause and how long to pause for. Pausing is a highly effective technique if used at the right time.

- Pause at the start of your presentation, to build suspense.
- Pause when you want to emphasize a serious emotion.
- Pause when you're presenting a key point and you want to repeat it.

- Pause if you want the audience to reflect on something.
- Pause when you're setting up a joke.
- Pause if you're listing several items and you want each to have dramatic impact.

Personalizing Your Presentation

If *anyone* can give your presentation, than it's not personal enough. Everything you present will be far more interesting if flavored by your own personality, experiences, and examples. Otherwise, your value, as a presenter, will likely be about as high as any other technician. What makes you the best presenter on your topic is *you*. The following tips remind you to make the most of your own personality and talent:

Everything you present will be far more interesting if flavored by your own personality, experiences, and examples.

- Be passionate about your topic.
- Use positive language; never use any vulgarity, profanity, racist or sexist remarks.
- Dress professionally, comfortably, culturally appropriate, and better than the general audiences.
- Hold the highest standard in personal grooming; offensive odor or smoker's breath is unacceptable.
- Observe protocol; loud voices or put-downs are unacceptable. Say something good or not at all.
- All accessories (jewelry, briefcases, handbags, etc.) should be classy, modest, and unobtrusive.
- Use portable phones and laptop computers tactfully, if at all, in social or group situations.
- Be polite and empathetic; practice civility and smile often.
- Answer questions straight; don't give run-on answers.
- Shake hands firmly and call people by name.
- Keep to your agreements and be honest.
- Listen to others carefully; be an active listener.
- Honor the culture of your audience with your gestures, habits, references, words, introductions, materials, and closings.

The Company You Keep

Know who the other leaders in your field are and associate with them. If your topic is brain research (like mine is) then you need to know the 50 or so top names in that field. Not only do I refer to them by name and institution, but I bring in samples of their books, newsletters, and notes I've taken from phone conversations with them. My credibility goes up because I have put myself in the company of the stars. One word of caution: if you're going to do "name-dropping," get your names, pronunciations, and facts straight. I have watched other presenters die a slow death in front of an audience when they've mispronounced a colleague's name or misrepresented their work.

Anchoring the Room

An anchor is a powerful stimulus-response mechanism. For example, you may get hungry just by wandering into a kitchen. Fast food companies entice you to hunger by the mere sight or sound of their logos and ads. Does the name "Pavlov" ring a bell? You can use this powerful tool in your course to increase understanding with your participants. Use a different personality or "hat" to emphasize different things in different quadrants of the room. For example, in smaller groups, have a large personal area or territory that is "approachable." Then have a smaller area that is your strong "credibility" spot. Go there when you need to give directions or make a serious point. In a larger group, it's reversed. Use the largest territory for your credibility voice, and a smaller area for your approachable voice. When your voice changes, the audience will feel more comfortable in raising their hands. You may also want to have a humor area or storytelling area. Four is probably the maximum amount of areas you'll want to "mark out" in your room.

As a presenter, you wear many hats including the expert hat, the disciplinarian hat, the friend hat, the storyteller hat, the coach hat, and the counselor hat.

As a presenter, you wear many hats including the expert hat, the disciplinarian hat, the friend hat, the storyteller hat, the coach hat, and the counselor hat. We all use a combination of non-verbal strategies—various voices, gestures, and "hats"—in our presentations. The important question is, "Are you systematically and purposefully using them?" Presenters who adjust their levels of authority systematically and consciously at the appropriate times, will be more effective. They will be heard, understood, and enjoyed more by their audience than those who don't; and your credibility will soar.

Purposeful communicators have fewer discipline problems and experience less stress and frustration. Why? They don't contaminate various areas of the room by mixing up the verbal and non-verbal messages. Mixed messages will create confusion among participants. Confusion means you will be perceived as incompetent. Your audience will also think of you as unfair if your voice and behavior are not consistent to the area of the room in which they are accustomed to seeing and hearing a specific instruction. For example, when you are telling a joke, go to a specific spot–your "joke corner"–and speak from there in a specific tonality and tempo. When you are getting unusually serious, go to another part of the room and speak from there. This strategy "anchors" the spot to what you are saying. You have created an association–a stimulus-response–with the location and type of message you are sending.

Over time, with repetition, you'll be able to simply walk to a part of the room to activate a desired reaction. Even if your jokes are bad, if you are systematic in going to your "joke-telling corner," you'll get more laughs than if you tell a joke from the same spot where you were lecturing earlier. The brain is triggered by location recall. Whatever happened in that area previously will flavor the current interaction.

Keeping Your Word

As a presenter, your integrity is a cornerstone of the relationship between you and your audience. Keeping your word, therefore, is essential. Confidentiality ought to be respected at all times. If you ever have to break a commitment, be honest about it and negotiate an alternative plan with the person/people involved. Start on time, and finish on time. Make sure your ending time matches the audience's expectations. "We're supposed to finish up at 3 p.m. Usually I run overtime, but today, I'll make sure we finish up by no later than 2:55 p.m. Is that a deal?" Be accountable. And acknowledge participants for keeping their word and participating with integrity, as well.

As a presenter, your integrity is a cornerstone of the relationship between you and your audience.

Summarize Often

People are more trusting when they know a presenter has thoroughly planned the learning process with a clear beginning, middle, and end. Therefore, make your plan explicit. Don't make the mistake of thinking the audience can read your mind. Though, you may have done this training so often you can do it with your eyes closed, don't forget, this is likely your participants first time through. Take the time, every hour or so, to re-orient the audience with what you've done so far, where you're at in the schedule, and what's next.

I call this the "you are here" update. If you've ever been to an unfamiliar shopping mall and stood in front of the store directory and map, you know the importance of the words "you are here" to orient yourself. This is a universally reassuring experience. Remember that the more often you orient and reassure your audience, the more likely they are to trust you.

Walking the Walk

Speaking of orienting your audience, let's take a moment right now to review the most important things to remember from this chapter thus far:

- You cannot enforce credibility; empower your audience and they will see you with trusting eyes.
- Use only professional quality materials and visuals.
- Organize your presentation with an obvious beginning, middle, and end; make your plan explicit.
- Incorporate your qualifications and credentials into your presentation.
- Be aware of how your body language impacts your message.
- Use a variety of voices in your presentation depending on the type of message you want to send.
- Develop your own style; add your personal touches, passions, and character to your presentation.
- Humanize your presentation; share other's success stories and your own personal examples.
- Stay informed in your field of expertise; subscribe to the industry newsletters, journals, etc.
- Exhibit a professional command of your subject area; refer to the other experts in the field.
- Be culturally sensitive; tailor-fit each presentation to the specific audience.
- Provide your audience with up-to-date and accurate content; cite your references.
- Be open to feedback and questions; create a safe environment for all participants.
- Involve the audience in their own learning; provide choice, flexibility, and respect.
- Acknowledge others who make your work and success possible.

The Accuracy Imperative

Research your data to ensure that you are providing information which is:

- ◆ Accurate
- ◆ Relevant
- ◆ Useful
- ◆ Up-to-date
- ◆ Consistent with the trends that are shaping society

Make sure you distinguish between opinion and fact; distinguish between personal experiences, what someone has told you about, and what you've read. Always quote your sources and give credit where credit is due. Better yet, provide a handout which lists your references and follow-up resources. This simple act will enhance your credibility tenfold.

At all costs, respect the emotional, physical, psychological, and spiritual states of your participants. Their beliefs, opinions, attitudes, and experiences are valid.

Earning Respect By Giving It

At all costs, respect the emotional, physical, psychological, and spiritual states of your participants. Their beliefs, opinions, attitudes, and experiences are valid. You may not agree with them, but to try to change their mind about something is risky. It is far better to lead a group into an experience which allows them to draw their own conclusions. If you will be facilitating an experience that may be out of some of the participants' comfort zones, build up to it slowly. Take intermediate steps, role-model desired behaviors and attitudes, and give them an out. Always make it clear that it is okay to "pass" on an activity if they don't feel comfortable with it. This is especially important when you are dealing with potentially emotional or very personal subject areas. Also, be sure to ask for group consensus if you wish to make changes to the agenda (i.e., breaks, lunch time, start or end times, etc.).

Handling Audience Questions

How you handle audience questions will powerfully influence your perceived credibility. Make sure that in the first half hour of your presentation you allow for some kind of interactions with the audience. Why? It's such an easy way to establish yourself as the expert. On the following page five simple guidelines are presented for answering questions in a way that boosts credibility.

Guidelines for Handling Audience Questions

1. Let the audience know in advance when they can ask questions.

2. Repeat all audience questions, if not word-for-word, then close enough that you are able to confirm the asker's intent.

3. Position yourself so that, spatially, most of the audience is between you and the speaker.

4. Look at the asker when you begin to answer and when you're finished. During the middle of your answer, glance at other audience members.

How you handle audience questions will powerfully influence your perceived credibility. Make sure that in the first half hour of your presentation you allow for some kind of interactions with the audience.

5. If you don't know the answer to the question, say so. But don't make a big deal out of it. Simply say, "I can't give this question the justice it deserves, but I'll do some digging and see if I can't recommend a resource for you." Or, "That's a good question and I don't know the answer to it." Or, "Sorry, this one's outside my expertise." There is no shame in not knowing the answer to a question. No one can know everything. If anything, answering honestly that you don't know the answer will give you some points in the credibility department.

Credibility can be achieved without implementing *all* of the suggestions in this chapter. To inspire credibility you don't have to do everything right and be the top authority on the subject, too. Many credible presenters are better at some things than others. You are human; you can expect some imperfection. This chapter does, however, represent an ideal to hold yourself up to.

Engage Your Brain:
Planning for High-Caliber Credibility

How will you incorporate your qualifications into the opening?

What body language habits do you have that are effective? Which ones do you want to change?

What voices do you currently use? Do you wish to expand your range? How might you go about this?

What is unique about you? How do you incorporate your individuality into your presentation?

SECTION THREE: Essential Sparks

CHAPTER 8

From Good Rapport to Raving Fans

Rapport is the mysterious "chemistry" that tells you if your audience identifies with you. More technically, it is a distinct physiological state of positive responsiveness. When a presenter has rapport with their audience, learning takes place effortlessly. Without it, frustration and ineffectiveness prevail. An audience does not, necessarily, need to *like* a presenter to be in rapport with them, but they do need to *feel* attended to. Responsiveness is optimized when a presenter shifts their frame of reference to match the participants—when you enter their world and see, hear, and feel things the way they do. When you've mastered the art of rapport, chances are you won't *wonder* whether your audience likes you or not, they *will be* your biggest fans.

Presenters who have achieved rapport with their participants have likely validated their feelings and enhanced their sense of importance either consciously or unconsciously. This ability is as paramount to a professional presenter as balance is to a tight-rope walker. Top-level trainers, like successful entertainers, have elevated rapport-building to an art form—able to achieve it with nearly anyone anytime! You, too, can master the techniques that make this possible. This chapter will show you how to captivate your audience from the start, and turn them into raving fans by the close. Read on if you're ready for this powerful result.

- *Calibrating Rapport*
- *Rapport Is Achieved By Matching Mind-Body States*
- *Establishing Group Rapport*
- *Personality Patterns*
- *Non-verbal Strategies*
- *Verbal Strategies*
- *Personal Acknowledgments*
- *Establishing Common Ground*

Brain Connection

Sensory Acuity Helps In Calibrating Rapport

The first step to mastering the art of rapport, is to develop a consistent awareness of when you are, or are not, in rapport. This awareness is called calibration, and it provides a means by which to gauge the impact of your actions on others. Highly developed sensory acuity helps in the calibration process as it is important to notice changes in skin color, movements of micro muscles, breathing, physiology, and posture as well as tonality, sensory predicates, tempo, pitch, and volume of vocal expression. The second step is developing flexibility and options for responding appropriately once you've calibrated the audience affect. Of course, calibrating the audience is not something that is done once and is then done. It is a process of "taking the temperature" of the group consistently throughout the training.

Rapport Is Achieved By Matching Mind-Body States

Rapport is not some intuitive, elusive, or magical state; it is a physiological response. Gaps between you and your audience can be closed by matching physiological states like breathing, posture, gestures, or physical proximity. Matching internal states like curiosity, apprehension, enjoyment, or satisfaction also influence rapport. While rapport may seem mysterious, on a biological level, it is simply achieved by matching mind-body states.

Rapport is not some intuitive, elusive, or magical state; it is a physiological response. Gaps between you and your audience can be closed by matching physiological states like breathing, posture, gestures, or physical proximity.

Establishing Group Rapport

There is a difference between building relationships with individuals and building relationships with groups. When your audience reaches a size beyond 10 or 15 people, it is no longer yours, but rather the "group's group." In other words, the group takes on it's own energy and culture. It is critical to pay attention to the group culture as it is being established. Who are the leaders in the group? What backgrounds are represented? What is the general mood? Why are you together? Before the group has cemented it own culture, you can influence it. But you'll never completely control the group, nor would you want to. A resentful group is a presenter's nightmare!

Here are some things you can do to develop relationships within the group. Be interested in your audience instead of trying to be an interesting presenter. Greet them at the door with a smile, handshake, or hug—whichever is appropriate. Give warm, sincere, and authentic greetings that convey real caring and interest in every participant. Continue these practices throughout the year. Being a caring and loving presenter will, above all, positively influence the group culture and lead to raving fans.

Personality Patterns

Audiences want to feel personally connected to the presenter. They want to know if you can appreciate their predicament or situation. Sometimes they just want acknowledgment for showing up. To ensure this happens (it does build rapport), you'll want to identify who is in your group right away. Your audience may all have requested, or even demanded, to attend. If so, you're either very lucky or very good. Most of the time, you'll have participants with a variety of motivations and intentions. They usually include the following personality types:

Know-It-Alls:

These participants think they don't need to attend because they already know everything. They think they've heard every theory, tried every strategy, and that it is mostly all bunk anyway. Say to the audience, "I know that many of you have had a great deal of experience in the area we're covering today; and, chances are, you are already doing just about all the right things. However, if you get some validation on what you're currently doing and pick up one or two good ideas, will this training be worth your time?"

Travelers:

These participants are at your presentation because they like novelty. They'll sign up to go anywhere or do anything different. They don't really want to be in your seminar, they just prefer it over the alternative. They may want a change of scenery or even to meet someone new. Say to the audience, "I know some of you are here just to check things out and enjoy life. You mostly want to have a good time, so I'm glad you came. We'll have fun today."

Give warm, sincere, and authentic greetings that convey real caring and interest in every participant. Being a caring and loving presenter will, above all, positively influence the group culture and lead to raving fans.

Prisoners:

These participants were sent to your presentation by someone else. They came against their will–kicking, scratching, and biting. They may be resentful or simply resigned. Generally, they'd rather be almost anywhere else than your talk. Don't take it personally. Say, "Every now and then it's someone else's idea that gets you to go somewhere. Who here fits this description? This means you're not responsible for coming today. Remember though, you are responsible for what you leave with."

Students of Learning:

These participants are the consummate learners. They're usually pretty focused, attentive, and eager to learn. They often arrive early and stay late. They take notes and lead discussions. They are the most likely participants to implement steps or take actions as a result of your presentation; however, be forewarned, some participants appear at first notice to be students of learning, but are actually disguised travelers primarily looking for a good time.

Whatever characters comprise your group, keep in mind that there's no win for you in always having an easy audience. You'll improve faster, become sharper, and get paid more if you become good at working with the difficult to reach participants–the prisoners, travelers and know-it-alls. This is when rapport-building skills really count. However, avoid prejudging even the so-called "worst" groups. Many times, they have turned out to be my favorite audiences. The most recalcitrant skeptics sometimes turn into the strongest zealots.

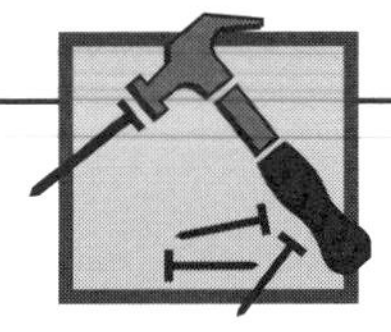

Non-Verbal Tips & Tools

Once you have begun presenting to a group, you'll realize there are a variety of personalities to contend with in building rapport. The following strategies will make a positive difference:

- From the very start, smile and show your audience you like them.
- Establish individual rapport with key persons before the session even begins officially.
- Once you are in session, identify the leaders in the group and start by establishing rapport with them.
- Match the breathing rate of the person with whom you're establishing rapport; watch for the rise and fall of their shoulders.
- Notice gestures such as a tapping foot, a flicking pencil, a rocking posture or similar methodical movement. Then begin your own gestures of a different type, using the identical tempo.
- Notice posture (i.e., relaxed, slumped, or upright), then match it exactly. Also notice if the legs are crossed or arms are folded and do the same.
- Match or mirror facial expressions along with eye movements and patterns.

How do you know when you have established rapport through non-verbal means? Two ways: First, become the leader instead of the follower and notice if the participant follows your behavior. For example, if you are tapping your foot to match a participant's pencil tap, quicken the pace and notice if the participant follows suit. If so, you have established strong non-verbal rapport. If not, try another method, or do the same one a bit longer or differently. At it's simplest, if the audience is responsive to your presentation, than you have successfully established rapport.

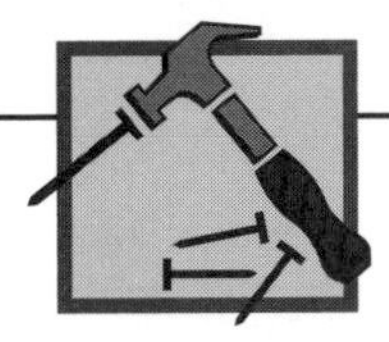

Verbal Tips & Tools

As you incorporate verbal rapport strategies into your presentations, consider both content and style. Content is meaning and word selection. Style is how the content is expressed.

Content

- Be happy to see your audience. Tell them, "I'm glad you're here. It's great to see you."
- Use the same words as your audience. For example, if a participant uses superlatives like "cool" or "great," you'll build rapport by using these same adjectives.
- Use an appropriate metaphor; for example, when talking to mechanics, relate to things mechanically. When talking to rural groups, use nature metaphors.
- Use matching predicates (i.e., visual, auditory, or kinesthetic). For example, if the learner says "I see," then use visual predicates like "that looks good" in your conversations with them. Audiences tend to favor certain predicates which relate to the physiological state they're in (how they are at the moment) or their primary representational system (favored thinking style: pictures, words or feelings). Occasionally, you'll encounter a participant who represents their world by taste (gustatory) or by smell (olfactory) or digitally (no preferred sense).

Participants in a visual mode will often say, "I see what you mean. The picture is clear to me now." (note references to visual mode: see, picture, clear.) Participants in an auditory mode will often say, "Listen, this sounds good to me." (note auditory references: listen, sounds.) Participants in a kinesthetic mode may say, "I feel like I'm up against a wall. This is rough!" (note kinesthetic references: feel, up against, rough.) Someone in a gustatory or olfactory mode may say, "That's a tasty idea. Here's a yummy solution to what could have been sour grapes." (note references: tasty, yummy, sour.) Participants in a digital mode use unspecified predicates such as: "From what I know, this makes sense to me. I believe it's a reasonable, thought-out solution." (note generalized references: know, sense, reasonable, thought-out)

If a participant says, "I'm feeling stuck," you might reply, "relax and let's try to get a handle on it." Or, if a participant says, "This doesn't ring a bell at all. I can't tell what it says." You might reply, "You sound as if you're not quite tuned into this. Here's something that may click for you." These simple replies impact the participant in a subtle but important rapport-building way.

- Listen to the pace, tempo, and rate of delivery. If it's fast, then you can gain rapport by also speaking quickly.
- Listen for the tonality, intonation, and range. Is it treble, nasal, bass, gruff, whining, sing-song, or monotone?
- Listen for volume variances and speak at approximately the same level of volume.

Personal Acknowledgments

Acknowledging your audience is an excellent way to build rapport. Audiences give their time and attention and deserve to be acknowledged and appreciated. Few presenters do this, and those who do, often give a perfunctory "thanks" to the audience. Say it with your heart while being congruent with your body. An acknowledgment may simply be, "Good morning, and thank you for being here. I appreciate your time and attention and plan to make today worthwhile." This is critical: Be sure to sincerely acknowledge your audience every single time. It is truly a privilege to learn and grow together.

Acknowledging your audience is an excellent way to build rapport. Audiences give their time and attention and deserve to be acknowledged and appreciated.

When audiences feel close to you, they are more likely to like you and be in good rapport with you. The following are some ways to increase closeness with your audience:

- Observations ("Beautiful briefcase.")
- Opinions and beliefs ("This cold is terrible!")
- Information sharing ("An article I read in *Newsweek* last month referred to...")
- Feelings ("I feel very nervous about ...")
- Dreams, goals, needs, wishes ("Someday I'd like to write the Great American Novel.")
- Activities (disclose something personal: hobbies, pets, trips, interests, shopping, concerts or recent learning.)
- Relate your life to the particular group (i.e., In a literary group, talk about your own writing; in a sports group, talk about your own fitness program, etc.)
- Relate something relevant about your past. (i.e., Tell a story about your fear of presenting when you first started—if it's true.)
- Relationship sharing (Talk about important people in your life—those who have influenced you the most, and why.)
- Ask what's going on in your participants lives.

Establishing Common Ground

Common ground refers to information that is stable and shared between you and participants. It is a fancy word for "what we have already acknowledged as true." Establishing common ground in a group situation creates rapport because it provides the audience with a sense of sameness and comfort about you as a person. After an epic event such as an election, a moon walk, or a catastrophe, for example, people experience a bond of commonality that assumes they had the same experience; thus, a common base of communication forms. You don't have to be alike, necessarily, to share a bond; perhaps, you merely see one thing the same, like you both dislike chocolate, or you're also a Capricorn, or the ocean is your sanctuary, too. The more people can identify with you as a person with flaws and imperfections, identifiable characteristics, and personality traits, the more they are likely to trust you.

The relationship you develop with your audience is the single most important thing you do to encourage learning. A power approach—using manipulation and threats to control a group—will most certainly backfire and reduce rapport. An empowered approach, on the other hand—influencing through the positive favorable relationships you have developed—creates an atmosphere of respect and motivation. Rapport is, indeed, a tell-tale sign that mirrors back to you your effectiveness as a trainer—that is, if you're willing to look.

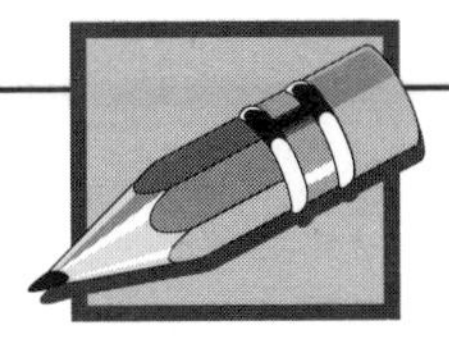

Engage Your Brain:
Planning for Raving Fans

How have you gone about building rapport with participants in the past? What verbal and non-verbal strategies have you successfully used?

What do you have in common with your audience? How might you make your similarities known?

What activities have you planned to help you and your audience get to know each other?

How might you incorporate personal acknowledgments into your next presentation? How will you make the audience feel important and validated?

Long-lasting learning is generated by going "internal." We can take information in better when it's not forced on us by an outsider, and when we can process it in our own way.

–Eric Jensen

Introduction to Brain-Compatible Learning

CHAPTER 9

Balancing Attention and Down Time

Many presenters pursue their audience's attention as if it were the Holy Grail. Even star presenters—those who earn the big bucks—often hold their audience's attention captive for hours at the expense of learning. They don't realize that the human brain is not designed for continuous focus. Even a two-hour movie has highs and lows built into it (and commercial breaks). The most effective presenters seek participants attention only at critical times. This chapter explains how to make the most of the brain's up and down times in the course of a brain-friendly presentation.

Biologically, we are designed to maintain focused attention for only short snippets of time. From an anthropological perspective, our survival would be at risk were we to focus too long on any one person or thing. To remain safe from predators, humans had to be able to shift their attention rapidly. We still have predators today–they've just changed forms. We have responsibilities, demands, and other people who also need our time and energy. Current brain research tells us that our brain is quite busy even when our attention is not narrowly focused. Known as down time, the human brain requires this non-focused reflection time to process information for meaning-making, organization, and future recall. Learning does not occur without it.

Since, it is natural for the human brain to move through cycles of high-low energy, input-output, and absorption-processing times, we need to organize our presentations so that participants do not experience conflict with their biological needs. This is the first step. The second step is understanding when it is most important to have your participants' attention, and how to maximize attention at these times. And the third step is knowing how to facilitate the effective use of audience down time.

Key Topics

- *Attentional Biases Drive the Brain's Focus Patterns*
- *Critical Times to Get Attention*
- *Four Principles That Impact Attention*
- *Attention-Getting Openers*
- *Establishing Rituals*
- *Tried and True Presentation Rituals*
- *Attention Impacters*
- *Strategies for Engaging Participants*
- *Sharing Your Vision*
- *Reasons for Down Time*
- *How Much Down Time Is Enough?*
- *Suggested Down Time Activities*
- *Time for a Change in Thinking*

Brain Connection

Attentional Biases Drive the Brain's Focus Patterns

Our brain has three attentional biases, say researchers: 1) The novelty of high contrast (anything out of the ordinary); 2) The bias for pleasure ("New miracle solution for lethargy and depression; details tonight at 11 p.m."); and 3) The bias of threat—possibility or avoidance of harm ("Your money or your life; hand it over.") When you utilize these biases to maintain attention, your efforts will be rewarded by better audience focus. However, the brain also requires brain-breaks every 15 to 20 minutes, so engage and release attention accordingly.

When to Get Attention

The five critical times to seek attention, as a presenter, are (1) when you're opening, (2) when you're closing, (3) when you're giving directions, (4) when you're addressing safety procedures, and (5) when you're making a key point. These are the times to use your highest-level creativity for gaining audience focus. However, remember that if you don't give participants time to process and reflect on what you've presented every 10 to 20 minutes, they will take it anyway. Whether you facilitate optimal utilization of down time or they take it by "daydreaming" or talking at inopportune times, it is statistically improbable that your audience will stay attentive 100 percent of the time. So let's work with the brain rather than against it. When it's time to have your audience's attention, keep the following four principles in mind:

Whether you facilitate optimal utilization of down time or they take it by "daydreaming" or talking at inopportune times, it is statistically improbable that your audience will stay attentive 100 percent of the time.

How to Get Attention

1. Provide Contrast

Offer information that is different or a change from the existing status quo. Examples include, topics that are beyond the norm, taboo, opposite of standard, etc. (i.e., "How To Lose Weight Without Trying," rather than, "Shed 10 Lbs. In 10 Days.").

2. Provide Novelty

Evoke states of curiosity, interest, suspense, awe, surprise, ah-ha! Examples include, a dramatic pause, an unusual prop, or an interesting piece of music.

3. Provide Pleasure

Evoke states of anticipation, hope, security, fun, acceptance, and satisfaction. Examples include, a smile, a cartoon, a friendly greeting, or a joke.

4. Avoid Harm

Offer ways to avoid states of anxiety, worry, fear, ridicule, and hurt. Example: the promise of a benefit to be gained by listening to your talk (i.e., "After taking this seminar, you'll master all fear of public speaking.").

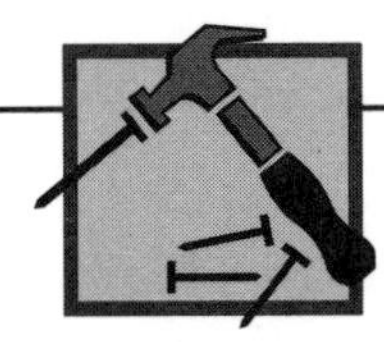

Attention-Getting Tips & Tools

- Be introduced by someone else, or by an audiotape, or video.
- Hold up your finger to your lips vertically.
- Put on a special hat.
- Do a charade, mime, or magic trick.
- Say, "my next statement will dramatically affect your day."
- Give a coded message.
- Use puppets.
- Announce some good news.
- Hold up an unusual object or picture.
- Conduct a science experiment.
- Use unusual lighting.
- Use music or other fanfare.
- Facilitate a round of applause.
- Make a strong statement.
- Thank the audience.
- Elicit audience curiosity with a question.
- Play an instrument or use a whistle or gong.
- Show a powerful video excerpt.
- Get into a strange position.
- Speak from an unexpected location in the room.
- Use a rhythmic clap.
- Use physical engagement: Ask everyone to change seats with the person next to them.
- Activate with novelty–an unusual costume, voice, or action.
- Ask participants to give partner-to-partner affirmations: "Turn to the person nearest you and welcome them with a smile!"
- Create fun group slogans. Train everyone to say something on cue that pulls the whole group together like, "Learning is fun!"
- Offer a powerful metaphor that encapsulates your message in a few words.
- Play a game of "Simon Says" with the audience.
- Share a brief story about something that relates to your topic.
- Use "loops" or incomplete actions or words that act as cliffhangers to hold attention. For example, you might say, "There are three reasons why you might be interested in this topic. The second reason is... and the third reason is..." Save the first reason for a few minutes to pique their curiosity.
- Provide immediate WIIFM- "What's In It For Me?
- Gather information: ask the audience what city they're from, business, or organization.
- Open with three key words you'd like the audience to remember... and they will!
- Create and activate a "start-up" tradition or ritual that is repeated on cue.

Establishing Rituals

Rituals are events that happen predictably: weddings, birthdays, graduations, funerals, celebrations, a favorite TV show, a vacation, or Friday night date night. Usually ritual follows an expected pattern of events. For example, action A triggers action B. When I raise both arms above my head, you stand and shout "yes." When several rituals are grouped together, you have a routine. Your morning ritual or routine, for example, might be to get up and shower, have a cup of coffee or orange juice, eat a bowl of cereal, read the newspaper, then finish getting dressed, and head off to work. It happens every day and is quite predictable.

Rituals emerge quite naturally in many trainings or seminars; however, when you consciously and purposely facilitate rituals, you can maximize their positive effects.

In the context of learning, a ritual is a predictable event based on the preceding event. In the course of a 6-hour learning day, 3 to 10 rituals ought to be incorporated. These can provide a sense of anticipation (an opening ritual), a sense of celebration (when tasks are accomplished), or a sense of closure (at the end of a day). Rituals emerge quite naturally in many trainings or seminars; however, when you consciously and purposely facilitate rituals, you can maximize their positive effects. The following are rituals with which I have had success:

Tried and True Presentation Rituals

- For a multiple-day course, start each day with the same song.
- Open each day with the same introduction like "Goooo-oood Morning! Welcome to..."
- Facilitate a "Yes" clap at the end of each 90-minute segment preceding a break.
- Encourage high-fives after a paired or group pair-share activity.
- Use audience-generated affirmations: "Turn to the person nearest you and say, 'Great job!'"
- Use a real "round of applause" (hands moving in a circle while applauding) to celebrate a contribution.
- Each attendee gets introduced with the same triple clap and "whooosh" motion.
- Offer a welcome-back-from-lunch joke.
- Facilitate a celebration at the end of the day.

Once you've established a ritual for getting the group started, a nonverbal cue is often sufficient to signal that it's time for the group to begin. Then, when the group is fully attentive, use a verbal opener. It is important to keep in mind that your opening words carry a lasting impact and influence on the flavor of the session, so choose your words well. This magic moment is open to immense creativity, surprise, and results. Plus, it's also a great way to set the tone for the rest of the day.

Personally, I like to open my presentations with an upbeat theme song from a hit movie. A movie production company has already spent millions of dollars creating a favorable impression with the public, so why not take advantage of it? Make eye contact with the audience and do any of the following: begin clapping, raise your hand, hold up an interesting object, motion towards the clock, stand fully straight and attentive, open your mouth and pause, have a participant get the attention of others for you, move to the center of the room, stand in a designated spot or an unusual spot, or look anxious and ready to start.

Rituals break up monotony, wake the brain, reinforce group cooperation, and provide affirmation and/or a positive state changes. As you increase your arsenal of attention-getting strategies, remember that what gets the brain's attention is contrast and novelty. Anything that's different from what you're doing at that moment will probably command attention. Also, the promise of pleasure or threat of pain (or loss) will focus participants. That is, unless the strategy has been used so often that it violates the first rule and loses its novelty. There are, of course, countless ways to get attention, and I've only mentioned a small sampling. You have to find the ones that work for you.

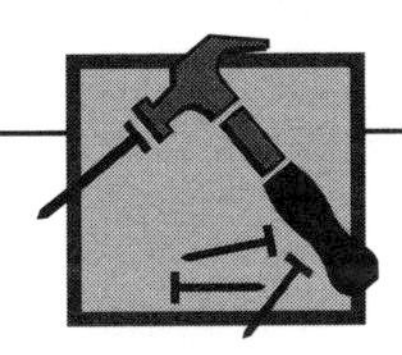

Attention Tips & Tools

- Movement
- Contrasting Sounds
- Aromas
- Increase in Catacholamines: Caffeine, Noradrenaline, Chocolate, Moderate Serotonin
- Intense Color
- Touch
- Changes in Brain Chemistry
- Emotional Content
- States of Joy, Fear, Surprise, Disgust, Anger, and Sadness

Produces <u>More</u> Attention	Produces <u>Less</u> Attention
Choice	Required
Content and Process	Content Only
Focus on Environment	Directed Activity
Utilization of Resources	Restricted Resources
Relevant	Irrelevant
Personal and Meaningful	Impersonal and Disconnected
Aligned With Participant Goals	Out of Context
Engaging	Passive
Emotionally Charged	Apathetic
Physical Activity	Sedentary Activity

Strategies for Engaging Participants

- Welcome and greet arrivees by name at the front door if possible.
- Shake their hands, be warm, and smile.
- Use positive body language and create positive expectancy.
- Acknowledge the audience for their time and attention.
- Solve an immediate problem they face (getting materials, finding parking, lunch, name tags, units of credit, something to write with, etc.).
- Give genuine compliments.
- Acknowledge participants for their commitment and reassure them of their value.
- Avoid giving long lists; break items into clusters of three or four and present them throughout the day.
- Wear a crazy costume like that of a literary character, a scientist, an inventor, or even a neighborhood character.
- Make a hot news announcement which can be authentic or made up.
- Incorporate real-life problems that directly relate to the audience.
- Employ special visuals, such as a large sign of something funny, mind-boggling, or poignant.
- Bring up participants—two or three at a time—and have them introduce themselves.
- Try out an unusual stage design, lighting, or backdrop.
- Innovate with wild decorations—flowers, plants, or ribbons.
- Immerse the room in powerful visuals—posters, props, or peripherals.
- Create a special event like an auction or announcement.
- Use unusually colored overheads or ones with cartoons.
- Take advantage of special CDs or tapes of movie themes: find out which movies are "hot" at the moment and use these.
- Announce novel ground rules that make your program unique like, "not listening to the presenter for the first two minutes."
- Make an unusual request, like write your name with your non-dominant hand.
- Ask participants to name what their expectations and goals are for the session.
- Ask participants to brainstorm goals: (1) verbally, (2) on paper, or (3) as a group.
- Put "stakes" in the presentation; elicit perceived or possible benefits and costs of not participating.
- Preview entire course at high-speed; pre-expose audience to topics using all the overheads and background music you'll be incorporating throughout the day.
- Take a survey: "How many of you had to travel more than one hour to get here? How many of you are here due to someone else's mandate?"
- Use brain activators like cross-lateral movements.
- Use positive learning suggestions; suggest that they'll absorb, enjoy, and use the material.
- Repeat a compelling quote that summarizes your whole presentation.
- Credibility: provide an unusual example that reflects your unique qualities as a presenter.
- Handle audience concerns: the schedule, parking, meals, bathrooms, and breaks.
- Hook your audience with a strong statement that evokes interest and challenge.

Sharing Your Vision

Share your vision with passion. Let others know what makes you tick and what your own dreams are. If you don't have a vision, discover or create one. A vision is basically your dream, or what your concept of the world would be like if everyone cared as you do. By sharing your vision *and* eliciting your participants' visions for their own lives, you do more than gain attention; You make your training fulfilling, purposeful and meaningful. It can be what enriches and puts joy in one's day. Shared visions can help create personal meaning, credibility, and a high standard for the day. Vision can change how the audience listens to the rest of what you say, too. After all, tasks without vision are drudgery; vision without tasks, but a dream. Both are necessary to the process.

Reasons for Down Time

There are, at least, three reasons why you must provide your audience with down time. For one, much of what we learn is unconscious; it happens too fast to process consciously. To understand it on a deeper level, therefore, we need time to reflect on it. We take in so much material visually (up to 36,000 images per hour) that in order to figure out what to do next, the learner must "go internal" and give up "external" attention. The brain continues to process information before and long after we are aware that we are doing it. As a result, many of our best ideas seem to "come to us from out of the blue."

Two, in order to really learn something, we need to create new meaning from it. Humans are natural meaning-seeking organisms. Since meaning is generated internally, external input conflicts with the possibility that learners can turn what they have just learned into something meaningful. That's why you can either have your learner's attention or they can be making meaning, but never both at the same time.

And three, after each new learning experience, we need time for the learning to "imprint." Research suggests that periods of purposeful down time, as an "incubation for learning" is the ideal. It may be down time, in fact, that's most important for new information processing. Learning can become more functional when external stimuli is shut down and the brain can link it to other associations, uses, and procedures. "This association and consolidation process can only occur during down time," says Harvard professor Alan Hobson. This elucidates the importance of allowing ten minutes of time or so for reflection after new learning. Writing in journals or discussing the new learning in small groups makes good sense for the brain.

Research suggests that periods of purposeful down time, as an "incubation for learning" is the ideal. Learning can become more functional when external stimuli is shut down and the brain can link it to other associations, uses, and procedures.

How Much Down Time Is Enough?

The amount of down time needed by your attendees varies. The more complex, challenging, or novel the information, the more down time is needed. The following general guidelines are applicable:

New Learners, Tough Material:

- 3 to 5 minutes of down time per 20 minutes of content; or 10 minutes of down time per 45 minutes of content.

Experienced Learners, Familiar Material:

- 1 to 2 minutes of down time per 20 minutes of content; or 5 minutes of down time per 40 minutes of content.

What's good for learning is simple: Seek your audience's attention sparingly and give them time to process.

Cramming more content per minute or moving from one piece of learning to the next quickly, virtually guarantees that little will be learned or retained.

Suggested Down Time Activities

- Journal writing.
- Leave the room for coffee or soda breaks.
- Note-taking time.
- Small group work with loose agenda.
- Lunch break.
- Video review.
- Listen to calming music.
- Afternoon break.
- Stand and stretch for a minute.
- Choice or flex time to choose an activity.
- Reflection time.
- On a multiple-day course, let the group out early to choose a reflection activity of their own.

Time for a Change of Thinking

The days are gone of the "hot shot" presenter who talks non-stop for hour after hour and thinks it's a good presentation. It's only good if you're hired to entertain and mesmerize. If you're hired to make a difference in people's lives, to inspire them, help them learn new things, and to apply that learning, you can't talk at people for hours on end. This is not how you maximize learning. What's good for learning is simple: Seek your audience's attention sparingly and give them time to process.

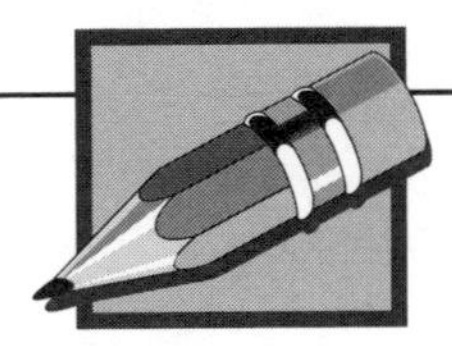

Engage Your Brain:
Planning for Attention and Down Time

How can you shorten the required attention time of your audience in your next presentation?

At what places in your presentation will you break for intermittent down time?

What down time choices will you provide participants?

What attention-getting strategies do you anticipate using at critical times?

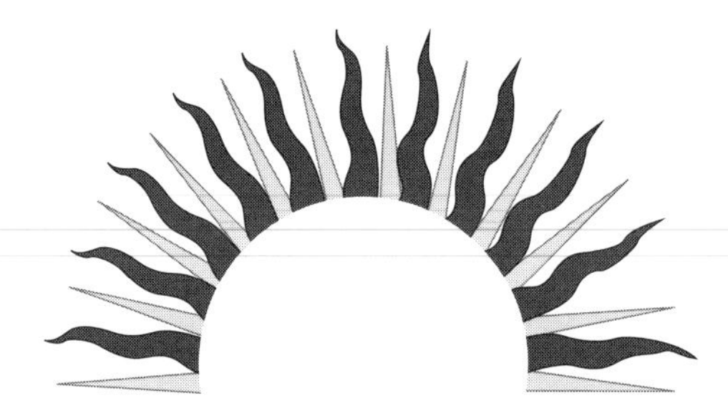

Happiness comes only when we push our brains and hearts to the farthest reaches of which we are capable.

–Leo Rosten

CHAPTER 10

Combustible Motivation

Close your eyes for a moment and consider what it would be like to have an audience that responded to your seminar with such enthusiasm that *they* appeared to be sizzling in their seats. Now close your eyes again and consider how it would be to have an audience like this *every time* you presented. This vision is *not* unrealistic. Rather, such combustible motivation is the *norm* in trainings where the primary barriers to participation—threat and high stress—have been eliminated. Though a moderate amount of controllable stress is good for learning, research has shown that lasting stress or threat shifts the brain into survival mode. In survival mode we are less capable of receiving and classifying information: Our pattern-detection, judgment, creativity, and problem-solving skills end up on the back burner while we deal with the more immediate and compelling survival needs. Thus, to achieve maximum potency in our presentations, we must make our training environments emotionally safe.

Naturally, what is threatening to one participant may not be to another. Since it is impossible to know the specific situations that trigger each participant's survival modes, it is best to error on the side of caution. Therefore, the following training conditions ought to be minimized if not eliminated completely: harsh opinions or criticism, evaluations or tests, having to perform publicly, a lack of resources, unrealistic deadlines, physical barriers, awkward groupings, potential failure, potential embarrassment, language barriers, uncomfortable room arrangements, and poor temperature control.

- *The Brain's Priority Is Survival*
- *Avoid Information Overload*
- *Identify the Group Culture*
- *Relevant Icebreakers and Low-Risk Activities*
- *Explicit Ground Rules*
- *Use Positive Rituals*
- *Emphasize Course Purpose*
- *Introduce Newcomers*
- *Handle Housekeeping Details*
- *Share Some of Yourself*
- *Certainty Affirmations*
- *Establish a Starting Point*
- *De-Mystify Vocabulary*

Brain Connection

The Brain's Priority Is Survival

A significant part of your brain will ensure that you learn, react, and adapt primarily for survival. The brain stem is the part of the brain that directs your behavior under negative stress and is the most responsive to any threat. When threat is perceived, excessive cortisol is released into the body causing higher-order thinking skills to take a backseat to automatic functions that may help you survive. Computer generated images show very clearly that under threat, excess anxiety, moderate negative stress, and induced learner helplessness, the brain reacts with increased blood flow and electrical activity in the brain stem and cerebellum area and decreased activity in the mid-brain and neocortex. These physiological changes cause more predictable, rote, knee-jerk reactions. Survival always overrides pattern detection and problem solving. This fact has tremendous implications for trainers.

To encourage motivation, participation, and active learning, reduce the risk of threat in the environment. Typically, threat can be broken down into three forms: 1) physical harm (or threat of); 2) intellectual injury (feeling helpless, stressed for time, overchallenged, underprepared, lacking resources or skills, or ignored); and 3) emotional injury (embarrassed, humiliated, disciplined publicly, or made an example of). Studies suggest that under any type of perceived threat, the brain reacts in one or more of the following ways:

- Loses its ability to take in subtle clues from the environment
- Reverts to the familiar "tried and true" behaviors
- Loses some of its ability to index, store, and access material
- Becomes more automatic and limited
- Loses some of its ability to perceive relationships and patterns
- Is less likely to exhibit higher-order thinking skills
- Loses some episodic/contextual memory capacity
- Tends to over-react to stimuli - in an almost phobic way

Studies confirm that low and moderate learning stress produces resilient learners and is better than no stress at all. The difficulty for presenters is that what is stressful or threatening to one learner may be harmless to another.

So, what's the ideal for learning? Studies confirm that low and moderate learning stress produces resilient learners and is better than no stress at all. The difficulty for presenters is that what is stressful or threatening to one learner may be harmless to another. Nevertheless, the best trainers have always found ways to produce low-threat environments. And their techniques are not surprising. The following strategies may sound like common sense but we now have biological evidence that reinforces the importance of them in the training environment:

- Never ask a participant to speak unless they volunteer or have been given time to prepare.
- Never mock or embarrass a participant, even if they made a frustrating mistake (like forgetting something).
- Never mock a culture, a language, a race, a lifestyle, or the way someone is dressed.
- Make sure everyone has access to clear instructions in a language they can understand.
- Avoid using judgment labels or stereotypes (i.e., slow learner, lazy, blond, air-head, etc.).
- Use words like "please" and "thank you," as well as, "I'm sorry."
- Ensure that all participants have the necessary equipment (including paper and pencil) and access to resources.
- Ensure that everyone has understood the directions and assignments given by repeating them and posting them.

Avoid Information Overload

To increase the likelihood that the audience will engage in your presentation, avoid too much information. Why? People want value and meaning, not information. People want to connect with others and have fun. Their lives are already full of faxes, modems, pagers, e-mail, phone calls, web sites, mandatory meetings, handouts, junk mail, and more meetings. Give them a break! Present a small bit of data, then let them process it. They can do this in small groups, pairs, or as a large group. Do not talk more than 10 to 15 minutes without facilitating some kind of audience interaction. Put yourself in their shoes and you'll realize that you don't need to overwhelm them with facts. Quite simply, make your presentation relevant and engaging and build in processing time.

Identify the Group Culture

Every group over time establishes its own culture or set of expectations (spoken or unspoken). You, the presenter, will be perceived as either fitting into their group culture or not. As the presenter or leader, you will probably influence the norms early on; however, at some point a departure is usually made between audience and presenter. At this time they will decide whether you understand or represent them adequately enough that they can relax and fully participate. Instinctually, their question will be, "How well does this 'leader' represent us; can we trust him/her?" Knowing this dynamic exists in all groups, you can supersede it by being prepared for it and working within the framework the group ordains. As if you are preparing for an interview, ask yourself the questions the audience will likely ask.

Every group over time establishes its own culture or set of expectations. Knowing this dynamic exists in all groups, you can supersede it by being prepared for it and working within the framework the group ordains.

In gearing your presentation for the group culture represented, be clear that what's appropriate for one profession, gender, geographic region, background, experience level, or education level may be very different than that of another. A presentation that is appropriate for teachers, for example, may not be appropriate for business executives. A topic geared to factory workers is likely to be very different than the same topic presented to design engineers. Customer service reps will probably want a different timetable and agenda than middle management. A seminar designed to motivate an all-male sales force will probably look very different than a seminar meant to motivate a group of female health workers. You will also likely find an enormous difference between geographic areas represented. For example, a group that consists primarily of Northern Europeans will respond and participate quite differently than a group of primarily Southern Europeans. The level of interactive engagement you get from a group of mostly African-Americans will likely be much higher than the engagement you get with a group of mostly Asians. Anticipating these differences and gearing your presentation accordingly will ensure the highest level of audience comfort, trust, and participation.

Relevant Icebreakers and Low-Risk Activities

Icebreakers encourage involvement because they allow the audience to participate without feeling threatened. Rule number one about icebreakers is, they must require little or no risk to the audience. Rule number two, they must serve a genuine purpose.

Icebreakers encourage involvement because they allow the audience to participate without feeling threatened. Books for trainers devoted entirely to icebreakers are on the market but most of them are a waste of time. Too often the activities suggested are unrelated and irrelevant to your specific training. Today's sophisticated participants don't want to invest any time at all on a silly game that asks them to figure out the name of a movie star written on scratch paper and taped to their back. Make your icebreakers relevant and short. And never insult your audience. It takes too long to win back their trust. Rule number one about icebreakers is, they must require little or no risk to the audience. Rule number two, they must serve a genuine purpose. If you can't explain why you're doing something (besides using it as a mixer), you probably need to find a more relevant alternative.

In seeking high levels of participation, start out with very low-risk activities and simple interactions and slowly engage participants over the course of the training in more complex and higher-risk exercises or questions that require an explanation. To start, ask simple close-ended questions like the following examples:

- Who is here from out of town?
- Who has been in this field for 10 or more years?
- Who thinks yes?
- Who says no?
- Who says, "I don't care?"
- Who came here because it was required of them to come?

Another simple, low-risk activity to edge your participants into higher-level involvement is to have them design a nametag. Provide them with colored pens, stickers, etc. to inspire their creativity. You can ask them to include three descriptors or adjectives to describe themselves (i.e., computer-whiz, mountain climber, class clown). A twist on this task is to ask them to write their name on the front of their workbook using their non-dominant hand. This activity usually brings out the kid in people and inspires a laugh. Other warm-up activities to inspire participation follow:

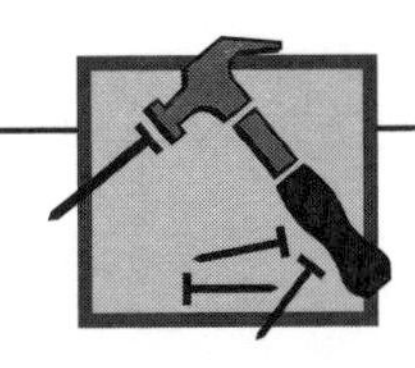

Warm-up Tips & Tools

Introductions

Ask participants to introduce themselves. There are various ways to facilitate this. You can have them expound on their nametag descriptors. You can have them do a mind-map and share it with the group. Give participants a few minutes to learn as much as they can about another participant and then switch. Participants can come up in a group and introduce themselves (this is much less threatening than coming up alone). Or you can go around the room and ask each person to say where they work, what they do, and something they're passionate about. However you approach it, introductions are a key element in getting participants to relax and open up to the group process.

Team Goals

Have pairs or teams create goals for themselves and design a chart to track their progress. Have them share their work with the larger group.

Transition Time

Provide transition activities that prepare the mind, body, and soul for learning. When you look out at your audience, do you see them as individuals for whom getting there might have been stressful or challenging? The complex web of circumstances we face as individuals with competing priorities and commitments makes essential some kind of transition process that puts everyone on even ground. Transition activities attempt to neutralize that stress, create a cohesive purposeful environment, and open up the mind and body for the learning at hand. Transition activities can be anything from a guided visualization to a time for "checking-in."

Physical Activity and Movement

Anytime you facilitate a movement activity, you are embedding learning on a cellular level. Physical activity can also lessen stress and alter mind-states. Stretching or walking are non-threatening ways to increase vitality and wake up the brain. Physical activity can be done in small groups to make it more manageable. Have the small groups choose their own leader. An activity I frequently incorporate in my trainings is pair-walks. Everyone finds a partner and takes a five minute walk outside (if weather permits). I sometimes assign a topic, and other times allow participants to choose one. Another basic movement activity is to ask participants to switch seats with the person next to them.

Small-Group Discussions

Giving participants the opportunity to talk with their peers about the material is highly productive. This allows them to involve more senses, to discuss things that are bothering them, or to get clarification or ask questions in a non-threatening atmosphere.

Journal-Writing Time

This activity can be conducted either formally or informally with either an assigned topic or not. After a few minutes of writing, some participants may want to share what they wrote or what the experience was like for them. This is optional. A variation on this strategy is to create an activity that participants can do at the door on the way in. It could include having participants write down on a piece of paper any negative feeling or problem they may be experiencing, then throw it in the trash.

Continued...

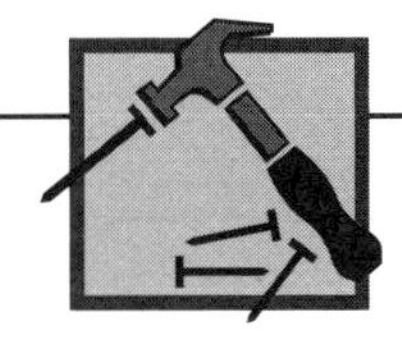

Warm-up Tips & Tools

Continued...

Apprentice Time

Ask participants to write an area of personal expertise on their nametag. People like to exhibit and talk about what they know most. If a portion of the group needs to be "brought up to speed" in a skill or content area, pair up participants accordingly.

Case Studies

Use scenarios from real life experiences—case law, business scenarios, or a simple customer service interaction. This provides the group with an opportunity to analyze motives, behaviors, values, actions, and consequences. The learning can be quite valuable if the discussion is facilitated by an experienced leader.

Fishbowl

Have participants form a smaller circle within a larger circle with their chairs. The inner circle discusses an issue and the outer circle listens and observes. Afterwards, the outer circle discusses what they observed and asks questions of the inner circle. The roles are rotated so that everyone experiences both the inner and outer circle.

Focus Sessions

A small group is asked to evaluate something. Often used by business enterprises to judge the reaction and/or reception of a new product or proposed change with a sample group. Focus groups work best with a covert leader who helps direct the communication and maintain the focus of the group.

Childhood Games

Many childhood games can be adapted to adult audiences with great success. Most everyone knows how to play them, so you don't have to spend a great deal of time on instructions. They are low risk because everyone knows what to expect. Some of the games that I use are: musical chairs, ball toss, bingo, quiz shows, and horseshoes. The secret to getting audience buy-in is to incorporate your topic area, create a clear and relevant purpose, and then make that purpose explicit. I have seen conservative, "case-hardened" audiences truly enjoy a childhood game when approached this way.

Jigsaw Groupings

Teams with a team leader are each seated in a separate area of the room. They are asked to brainstorm a topic and to record the ideas on paper. After the time limit is reached, the team members move to a new group of their choice, but the leader stays put. The new teams are then asked to add to the list the leader has maintained. Eventually everyone returns to their original team to re-examine their improved lists and to refine the ideas even further.

Polling

Ask for an "in-house poll" on a topic; this can be done using any or all of the following modalities:

- Verbally— by saying yes or no
- Kinesthetically—with a show of hands or standing/sitting.
- In Writing—by ballot or questionnaire; then share the results with the group.

Explicit Ground Rules

In any situation—whether playing a sport, a board game, or problem solving in a group—people aren't likely to willingly participate until they understand the rules. If you want your audience to participate, you need to let them in on the ground rules first. Can they talk during the presentation, go to the bathroom, or sit in a different seat after the break? What happens if they're late, forget their notebook, or have a concern? What about cell phones, pagers, dress standards? Everyone brings their own set of expectations into a learning situation and the more you handle them head on, the fewer problems you'll have later.

In my workshops, I call the ground rules "guidelines" or "ten ways to succeed in the course." Instead of reading the guidelines to the audience or putting them in a workbook where they may go unread, I ask participants to read them to each other. The directions go like this: "Please stand up, find a partner and decide who is odd and who is even. Odd numbers read odd numbered guidelines, and even numbers read even numbered guidelines." Then to make it more interesting, I add a twist: "Read them with as much enthusiasm as you can muster." Or, "Use a made-up accent. When you're done, have a seat." Involving the audience in this small way makes otherwise boring material enjoyable.

In any situation—whether playing a sport, a board game, or problem solving in a group—people aren't likely to willingly participate until they understand the rules. If you want your audience to participate, you need to let them in on the ground rules first.

Also consider whether you want participants to be involved in choosing the rules or guidelines. If possible, it is a good way to get buy-in; however, it may not be realistic. Your decision on this matter may be influenced by: How much time you have; The age of your participants; The experience level or language skills of your participants; The type of training or seminar it is; Whether participating in the training or seminar was mandatory or optional.

Use Positive Rituals

A ritual is an activity which is consistently triggered by an event. In other words, when A occurs, B always occurs. For example, if you do a roll call everytime you start class, this becomes a ritual. A routine is, merely, a group of rituals clustered together. Most of us have a morning routine to get ready for work.

If you chew gum often, but not at any particular time of the day or day of the week, this is not a ritual. A ritual is predictable. In today's world, with so much change, it's very reassuring and comfortable for learners to experience rituals and know the routine. Rituals and routines lower stress. Some examples of effective learning rituals follow:

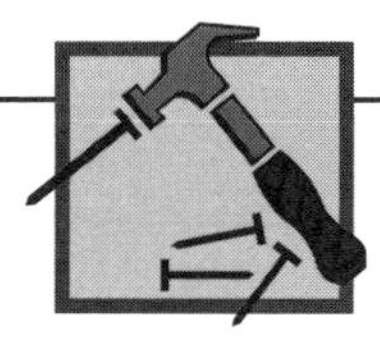

Tips & Tools for Learning Rituals

- Greet participants at the door with a smile; use their name if possible.
- Start the course each day with the same rousing or inspirational song.
- Open the day with call-responses: like "Goooo-oood Morning to You!
- Do a "Yes" clap at the end of a 90-minute segment right before the break.
- Do high-fives after a paired activity or group pair-share.
- Take a short walk with a partner to share insights.
- Use affirmations: "Turn to the person nearest you and say, 'Great job!'"
- Use a real "round" of applause (hands moving in a circle while applauding) or do an audience wave (standing and sitting one row at a time in synchronization).
- Ask teams to do a daily self-assessment.
- Invent a cheer to do after participant introductions.
- Share jokes at the lunch break.
- Use the same "call-in" or music to bring participants back after a break.
- Stretching: Ask participants to stand up, join their team or pick a partner and face each other. Play relaxing music and do slow deep breathing to oxygenate the body.
- Mind-mapping can be a daily ritual. Ask the participants to make a mind-map of yesterday's learning from memory.

Emphasize Course Purpose

Early on in your presentation share with your audience the direction you're going so they can feel good about going along. Emphasize both your purpose and your goals. A goal is an end point; a purpose is a direction or territory. Once participants know the purpose of the course, they will have the criteria necessary to evaluate it as you proceed through the training.

Introduce Newcomers

If somebody new has entered the training, whether they're a late-arriving attendee or a guest speaker, introduce them. One of the essential keys to creating an emotionally- and psychologically-safe environment is to ensure that participants feel informed and comfortable. This is how you build trust. To keep the audience in the dark leaves wide open a door to the imagination: Is it a parole officer, an FBI agent, a parent, a doctor? When you introduce your guests, make sure you also let them speak (even if it's just to say hello) so that participants can get a feel for who they are and why they are visiting the group.

Handle Housekeeping Details

Housekeeping refers to the personal information or logistics participants will need to know, such as, the location of the rest rooms, telephones, and soda machines, breaks times, classroom eating protocol, etc. Other questions that will likely surface are cell phone/pager protocol, credit for the course, necessary materials, length of breaks, close-by restaurants, evaluation forms, etc. Consider outlining all this information in a handout; key items like bathroom location should also be announced. Having logistical information at their fingertips allows participants to relax and sink into the learning process.

Share Some of Yourself

Share with the participants what you bring to the party. How are you feeling today? Anything exciting happening? While it's preferred that you share something positive, it's okay to share something negative as long as you don't dwell on it. You may share explicitly (just tell them!) or implicitly (demonstrate). Share the qualities within yourself that you bring to the group. Examples are commitment, enthusiasm, and love of learning. Sometimes a story about yourself (that's short and to the point) is a great way to allow others to feel comfortable in participating. I've had a positive response to sharing events that are powerful and true from my childhood. As a new presenter, I didn't share childhood stories because I thought who cares? It took me a few years to realize the value of sharing. People like to feel they know you—not just the professional you, but the personal you, too.

You may find great value in the use of certainty affirmations. Tell your participants with certainty and congruency that they will *learn and implement easily what they learn.*

Certainty Affirmations

You may find great value in the use of certainty affirmations. Tell your participants with certainty and congruency that they *will* learn and implement easily what they learned. It might be something as simple as saying, "Everyone loves a boost of confidence. Turn to your neighbor and say, 'This will be fun!" Or, "You're a great learner." It's much easier for participants to feel like they'll succeed in the midst of such certainty.

What if you have participants that might not learn well? Stay positive. You can still believe that your car will get to the grocery store even though you know that someday, sometime, your car will break down. The possibility of failure should never deter your confidence. If you communicate uncertainty and hesitancy to your participants, it will negatively impact their ability to learn, guaranteed. In short, any doubts on your part will likely become a self-fulfilling prophecy. As a professional, you can't afford a negative thought.

Establish a Starting Point

A common problem experienced by many trainers is that participants have varying degrees of experience and knowledge. They can either feel overwhelmed if the material is too advanced and presented too quickly, or bored if the material is too basic and presented too slowly. One way to offset this dilemma is to start the session with a simple activity that allows participants to make explicit their level of expertise on the topic. Ask participants to either list or mind-map their experience or knowledge in a way that makes sense to them. Collect the lists and maps and review them during the first break if possible. Besides giving you a broad overview of the group's experience, this exercise provides participants with a starting point. And with this information, you can more accurately respond to individuals and the group itself.

A common problem experienced by many trainers is that participants have varying degrees of experience and knowledge. One way to offset this dilemma is to start the session with a simple activity that allows participants to make explicit their level of expertise on the topic.

De-Mystify Vocabulary

A surprising number of participants perform poorly in subjects simply because the terminology is a barrier to their understanding of the material. For example, with technology many participants have problems with terms like RAM, network, hard-drive, system folders, processors, extensions, software, and Zip drives. They can't provide a working definition of these terms even if they know what they are; or they often have a whole range of fears associated with the terms. To de-fuse technical terms or new vocabulary, create a mnemonic with a positive emotional impact. For example, to remember that RAM is simply computer memory capacity, offer "Really Awesome Memory." Sometimes, simply letting participants come up with a distorted picture, guttural sound, or activity associated with a specific term will embed the meaning in their memory.

Engage Your Brain:

Planning for Combustible Motivation

What relevant icebreakers and/or low-risk activities will you incorporate into your next presentation? How do they relate to your topic?

How do you plan to establish the ground rules with your group? Will you involve them in the process; if so, how?

Will you incorporate any learning rituals into your next presentation? If so, which ones and how?

What is the purpose of your next presentation? How will you convey this to the audience?

What personal example or story might you share with your audience to personalize your presentation? Is your example relevant to the topic, purpose, or theme of your session?

Honors and rewards fall to those who show their good qualities in action.

–Aristotle

CHAPTER 11

Body Language Secrets Illuminated

Far more information is obtained with the eyes than with the ears. If you say, "I'm excited," but you don't look excited, your listener isn't likely to believe you. This is why it's critical to pay attention to what impacts your audience the most—the unspoken element of communication, known as body language.

Key Topics

- *It's Not Natural*
- *Most Learning Is Nonconscious*
- *Study the Pros*
- *The Use of Videotapes*
- *Knowing Key Gestures*
- *Practicing Key Nonverbals*
- *Big Gestures for Big Audiences*
- *Hand Tips*
- *Working the Corners*

It's Not Natural

Anyone who tells you to "simply act natural" is not a very experienced presenter. It's not "natural" to stand in front of a large, occasionally hostile, group giving information to people who don't even know you. The body's natural reaction is to be fearful and anxious in such a situation. This does not mean, however, that you cannot override this natural response. But to achieve high-level success, you will need to learn some new behaviors and coping strategies. This chapter will illuminate some simple strategies that will ensure your message is received the way you intend it.

Brain Connection

Most Learning Is Nonconscious

Learning can take place both consciously (being aware of what you're learning) or unconsciously/nonconsciously (not being aware of what you're learning). The vast majority of learning, however, happens on the nonconscious level. Visually, the brain can process up to 100 million bits per second. Auditory information is processed at up to 20,000 bits per second. Kinesthetically, our tactile stream of data can exceed 10 million bits per second. With this kind of capacity, it might seem that the brain would be simply overwhelmed with information. Fortunately, we are designed to process only one form of sensory input, *consciously*, at a time. This means that while you may be aware of the content you are absorbing or conveying, you're probably not consciously aware of your body language. In fact, 99 percent of information is obtained and processed by the brain nonconsciously.

Study the Pros

As writers have always been advised to read the classics and study the style of their favorite authors, it is equally important for presenters to watch and study the techniques of their favorite professional speakers. Observe what they do with their hands. Learn how they position themselves in relation to the audience. How much space do they use up? Where do they stand? How long do they stay in one place? Do they hold or use a clip-on microphone? Are they always in the front or do they move to the sides of the room? Do your own personal study! You cannot achieve high-level success until you have a very clear picture in your mind of the standard you want to achieve. For example, when I began presenting I really didn't know what to do with my hands. Then, I did my own study with the pros as my subjects, and the issue was quickly resolved. The secrets I discovered will be illuminated in a moment—stay tuned!

As writers have always been advised to read the classics and study the style of their favorite authors, it is equally important for presenters to watch and study the techniques of their favorite professional speakers.

Study Videotapes

If you don't have the opportunity to observe a number of top-level professional presenters in person, watch them on television or videotape. The value, of course, in studying videotapes is that you can stop action, rewind, and review as much as necessary. This technology makes learning easier. The possibility for mastering a technique observed over-and-over again on video is much greater than mastering a technique observed once very quickly.

Use Key Gestures

To say, "It's not my style to use gestures," is a mistake. We all gesture to one degree or another when we speak. In fact, an enormous amount of information is communicated this way. Ideally, you'll learn to use your gestures to your advantage. That is, ensure they are in alignment with your spoken message. As your conscious awareness regarding body language increases, you will discover what gestures come naturally to you. Some classic gestures and their meaning are described on the following page.

Key Gestures

Palms Up

This gesture invites the audience to do something (i.e., stand up), or emphasizes a question (i.e., "What's going on?").

Safe Pose

Like the hand motion baseball umpires use at home plate, this gesture is used by a presenter to signal "no way." It is done with arms extended, palms down, crossing each other quickly again and again.

Palms Out and Facing Forward

Like a traffic cop uses to control drivers, this signals the audience to "stop and pay attention."

Chopping Motion

The edge of the hand is used in an up-down motion. Perfect to symbolize the end of something.

Make a Fist

This gesture ought to be used briefly and sparingly to retain its value and intensity. I use it to symbolize a victory cheer, like one that goes with the saying, "Yes!"

Palms Down

This gesture is often used to invite the audience to settle down or have a seat.

Pointing

Pointing ought to be used sparingly with pointing at audience members avoided. Therefore, your options are to point to yourself, an imaginary person, or at an object.

Critical Nonverbals

Numbers

If you say you're going to present three key ideas, be sure to show three fingers. It sounds obvious, but such a phrase is often presented with no gestures or the wrong ones.

Size

If you say something is huge use widely outstretched arms. If you say something is small, show a tiny thumb and forefinger.

Position

If you say something is over there, use your hands to demonstrate the distance. If you discuss two ideas, always stand in two different places to illustrate their differences.

People

If you refer to yourself or another person, point towards yourself or away, respectively.

Action Steps

By making a habit of using common traffic signals in conjunction with your verbal messages, you establish consistency in your nonverbals (i.e., stop, pause, start, or wait for the next instruction).

Big Gestures

The bigger the audience, the bigger the gestures ought to be. Broadway performers, for example, practically have to shout their lines and really exaggerate their movements on stage. Why? Because though a television camera can create a close-up image that can be viewed easily, stage productions don't have this luxury. From where you're presenting, the audience may be 25 to 100 feet away. Subtle gestures from this distance are impossible to see, so exaggerate them. Highly restrained or timid presenters appear to be less than passionate about their topic. This, of course, is less preferable than the possibility of seeming overly dramatic.

The bigger the audience, the bigger the gestures ought to be. From where you're presenting, the audience may be 25 to 100 feet away. Subtle gestures from this distance are impossible to see, so exaggerate them.

Hand Tips

You probably don't worry about what to do with your feet or your eyes; the most common concern among presenters is what to do with your hands! What you want *to avoid* is nervous reactions or fidgeting, hands at your sides, or in your pockets for more than a few seconds, and grooming or scratching gestures while on stage. If you're compelled to do any of these, find a reason to walk off stage or offer a break. What you do *want to do* with your highly exposed hands is the following:

- Engage one of them. Hold something in one hand (like a microphone or prop) and gesture with the other.
- Use both hands to gesture at the same time if you want to emphasize an important point, but use sparingly to maintain emphasis.
- Steepling: Hold both hands approximately chest high loosely together with fingers spread and pointing to the sky.

Work the Corners

If you are given a small room with a small audience, your job is easy. Your real test will be in an odd-shaped room with a large audience. If this happens, make sure you either have a long microphone cord (50 to 100 feet) or a wireless lapel microphone. Open your talk from front center stage just a bit to the audience's left or right; and during your presentation walk from side-to-side speaking directly to all of your listeners. The important thing is to break out of the front of the room "box."

Presenters generally favor one side of the room over the other. To avoid speaking to only one-half of your audience, change your room position often, standing, for example, near the corners of the room. Most importantly, don't stay in only one place. Your entire audience wants to feel important and included. You can achieve this simply by getting physically closer to them.

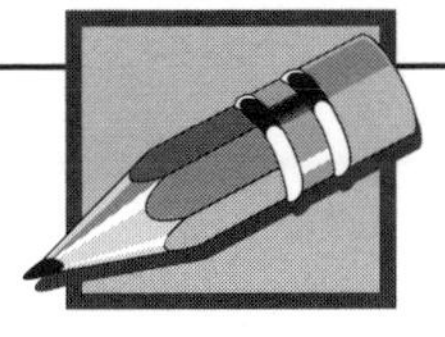

Engage Your Brain:
Planning for Effective Body Language

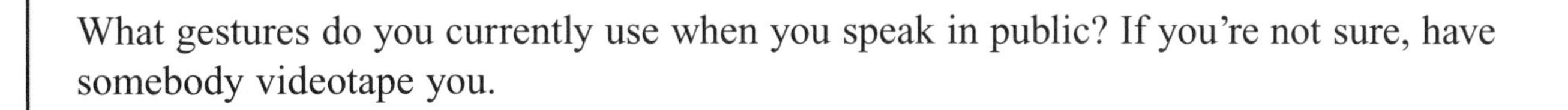

What gestures do you currently use when you speak in public? If you're not sure, have somebody videotape you.

What gestures or nonverbals do you think would be more effective, if any? How will you practice them to achieve mastery?

What room and audience size will your next presentation likely be? What strategies will you use to ensure all participants feel spoken to directly?

Optimism is essential to achievement and it is also the foundation of courage and of true progress.

–Nicholas Murray Butler

CHAPTER 12

States for Optimal Learning

States are distinct, measurable, biological moments. For example, there are states of curiosity, anger, apathy, frustration, or celebration. A state is a snapshot; whereas, a mood is a motion picture. State changes can often be achieved by simply ingesting food or drink, changing a posture or position, or interacting with someone new. States are so important to us that a change of state is the only thing people pay money for! We buy food or go out to to a restaurant to end a state called hunger. We buy new clothes or a new car or new home because we're not satisfied with the state we're in presently. We pay for a state change when we go to the movies, the amusement park, a museum, and on vacation. The following are common ways we change our mind states:

- Eating or drinking
- Playing a game
- Watching TV
- Sleeping
- Visiting with friends
- Exercising
- Intimacy
- Travel

When you say you are depressed, this is a state. Disbelief is a state. Being in love is a state. And curiosity is a state, as is anger, jealousy, inspiration, lust, apathy, and abandonment. While our state is just a snapshot of the moment, our personality is comprised of zillions of states added together like a long-running movie. Unless you're catatonic, everyday is a series of thousands of states. If most of your states are confident, grateful, resourceful, excited, and positive, people say you're a happy person.

Key Topics

- *Learning Is Strongly State Dependent*
- *The Biology of States*
- *Why States Are Critical to Success*
- *How to Read States With Accuracy*
- *Preventing Problems With Listening States*
- *Read Emotions First*
- *Managing States*
- *Gradient*
- *States Mediate Meaning*
- *The State of Knowing You Know*
- *Differences in Learners*
- *How to Trigger Convincer States*
- *Use of Humor*
- *Use of Time References*
- *Managing Your Own States*

Brain Connection

Learning Is Strongly State-Dependent

Each brain state carries with it a characteristic biological report card. It is likely to consist of the electrical report (the EEG), blood flow (measured by blood pressure and pulse), learning efficiency (evidenced by the specific usage of glucose as shown in PET scans), the dominate lobes involved (functional MRI), respiration (breathing rates), stress levels (amount of cortisol, vasopressin, etc.) attention levels (amine-choline ratios), and general energy levels (nutritional analysis). Research suggests that each brain state carries with it a corresponding set of behaviors. For example, an alcoholic state of drunkenness is associated with poor motor control, slurred speech, and distortion of reality. An optimal learning state of curiosity, motivation, and excitement is associated with brighter individuals. As a presenter, the better you are at productively managing participant's states, the more they will learn and enjoy the learning.

The Biology of States

States, as discussed in the previous Brain Connection section, can be measured many ways. One way is to measure the levels of certain chemicals in your body. Adrenaline, caffeine, noradrenaline, amphetamines, and epinephrine are all variations of the same chemical structure we call amines. Greater numbers of amines like the naturally occurring dopamine or adrenaline in your brain usually equate to more attention and arousal. Medications like Cylert, Dexatrin, or Ritalin serve the same purpose. Thus, states are determined by the chemicals in your system.

Another way to measure states is with an EEG (electroencephalograph), which measures the electrical activity in CPS or cycles per second of the brain. The slower the brain waves, the more relaxed you are. The higher the CPS, the more intense your states. Learning can occur in many different states. One is not necessarily better than another. It depends on what you're trying to accomplish.

Research suggests that each brain state carries with it a corresponding set of behaviors. An optimal learning state of curiosity, motivation, and excitement is associated with brighter individuals. As a presenter, the better you are at productively managing participant's states, the more they will learn and enjoy the learning.

In the slowest state, delta (0-3 CPS), the brain does not learn. The next slowest state, theta (4-7 CPS), operates as the twilight zone between sleep and awake. Though this is an excellent state for meditation or sleep learning (if you're an auditory learner), it requires that you remain passive and inert. In alpha state (8-12 CPS), you're alert but relaxed. This can be a great state for receptive learning like reading, watching, or listening. But for active learning, beta (12-25 CPS) is best. This is the optimal state for conducting debates, hands-on learning, group discussions, question and answer time, problem-solving, and brainstorming.

Why States Are Critical to Success

A state is a moment in your mind-body history. Not surprisingly, every thought we think, action we take, and feeling we have is directly dependent on the state we're in at the time; thus, all our behaviors are state-dependent. Each state has within it a unique library of behaviors and memories. When you're happy, you can recall other times when you were happy. When you're mad at another person, you can usually recall all the dirty, rotten things they did to you in the past. When you are tired, you are not interested in doing exciting, motivational, active things. But when you have energy, you are more likely to participate. While this may sound obvious, it has profound implications in a training session.

States are so important to us that most participants will remember the states they were in and evaluate your session based on them much longer than any ideas they got from you. When we experience states, for example, of curiosity, hope, and anticipation, we feel the presentation was good. On the other hand, when we experience states, for example, of boredom, discouragement, resentment, apathy, frustration, or fear, we feel it's a bad presentation. It sounds simple, but it's true! States run our lives; they are the report card of the quality of our lives. Good presenters are good at managing states. The very best presenters, like Zig Ziglar, Tony Robbins, or Charlie Jones masterfully manage audience states; they usually get paid the most, too.

Good states for learning are usually states like curiosity, anticipation, suspicion, confusion, hope, affirmation, surprise, pleasure, and confidence, and low to moderate stress or challenge. Bad states for learning include fear, frustration, anger, threat, and apathy. While you don't have absolute control, you certainly have influence over the states of your audience. If your audience is not in a receptive state for learning, change the state. Before you can manage learning states productively, however, you have to be able to read them accurately.

How to Read States With Accuracy

A person's body language is strongly representative of their state. Below are listed some of the common postures and gestures you will observe in participants and the general meaning of each. Though these conclusions represent only generalities, they will help you to better read your participants' states over time.

Reading States

- *Legs uncrossed:* openness, receptive, macho, or cold
- *Head scratching:* puzzled, nervous, or impatient
- *Tugging on the ear:* ready to interrupt or lend an ear
- *Touching nose or jawbone:* doubt or contemplation
- *Open extended palms:* explaining a generous offer, openness, disbelief, or frustration
- *Hands on lips:* impatience, silence, or deep thought
- *Hands on knees or leaning forward:* readiness, stretching, impatience, or attention
- *Clenching fist:* power, anger, or control
- *Wrinkling forehead:* confused or puzzled
- *Hands in pockets:* hiding meaning, relaxed, or cold atmosphere
- *Shrugging shoulders:* uncertainty, negative, or tight neck
- *Hands clasped behind back:* authority, humility, or service
- *Looking downward:* deep in thought, bored, or feeling emotions
- *Steepled fingers:* confidence, boredom, scheming, or a barrier
- *Palm down, flat on chest:* struck by a thought, honesty, or defensive
- *Fidgeting:* frustration, irritation, upset, or boredom
- *Eye contact:* interest, anger, boredom, or distrust

Use all of your sensory skills to listen and determine states; notice the following: 1) flush in the face or neck; 2) dilation of pupils; 3) changes in skin (i.e., goose bumps); 4) twitching of ears, nose, throat, hands or legs as a response to an emotion filling the body; and 5) the obvious visual clue of tears which may signal sadness, anger, relief, frustration, or joy.

The eyes may have an increased blink rate or twitch when the speaker moves into either highly emotional messages or when they are reliving an experience or lying about it. The eyes may also squint when the intensity of the message increases. The mouth provides excellent clues because it is also delivering the content. Watch for tightened lips, narrowed jaws, frowns, smiles, held-back laughs, or lifted lips. An astute observer will also notice the breathing rate of the speaker. As the breathing rate quickens, you may guess the speaker is experiencing some anxiety, excitement, or other stimulating emotion.

How you listen to others can make the difference between whether they choose to become a disruptive force or an ally. Monitor your own state to prepare yourself for listening.

Now, let's reverse the idea of the list above. Instead of the body language first, now you get the states first. the following examples present common bodily reactions (states) and how they can be interpreted.

- ***Fear:*** restricted breathing, tightened muscles, a closed body posture
- ***Anticipation:*** eyes wide open, body leaned forward, breath held
- ***Curiosity:*** hand-to-head, facial expression wrinkled, head turned or tilted
- ***Apathy:*** relaxed shoulders, slumped posture, slowed breathing, no eye contact
- ***Frustration:*** either expressed or suppressed, possible fidgeting and movement, or tightened muscles, and shortened breathing
- ***Self-convinced ("I know I know it"):*** shift in breathing, leaned back posture, body rocks, tilts, or rolls

Are these 100 percent accurate? No, they are merely generalizations. The key to reading body language is calibration. Observe closely, then check it out. Avoid assumptions; ask questions. Don't get attached to hard and fast rules about body language because there are always exceptions to the rule. Try something, check it out. Calibrate, calibrate, calibrate.

Prevent Problems With Listening States

Sometimes an audience is in a negative mindset when they arrive. Maybe they had unexpected traffic or parking problems, or got lost, or had to wait in a long line, etc. Or, perhaps, busy staff members neglected to be customer service oriented. One particularly big mistake is not listening to a participant's gripes early on. When people don't feel listened to they get frustrated and angry. By reading a participant's state, you may be able to address the problem early and minimize the damage to your group.

How you listen to others can make the difference between whether they choose to become a disruptive force or an ally. Monitor your own state to prepare yourself for listening. Before you put yourself in the position of listening, ask "What state am I in right now?" If there's an unexpressed emotion inside you, it may create a distorting filter for the message. When you are angry you hear differently than if you just won the state lottery. Find a way to set aside your personal feelings so that you can go about listening to others and reading their states without the added filter. Here are two different kinds of listening styles. Each of them embodies a different state.

Emotions come first, then content. In our culture we don't usually learn to listen to others with empathy or to listen with minimal responses; yet, to do so is extremely important to good communication. Empathetic listening allows you to simply "be there" in partnership with the speaker.

The first is empathic listening which is a response to emotional states; the second is precision listening which is a response to content. In both approaches your outcome is discovery. With empathetic listening you allow the participant to become more visible; with precision listening you allow the content to become more clear. The key is knowing which one to use; and then to use it effectively.

Read Emotions First

Emotions come first, then content. In our culture we don't usually learn to listen to others with empathy or to listen with minimal responses; yet, to do so is extremely important to good communication. Empathetic listening allows you to simply "be there" in partnership with the speaker. It is especially important to use empathetic listening when someone is speaking about something emotional. For example, "I am so sad... my best friend was hurt and is in the hospital." Your response might be "Oh... I'm so sorry..." It would not be, "I, too, was hospitalized a year ago after..." This idea here, again, is to bring out the emotions and experience of the speaker, not the content. Notice the listener did not say, "which hospital" or "when are visiting hours?" Empathetic listeners will exhibit the following behaviors:

- They will listen for the feelings behind the message.
- They will let the speaker know they are listening and care.
- They will avoid interruptions or lengthy comments.
- They will listen for the relationships in the speaker's world.
- They will be an "invisible" listener and make the speaker visible.

Most listeners are so into their own world, they rarely experience the speaker's world. Untrained communicators have only one mode of communication—that of relating the message to their own lives. Resist that temptation and listen to the speaker as if you were in their shoes—living the experience yourself. Only then can you truly be empathic.

Listen for the participant's state changes. As valuable as the content of the message may be, learn to tune into the feelings of the sender. Often feelings are a more accurate clue to true meaning than words. Emotions are not easily hidden and there are many ways to spot them. A speaker's voice can provide subtle and not so subtle clues about their emotional state. As children, we became very tuned into the differences in our parents' voices. Beyond the obvious clue of volume, cracking of the voice, a drop in energy level, and a change in tone all signaled that an emotion had been triggered. States run people's lives. When you realize how important this concept is, your priorities may shift in your training sessions.

As a presenter, you have the responsibility to walk the fine line between managing states and controlling others. Make sure that you are always building relationships first so that there's a give and take, and participant buy-in or agreement in the process.

Managing States

The younger your participants are, the more responsibility you have to manage their states. If you're working with adults over a period of time, teach them to manage their own states. If both trainer and participant are effectively managing learning states, the result will be an optimal learning environment.

As a presenter, you have the responsibility to walk the fine line between managing states and controlling others. Should you always get the group to do what you want them to do? Should you enforce your own way as the right way? Should you always change participants' states to good ones? No. If you overdo it, your audience will feel manipulated and resentful. Make sure that you are always building relationships first so that there's a give and take, and participant buy-in or agreement in the process. Sometimes an individual feels better being left alone. Their issue may be very personal. Use your skills to manage states with discretion. Most of the time, people want to be in a good state. But that never gives us, as presenters, the right to cross over the line and intrude in their lives. Use state-change strategies cautiously and you'll keep the quality of learning up while retaining the respect of the audience.

There are two approaches for triggering state changes: by changing thinking or physiology. To affect a change, for example, in a participant's feelings of depression you might ask a question that triggers their thinking: "How would you feel if you just won the lottery?" To affect a change in someone, for example, who is slumped in their chair, you might suggest they go for a short walk or announce that it is time for a group stretch break. Just the change in posture, eye patterns, breathing, and/or movement can change a person's state. Anytime your audience begins to lack energy or concentration, or seems bored, what do you do? Change their state, of course!

As a presenter, building rapport and good relationships runs neck-and-neck in importance with effectively managing audience states. When you observe a nonproductive state in a participant, a change in their existing state or a pattern interrupt will allow something better to follow. The form of state change or pattern interruption can be nearly anything that breaks the routine.

It can be as simple as saying: "Write this next idea down, it might be the most important point today." The simple act of writing can be a state change. Or, use a surprise, a prop, a new sound, or a change of character or visuals in the room. Humor also works, as does activities. Have participants change seating, stand, switch groups, pair-off, or play a quick game of Simon Says. You may also want to involve them in decision making so that they are more willing to participate. This can be accomplished through discussion, a suggestion box, or with group activities. Not only will the participants like the result of these state changes, you're likely to have fun with them, too. All of the following suggestions can help break up static and unresourceful learning conditions:

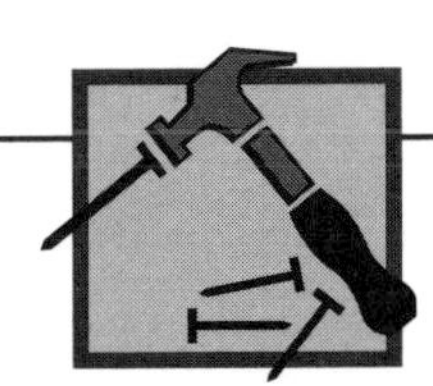

State Change Tips & Tools

- Change of speaker's location in the room
- Post affirmations
- Wear special hat/clothes
- Make faces
- Use familiar expressions
- Use special gestures
- Incorporate videos/overheads
- Do mime
- Stand on a chair or table
- Point to something
- Use visualization exercises
- Stand still
- Mind-Map material
- Turn your back on the group
- Hold up an object
- Change of lighting
- Read with passion (out loud)
- Laugh or tell a joke
- Sing or use a whistle
- Incorporate group work
- Change tonality
- Provide positive affirmations
- Play music
- Use metaphors or stories
- Ask questions
- Use partner presenting
- Facilitate a group discussion
- Have participants present
- Repeat what was just said
- Scream, pause, be silent
- Use sound effects
- Knock on door or desk

Continued...

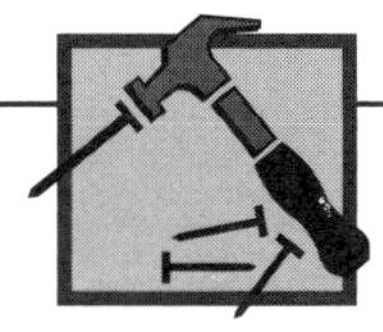

State Change Suggestions

Continued...

- Do a magic trick
- Leave the room
- Conduct a stretch break
- Play ball toss or footbag
- Drink water
- Change seats
- Do cross-lateral or brain-gym activities
- Play Simon-Sez
- Invent new ways to shake hands
- Incorporate role play or theater
- Offer hands-on learning
- Use several names
- Repeat after me
- Bring in potpourri
- Food
- Flowers
- The smell of popcorn or fresh bread
- Do deep breathing
- Go outside or to a new room
- Move chairs
- Stomp feet
- Sub-divide groups

Note: Almost anything can change a state. Decide what's appropriate for your particular audience and circumstances.

Gradient

The concept of gradient, when used by presenters, means to consider the "end state" you want to achieve with your audience first; then, take them there in small steps or a gradual gradient. For example, to get your audience to participate in a very extroverted activity, first ask them to take a deep breath and set their things down. Next, ask them to stand and look for another person about their own height. You can lower your voice to a whisper so they have to lean forward to hear you. This simple sequence will work better than asking your audience, for example, to "please prepare to do trust-falls in groups of five each."

States Mediate Meaning

You've probably heard someone say, "She sees everything through rose-colored glasses." Or, "Nothing will make him smile." These statements reflect how a person's state mediates meaning. For example, if you are in a depressed mood and someone tells you that you are getting a parking ticket, you might say something like, "I knew it was a bad day." On the other hand, if you're in a happy-go-lucky mood and someone tells you you're getting a ticket, you might respond, "Oh well, I was about due; no big deal." In this same way, a participant who is excited about learning will hear your directions differently than a participant who is bored with the session.

Anything you present is being filtered, altered, and influenced by the state of the participants. If you don't stay tuned into their states, chances are they won't get the full value of your presentation. Whatever state your audience is in will flavor the content and meaning of your message. So, what do we do about this? It's simple. Always put your audience in a good state before attempting to facilitate an activity, present information, or get buy-in. Let's say, for example, that you are about to give the group directions for a role play. If your participants are in a tired or bored state, the activity might sound like too much work, too risky, or a dumb idea. In an activated or curious state, however, participants are likely to think it sounds like fun. The following eight steps provide a framework for encouraging productive learning states in participants:

Anything you present is being manipulated, altered, and influenced by the state of the participants. If you don't stay tuned into their states, chances are they won't get the full value of your presentation.

Step 1: Preparation

Deep breathing creates a better state for listening—a state of curiosity and anticipation.
"Let's do something fun. First take in a deep breath and stand up!"

Step 2: Exploration

Explain the reason for doing whatever you're asking them to do.
"How many of you played musical chairs as a kid? And how many of you still like to have fun in one form or another? How about if we mix learning with having fun?"

Step 3: Who

Specifically address those being asked to take action.
"Everyone..."

Step 4: When

State when the "fun" starts.
"In just a moment, we'll..." Or, "In 60 seconds, we'll ..."

Step 5: What

State the specific course of action.
"Move your chair to form a big oval like the shape of a racetrack. Then wait for further directions."

Step 6: Restate

Clarify or restate directions in a different way.
"This means the chairs will be right next to each other facing each other in a big, elongated circle or an oval. You can put your things off to the side of the room on a table."

Step 7: Clarify

Ask for questions and feedback.
"Before we start this session, who wants clarification?"

Step 8: Call to Action

Make sure there is a congruent call to action.
"Ready?... get set, go!" (Keep this call to action the same each time.)

The State of Knowing You Know

When the learner knows they know something and they feel good about learning it, of course, they want to continue learning. This is not a reinforcement that comes from you. The self-convincer state comes from inside the learner, but you can certainly evoke it with the right activities.

The ideal ending state for a learning session is called the self-convincer state. The self-convincer state is a belief state and feeling state linked together—the belief that I know I know it, and feel I good about knowing it. This key state fuels the motivation to learn loop. It is a state of excitement, pride, and happiness. This state is an exact moment–a physiological, mental, emotional snapshot which resonates, "Yes... it was worth it!" The best presenters use this state to embed learning and further motivate participants.

Remember the movie *Home Alone*? In it, the main character, a 10-year-old boy, Kevin, is left home alone and burglars try to break in. As he foils their break-in attempts, his celebration state or self-convincer state is demonstrated by the physical motion of him clenching his fist and drawing it towards himself while saying, "Yes!" This was his way of saying, "I've succeeded and it feels good!"

When the learner knows they know something, and they feel good about learning it, of course, they want to continue learning. This is not a reinforcement that comes from you. The self-convincer state comes from inside the learner, but you can certainly evoke it with the right activities. This can happen in two ways: either you can evoke it in the learner, or they can evoke it in themselves. When the self-convincer state is learner directed, it makes your job easier. But, unfortunately, most people don't do it for themselves. They don't know how. You may have noticed that most learners are not really that confident. This is where you come in.

Criteria for Reinforcing the Self-Convincer State

The three necessary criteria to trigger the self-convincer state and reinforce learning are:

1. Dependent Modality:
The learner must get the learning reinforced in their own dependent modality: visual, auditory, or kinesthetic. To see, hear, or feel the information in the learner's preferred modality is critical to believing it.

2. Frequency:
Each learner varies in how many times they need to have the learning repeated in order to believe it and feel good about it.

3. Duration:
We all need a certain length of time before the learning sinks in. This length of time can vary from a couple of seconds to several hours.

Here's an example: A learner comes up to you and says, "How do you think I did on my project?" You say, "I'm real happy with it. It's your best effort yet." The learner thanks you and walks away. Ten minutes later the same learner comes up again. He asks a similar question about the project. This time you say a little more, but you virtually give him the same feedback. At one point, his eyes light up, and he is visibly pleased. Frequency and duration strikes again. He got what he really wanted: that "knowing that I know it" self-convincer state.

The Self-Convincer State Is:

A combined belief and feeling state–
"I believe it and I feel it."
It needs visual, auditory, or kinesthetic reinforcement
+ frequency + duration

The physiological signals are usually a nodding head, a smile, a deep breath, eyes shift downward, a weight change, change in posture, skin color change or any combination of these reactions. Perhaps, most notably, look for a learner's eyes to shift downward signifying that a feeling state has been accessed.

Differences in Learners

Some learners become sure of themselves (self-convince) too easily. They hear something once, never check it out, and believe it's true. Learners who self-convince too easily are often called gullible. There are obvious dangers in learners thinking they know something that they really may *not* know. In others, it's the opposite. They may need a frequency exposure of 10, or even 50 times before they believe they know it. The duration might be minutes or hours. Each person has their own combination to their lock. Those who are too hard to convince might be called skeptical or cynical. This is not necessarily bad; it's all context-dependent. For example, if a fire breaks out and someone yells, "leave the building," it's probably best to be gullible. Or, if you're a security agent at an airport and someone mentions the word "bomb," it's best not to be a skeptic. And, if you get a telemarketer calling you about a *free* vacation you just won to Las Vegas (you only need to pay a $49 transfer fee by credit card), it's best to be a skeptic.

How to Trigger the Self-Convincer State

To elicit a self-convincer state simply include all three conditions: modality, frequency, and duration several times a day—especially after each learning chunk. Doing a paired mind-map will do it or presenting to a partner will do it. Offer a variety of modalities, do it more than once, and do it for more than just a few seconds. Nothing will guarantee that a learner will "know that they know," but the following are some specific strategies for eliciting this critical learning state:

Triggers for the Self-Convincer State

- Conduct a work-related project.
- Assign learning logs or a diary of learning.
- Have participants peer present or work in teams.
- Incorporate self-assessment activities.
- Distribute certificates.
- Give credit to a participant for their good idea.
- Create a video or audiotape.
- Check against a rubric, chart, or pre-established criteria.
- Perform a play or skit.
- Assign mind-maps and have participants share them in small groups.
- Conduct celebrations with noisemakers or party poppers.
- Play partner-to-partner word association games.
- Incorporate learner-created performance reviews.
- Use simulation quiz shows.
- Use role plays.
- Incorporate cheers and rituals.
- Use team or individual charts.
- Assign projects that take time, are challenging, and require a variety of skills.

Remember to end each session on a high note. Use a special group gesture, a cheer, or a high-five. Allow learners to express their emotions in order to get the effect you desire. Even if they have to fake it at the beginning, their brain will get used to it and soon crave it like a drug. Acknowledgment and approval can be just as addicting, but in a positive way!

Use of Humor

Humor is one of the most effective state changers. Researchers at Tel Aviv University demonstrated that participants retained more information from lectures when humor breaks were interspersed throughout the presentation of content. At Indiana University, researchers found that key learning points that were followed by a humorous story were remembered better than those that were not. Other research suggests humor stimulates the reticular formation in the brain which brings out attentiveness and makes the learner more receptive to information. Many presenters who use humor report that they do it to increase audience rapport. Others say the laughter of the participants decreases everyone's stress and provides valuable presenter feedback.

Other research suggests humor stimulates the reticular formation in the brain which brings out attentiveness and makes the learner more receptive to information. Many presenters who use humor report that they do it to increase audience rapport.

Humor is appropriate when it is used to make a particular point, when the audience needs an energizer, or when you want to highlight an important point. Humor is not appropriate when it is racist, sexist, abusive, critical, or not empowering. Don't repeat a joke if it has the potential to insult or alienate someone.

Use of Time References

Time distortion is an important way of creating an environment of successful learning. Let others know that there is enough time to do what we need to do today. Give close-in deadlines for simple, rote, physical tasks. Give more open deadlines for tasks which require creativity. Do not tell participants that you're unsure whether there's enough time to cover the day's material; this creates unnecessary anxiety. They may feel they need to rush and in so doing risk not understanding. Rather, give participants a feeling that there is sufficient time for what needs to be done. Then, make sure that your schedule is flexible and honed to the time constraints of your presentation.

Along the same lines, use time cues in your opening to let the audience know what's coming. For example, "We have just three items to take care of before we start our main topic today." Or "In just a minute, when I start today's lecture..." or "As soon as we have completed our daily stretching and preview, we'll be starting..." Even if it seems as if you are running out of time, say with a smile, "You have all the time in the world, take three more minutes." With the anxiety-producing part of the statement counteracted by the abundance-oriented part of the statement, the message is humorous and not taken too seriously.

Positive suggestions are helpful when it comes to time references. For example, you might say something like, "Chances are, you'll find that the next time will be easier than this time and the time after that will be even easier." Or, "In no time, you may know this stuff cold." Or, "Will you be surprised when this material suddenly makes perfect sense to you!" Or, you may want to consider facilitating an extended visualization using full sensory responses to suggest successful usage.

Managing Your Own States

For a person to perform at their peak repeatedly, they must be able to maintain the states necessary for this level of concentration and focus.

It makes little sense for us to address the states of others without addressing our own states. The very best athletes have reached success not because they have more talent, but because they have learned to maximize their talents by managing their own states better. Yes, Michael Jordan is a great basketball player; and he manages his mind, mood, and attitude so well that we know he'll play well at every game. For a person to perform at their peak repeatedly, they must be able to maintain the states necessary for this level of concentration and focus. The following tips are used by many top performers in all fields to manage their states for peak performance:

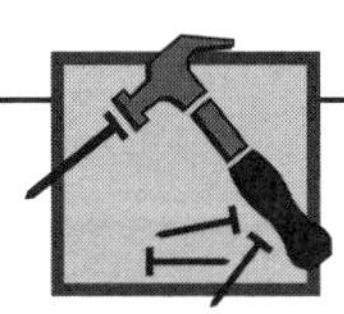

Tips & Tools for Managing Your Own States

- Maintain a high-nutrition diet.
- Make sure you are prepared, even over-prepared, for the task at hand.
- Learn the physiology of excellence; and use posture, breathing, and position to elicit that state.
- Use music that inspires you in your presentation.
- Avoid consuming alcohol or drugs up to 12 hours prior to your presentation.
- Wear clothing that helps you feel good about yourself.
- Manage your own self-talk; repeat the positives, not the negatives.
- Visualize yourself succeeding over and over again.
- Drink enough water throughout the day to stay hydrated.

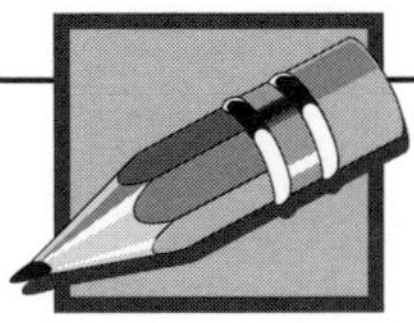

Engage Your Brain:
Preparing for Optimal Learning States

What states do you want to evoke in participants in your next presentation? How do you expect to do this? What problems might you encounter?

How will you elicit the self-convincer state in your participants?

How do you manage your own states? What strategies might you apply to better manage them?

To turn an obstacle to one's advantage is a great step towards victory.

–French Proverb

CHAPTER 13

The Art of Persuasive Presentations

Persuaders are the personalities who most often initiate change in the world. Persuasiveness is an art which begins with a compelling message. As an audience, we don't want information or opinions alone; we want to be moved by a compelling message. We want to hear someone who's passionate about their beliefs and work. In addition, we need the message delivered in such a way that it goes from being the presenter's message to being our message. This chapter highlights the tools top presenters use to master the art of persuasive presentations.

Key Topics

- *Congruency*
- *The Biology of Persuasion*
- *He Said, She Said*
- *Avoid Jargon*
- *Share Your Vision*
- *Use Sensory Rich Language*
- *Dramatize Your Point*
- *Incorporate Affirmations*
- *Engage Emotions*
- *Use Empowered Language*
- *Tell Purposeful Stories*
- *Share Success Stories*
- *Embed Key Words*
- *Change Your Frame of Reference*
- *Use Presuppositions*
- *Use Linkages*
- *Use Quotes*
- *Use Metaphors*
- *Use Round-Ups*
- *Elicit Increasing Commitments*

Congruency

One of the most critical elements for developing powerful persuasion skills is congruency. This is the skill of matching up your:

Voice	*With*	*Gestures*
◆ Tonality		◆ Facial expressions
◆ Tempo		◆ Eye contact
◆ Word choice		◆ Positioning in the room
◆ Volume		◆ Content of the message

A lack of congruency will kill your message; whereas, a fully congruent message will be perceived strongly. If your message is congruent, your audience will be much more likely to believe you. If it moves them internally, they will want to take external action. Practice your presentation and start to become aware of your tendency to match or mismatch particular words or phrases. Practice achieving congruency by observing yourself in front of a mirror, videotaping your presentation, seeking feedback from an objective observer, and audiotaping yourself.

Brain Connection

The Biology of Persuasion

Scientists have studied very little about the biology of persuasion. What goes on in the brain before and after someone is persuaded remains a mystery for the moment. We do know, however, that two strong variables are at work: 1) the neural networks that form critical thinking and belief systems; and 2) the physiological states of receptivity, motivation, and action that complete the second half of the persuasion equation. These variables may be modulated by levels of dopamine or serotonin (positive moods or receptivity) to some degree, and adrenaline (eagerness to take action), to a larger degree.

He Said, She Said

You don't always have to be the one on the "hot seat." One especially effective strategy for persuading an audience is to have someone else be your messenger. You can do this by asking a guest speaker, for example, to incorporate a particular message; or by telling a story whereby the character states the message; or by a strategic name dropping. For example, "someone" once said that people who read books on presentation skills are more curious, creative, and likely to succeed. Notice, I didn't make this statement; but "someone" did. A trainer I co-present with occasionally gets audiences to try out new things by telling them she has been asked by a research team to conduct an experiment with the group. The activity, of course, is the research team's idea, not hers.

A vision defines a world where things are different and better. People love to share in a successful movement and be part of a better world. The more defined and compelling your vision is, the more persuasive your message will be.

Avoid Jargon

One of the quickest ways to turn off an audience is by using jargon. Most audiences are too polite to stop you and say, "Hey! I can't understand half of your terms!" They're much more likely to just turn off. Always translate your presentations into language that everyone in your audience is sure to understand. Rather than "records management," say filing. It's not CPUs and RAMs, but computers and memory. When it is necessary to use technical terms, take a few moments to define the terms as simply as possible. Use participant's jobs or personal lives as the basis for your examples.

Share Your Vision

Who are you? What is your dream in life? What do you want to see happen as a result of your work? Martin Luther King gave a famous speech called, "I have a dream." Part of the persuasive power of that speech was that he gave us a "place to go." A vision defines a world where things are different and better. People love hope. People love to share in a successful movement and be part of a better world. The more defined and compelling your vision is, the more persuasive your message will be.

Use Sensory-Rich Language

The human brain craves high-level input and can make sense out of far more input than a traditional seminar or workshop can possibly provide. To fulfill the brain's need for sensory stimulation, plan your presentation with auditory, visual, and tactile stimulation in mind. Use classical music as a backdrop for speaking and popular music in the background during activities. Incorporate musical instruments. Use sensory-rich language when speaking. Use different dialects and accents to get the point across. It may be a Californian, Bronx, Shakespearean, Southern, Yiddish, Swedish, Italian, Australian, Indian, Japanese, or German accent. Wear interesting clothing. Pepper your language with words like salubrious, invidious, surly, or yeasty. Use a wide vocal range combined with a full range of gestures. Effective? Absolutely!

You'll notice that some participants appear to get the picture better when they see what you're talking about. What sounds good to others and really resonates for them, is the symphony of harmony and vibrations created by a really tuned-in speaker. But what it all boils down to is a firm foundation and a sense of feeling good. In the previous three sentences, the sensory language varied from visual (notice, appear, picture, see) to auditory (sounds, resonates, symphony, harmony, tuned-in) to kinesthetic (boils, firm, sense, feeling). All of these represent ways to reach different styles of listeners.

The human brain craves high-level input and can make sense out of far more input than a traditional seminar or workshop can possibly provide. To fulfill the brain's need for sensory stimulation, plan your presentation with auditory, visual, and tactile stimulation in mind.

Dramatize Your Point

To dramatize is to make bigger-than-life, to parade, or to be bold and flashy about a subject. Many presenters bring greater life and vitality to their messages by using costumes or bringing props for participants to feel, investigate, and ask questions about. One costuming technique is to have participants dress up like the subject they are studying. How fun it is to dress up like Aristotle, Queen Elizabeth, Booker T. Washington, Napoleon, Einstein, a Medieval peasant, Mark Twain, Florence Nightingale, an Aborigine, Churchill, or Newton! Or, perhaps, you wear a special hat that relates to your topic. This powerful medium ought not be overlooked.

Incorporate Affirmations

Positive affirmations used with repetition will influence the beliefs of your audience. Simple statements like, "I've done this course hundreds of times and my participants always get it; I am absolutely certain that each of you will totally master this," will spark your audience's confidence. Have them repeat key phrases after you. Ask them to repeat a key phrase to the person sitting next to them. Affirm that they will remember the key phrases they are repeating.

Engage Emotions

The days of boring audiences with a content-heavy stand-and-deliver style of presentation are quickly disappearing. Even computers can deliver content today in a way that is more engaging to the senses than this. So, what can you offer that a computer cannot? Emotions. The emotions you exude communicate strong nonverbal messages to your audience that influence and persuade. Don't be afraid to inject your presentation, therefore, with emotions like excitement, frustration, joy, hope, apprehension, and empathy.

There are many ways to engage appropriate emotions. The key is moderation. Show passion and emotion without making that the foundation of your presentation. Present with feelings, but don't let your feelings overshadow your content. If you become too maudlin about an issue, it can make the audience feel uncomfortable. It's okay to get teary-eyed about a topic, but uncontrollable tears create discomfort. Shouting, for example, for a *brief moment* will capture your audience's attention; however, more than this will likely turn your audience off. The following strategies will assist you in engaging audience emotions:

Engage Audience Emotions

- Tap into the audience's prior emotional experience with leading questions: "How many of you have had this experience...?"
- Use dramatic music to open, close, or highlight a point.
- Tell a personal dramatic story.
- Have an accomplishment celebration.
- Incorporate a physical activity, like a game, stretching, or role play.
- Personalize the material with relevant issues like health, money, family, and humor.
- Have participants work in teams or small groups.

Use Empowered Language

There is a happy medium for effective communication that falls somewhere between the way women and men have been socialized. Women have been brought up to be polite and people-oriented. Men, on the other hand, have been brought up to be assertive and task-oriented. The ideal is to have the capacity to "speak either language" depending on the situation. In general, however, it is best to use powerful language, but not in a bossy or pushy way. People who tend to qualify their statements with questions or neutralizing words will be perceived as ineffective, wishy-washy, or lacking confidence. For example, the following statement does not do a very good job of sparking confidence in the listener: "It seems cold in here, don't you think? I don't think I ought to stay." The same message, however, when spoken with commitment and confidence sounds more like, "It's freezing in here. I'm taking off." A person who asks permission for their feelings or needs to qualify them with the listener is perceived as indecisive and week. "I presented that okay, didn't I?" weakens the impact of a more empowered alternative like, "I really felt connected in that presentation."

Tell Purposeful Stories

Stories in and of themselves are neither good nor bad; their value is in how they are used, for whom, and for what purpose. Stories have the magical quality of transference, or the possibility for participants to apply the story's meaning to themselves. In general, stories that have a specific and clear message, and that are relevant to the discussion at hand, will have the most impact. The ones that are rarely useful are those which are told because the presenter likes the story, it makes the presenter look good, or it takes up time. Personally, I find most useful, stories of participants whom may have had difficulties, yet overcame them and succeeded. I often use Sufi tales with Nasrudin as the main character. Sufi tales meet most of my personal criteria: they are short, to the point, easily interpreted, and timeless. The following excerpt adapted from *The Exploits of the Incomparable Mulla Nasrudin*, by Idres Shah, provides an example:

Stories have the magical quality of transference or the possibility for participants to apply the story's meaning to themselves. In general, stories that have a specific and clear message, and that are relevant to the discussion at hand, will have the most impact.

> Nasrudin often took people for trips in his boat. One day a fussy professor hired Nasrudin to ferry him across a wide and dangerous river. As soon as they had departed, the professor asked whether the ride would be rough. "Don't know nuthin' about no weather," said Nasrudin. "Have you never studied grammar?" the professor asked. "No," said Nasrudin. "In that case, half your life has been wasted," replied the arrogant professor. Soon a terrible storm blew up. Nasrudin's rickety boat began taking on water. He leaned over to his passenger and inquired, "Have you never learned to swim?" "No," replied the Professor. "In that case, *all* of your life has been wasted, for we are about to sink."

Share Success Stories

For most people when they begin to hear a story, their conscious mind recedes. Perhaps, this is the result of childhood associations ("Once upon a time," as in a bedtime story) or the result of a mind-state triggered like, "Okay, here's a break from important course content that I'll need to know; I'll just think of something else for awhile." What this means is that the story is not usually received by the conscious mind. What's left is the unconscious mind which is making associations with whatever words you are using. If the words you use in your story are words like struggle, pain, problem, fail, impossible, and hardship, guess what the participant is left with? Only the thoughts and associations made unconsciously! Therefore, it is critical that your stories incorporate words like success, achievement, empowered, happy, overcome, joy, and ease.

In selecting the stories you will be sharing with your audience first ask yourself, "Does the lesson or thought I intend to trigger with this story support the overall purpose of this training?" And second, "Is the language positive and consistent with what I want participants to learn?" You'll get back what you give, so be careful what you give.

Embedded commands are simply messages woven into other messages which have a specific intended outcome. To build confidence in your participant's learning ability embed suggestions of confidence.

Embed Key Words

When words that conjure up feelings of success are incorporated into your storyline, participants don't know why, but they feel more confident and learning is easier. In the fields of therapy and hypnosis this is known as embedded commands. The participant is distracted by the story which may or may not be important; it is the vehicle for engaging the non-conscious mind while the presenter embeds the positive commands.

Embedded commands are simply messages woven into other messages which have a specific intended outcome. To build confidence in your participant's learning ability embed suggestions of confidence. For example, "Make sure that when you're doing your homework successfully tonight, you use the group handouts." Or, "Everybody who completes their project, whether they're confident of getting an A or not, should make sure that they have their name on it." While the participants are paying attention to the content of your message, their unconscious minds hears the affirmations of success that you've casually dropped in.

You can use embedded commands in many ways. As an example, you can ask your participants to do something while also giving them "suggestions" of confidence and resourcefulness. "While you are successfully and confidently putting your books away, remember to complete your assignment by Friday." What participants are paying attention to is your reminder that they have an assignment due on Friday. What they are actually hearing, even if it's subconscious, is that they are confident and resourceful.

If you want your audience to quiet down, for example, consider the suggestions embedded in the following statement: "Whether you think you've learned this topic well, or almost gagged on it, is a moot issue. I'm sure that the material has quietly become a part of you and, in fact, I may have to muffle your enthusiasm about it at a later time." Notice the references to silence (i.e., gagged, quietly, and muffle). Each of these words is entering the unconscious minds of participants.

Change Your Frame of Reference

Everything makes sense in its own context. To re-frame something means to give an idea or event a different context, a spin, or a new reference point. For example, being forced to attend a seminar would be perceived negatively by most participants, but to re-frame it, you might suggest one or all of the following: "You might meet someone new here today—someone who becomes very important to your life." Or "You may discover something new that really improves your work life."

The next time you are presenting and you get those blank stares looking back at you, try explaining the concept you are covering from a different frame of reference or perspective.

The next time you are presenting and you get those blank stares looking back at you, try explaining the concept you are covering from a different frame of reference or perspective. How would a blind person explain it or how would a deaf person explain it? How would a foreigner explain it? What about a handicapped person, an athlete, or a movie star?

Use Presuppositions

To ask a participant if they are willing to give a presentation to the group leaves you open to getting a refusal. If you presuppose, however, that the participant will do it, then your question becomes, "Would you rather give a presentation on Tuesday or a week from Tuesday?" This is the classic double-bind choice; you are committing the participant to an outcome. The value of binds is that they provide the illusion of choice, yet the options are actually narrow enough to maintain the intended value. Additional binding questions are highlighted on the following page.

Binding Questions

- Would you rather relax now, or in five minutes?
- Do you want to learn something new now, or later?
- Do you think you might be ready to succeed on the first section, or second one?
- Would you like to breath slowly and allow your eyes to gently close, or simply let your whole body relax with your next breath?
- Would you like to give your speech on a topic I choose, or one that you choose?
- Would you like to write a paper, or record your comments on an audiotape?
- I can pick a homework assignment for you or you can; which would you prefer?"

Linkages draw a relationship between otherwise unrelated events. Though we know that an actual relationship doesn't exist in real life between the sound of a presenter's voice and their participant's confidence level, the unconscious mind doesn't know or care about that, and it links the two items together.

The double-bind is a useful tool because it can give you what you want as a presenter, and the participant what they need, as a learner. You want to accomplish the learning objectives, and the participant wants some choice in how this happens.

Use Linkages

Linkages draw a relationship between otherwise unrelated events. As a language tool, it is most often used to connect sensory-grounded experiences with externally-oriented experiences. The simplest form is "A and B." For example, "you are now hearing the sound of my voice and knowing that your confidence will grow." Though we know that an actual relationship doesn't exist in real life between the sound of a presenter's voice and their participant's confidence level, the unconscious mind doesn't know or care about that, and it links the two items together. Since they bypass the conscious mind, linkages have the powerful capacity to affect behavior states.

The strongest form of linkage is cause and effect symbolized by "A causes B." For example, you might say, "As you begin to pick up your pencil and write, you'll be feeling more confident." Or, "Take in another deep breath and exhale as you feel your confidence surge."

Another form of linkage is "if A then B" format. This form involves giving participants a suggestion of confidence which they must accept if they do what you ask. For example, "Only quiet down if you're interested and curious about the next item on the upcoming test." "Stand up and stretch only if you're ready for a great weekend." "You may leave now only if you're more confident than ever before." Notice that you have given your participants a narrow behavioral choice.

Use Quotes

Using a quote is a simple way for you to say something that might, otherwise, make you feel uncomfortable, or might be less effective if directly stated. "Creative quoting" is a technique whereby you embed a suggestion into your presentation through a quote. For example, "This weekend I was talking to my friend about an idea that I had and you know what he said to me? He said, (look right at your participants), 'You're brilliant. I've never met anyone who could pick up things as quickly as you. You're the greatest.' Now, I don't know if he was 100 percent accurate, but it sure felt great!" What you just did was tell a story about your friend, but what was heard by the participant's unconscious mind was a direct appreciation and acknowledgment of intelligence and personal worth.

In the middle of a lecture you can use quotes to enlist the attention of your participants. If you are about to present an important point, you might say to your participants, "I remember when I was learning this material, the presenter said (raise your voice), 'pay close attention', keep an open mind, and you'll learn this easily.' Now, I'm not sure if that was the reason I understood it and was able to apply it in my life, but it likely helped." Then proceed with your lecture while participants pay closer attention and likely understand the material better.

Use Metaphors

The eminent psychologist Milton Erickson used to tell a story about going to work for the first time in this country and being faced with a foreign alphabet. He related the difficulty in what seemed like an overwhelming task and then how, over time, the letters became permanent images in his brain and became the basis for everything he read and wrote, thereafter. Because learning the alphabet is a universal example, it provides the perfect metaphor for something becoming easy that, when first faced with the learning, seemed very difficult or complex.

The following example is also a quote of Milton Erickson's: "When you were a very young child, and you first learned to crawl, you saw toes and table legs, and the world looked a certain way... and when you were able to stand up, the world looked different... and as you bent down to look through your legs, you gained a new perspective... then as you stood up, you had even newer perspectives—each of which gave you additional knowledge and resources." In this example, the metaphor also acts to reinforce the concept that growing and changing widens your perspectives.

"When you were a very young child, and you first learned to crawl, you saw toes and table legs, and the world looked a certain way... and when you were able to stand up, the world looked different... and as you bent down to look through your legs, you gained a new perspective... then as you stood up, you had even newer perspectives—each of which gave you additional knowledge and resources."
–Milton Erickson

Using metaphors is a powerful way to evoke change in your participants. They are easy to use, fun to listen to, and often long-lasting. The following presuppositions underlie the successful use of metaphor: that an individual wants to change and grow; that most of our life's behaviors are controlled by our unconscious mind; that experiences (even if vicarious) are as, or more, powerful an agent for change than didactic forms.

Use Round-Ups

Rounding-up is a process whereby material is reviewed, contextualized, and recycled or "rounded-up" regularly. When round-ups are used consistently, participants feel more confident with the material, and presenters feel more confident that they have been understood. To use this principle, simply remind participants where you started, where you are currently, and where you are taking them. This process anchors the learning and helps your audience perceive the big picture. You might use phrases such as, "Earlier, when we learned about A and B..." or, "You may recall that we said..." Or, "Given that we have covered the area of..." Master presenters round-up constantly. It's surprising how much better participants understand when they are provided with the overview to support the detail.

By eliciting increasing commitments with your audience, you are keeping them engaged. At this point, they are walking hand-in-hand with you, rather than being pulled along.

Elicit Increasing Commitments

A good salesperson knows better than to ask for the sale before they have made an initial presentation. It takes time to build trust, discover customer concerns, and develop an effective and appropriate response to consumer needs. A top salesperson affirms points of agreement throughout the presentation. Like a good salesperson, highly effective presenters use a similar technique. Seek agreement as you establish common ground with your audience. Start with simple things like, "Who has found this to be true?" As you develop rapport and trust with your audience, you can increase the intensity of your leading questions. For example, you might shift to, "How many of you have had this happen so often that you're ready for something new?" At the right moment, you can say, "If there was a way to do such and such, how many of you would be interested?" By eliciting increasing commitments with your audience, you are keeping them engaged. At this point, they are walking hand-in-hand with you, rather than being pulled along.

This chapter has included some powerful persuasion tools that will dramatically enhance any presentation. Practice a few of them at a time; like learning the alphabet, soon you will achieve mastery and they will become a natural part of your presentation style. Present your material with zest, commitment, flexibility, and compassion. Use the tools in this chapter, along with love and respect, and you will soon master the all-important art of persuasion.

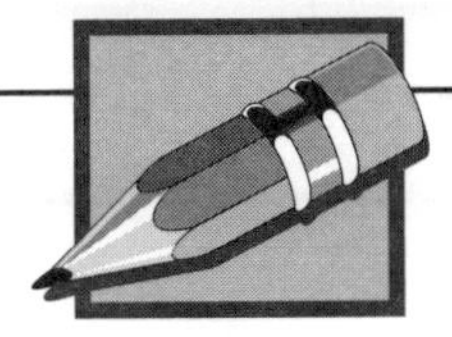

Engage Your Brain:
Planning for a Persuasive Presentation

In planning for your next presentation, how will you ensure your voice and gestures provide a congruent message?

What vision will you share with your audience? How will you dramatize your main points?

How do you plan on engaging participant's emotions? Will you be sharing any stories? If so, how do they apply to your message?

What other strategies presented in this chapter might you incorporate into your next presentation? How will you use them?

I know the price of success: dedication, hard work, and an unremitting devotion to the things you want to see happen.

–Frank Lloyd Wright

CHAPTER 14

Handling Hot and Spicy Audiences

The more you present, the better you'll get. The better you get, the more trainings you'll be asked to do. The more trainings you do, the more your reputation spreads. The more your reputation spreads, the more you'll be asked to work with hard-to-reach audiences. The more you work with resistant and indifferent audiences, the greater the challenges you'll face. There's no escape! You simply need to learn the skills of dealing with tough audiences to survive in the world of presenting.

While most presenters love to work with motivated, eager-to-learn audiences, this kind of audience will respond well to even an average presenter. Positive feedback from non-critical audiences may feel great at first. But, after awhile, you realize that your skills improve much faster when you are faced with a hot and spicy audience that challenges you. Resistant audiences provide excellent practice opportunities. This chapter provides practical strategies for dealing with the inevitable challenge of resistant participants.

- ***Resistance Is Best Handled With State Changes***
- ***Four Basic Principles***
- ***Red Flags to Avoid***
- ***Changing Shoes and Perspectives***
- ***Offer Extra Value***
- ***Let Your Modest Side Shine***
- ***Experiment Often***
- ***Resistance Breakers***
- ***First Aid for the Heckled Presenter***

Brain Connection

Resistance Is Best Managed With State Changes

Participants will exhibit a variety of biological states during a presentation. Resistant audiences may have a dozen legitimate reasons to be resistant–anything from lower levels of dopamine, depression, or forced attendance, to an uncomfortable physical environment. Use what you know about the brain to raise levels of dopamine, adrenaline, and serotonin. This includes incorporating forms of movement, music, controversy, and arousal. Rely on nonconscious influences. The states we definitely want to minimize are defiance, frustration, anger, apathy, and hostility. Our words, posture, tonality, position, facial expressions, and gestures all impact participant states. To handle hot and spicy audiences, we need to positively influence the chemical states of our participants.

Four Basic Principles

The first thing to do when encountering a resistant audience or participant is to remember the following four basic principles:

1. ***People are different.***
2. ***Trying to fix people is counterproductive.***
3. ***Stretch yourself.***
4. ***Enjoy the challenge.***

Our words, posture, tonality, position, facial expressions, and gestures will all impact participant states. To handle hot and spicy audiences, we need to positively influence the chemical states of our participants.

People don't wake up in the morning thinking, "I'm going to give our presenter a hard time today." Most likely, the resistant participant has been influenced by some negative experience either related to the seminar or not; and they need a state change. It's not your job to fix others; however, all of us can be positively influenced by a simple state change strategy. Suggestions for changing participants' states are provided throughout *Sizzle & Substance*, but the subject is covered comprehensively in Chapter 12. It is often resistant audiences that challenge you the most, uncover your weaknesses, and ultimately facilitate your growth.

Red Flags

When you're working with resistant audiences, there are plenty of things to do right: keep your word, offer real value, include the participants in your presentation, etc. But there are also a few red flags to avoid, like the following:

- Assuming you know about the audience when you don't.
- Being arrogant or acting like the great expert.
- Not knowing the community culture or local business culture.
- Not determining what your audience already knows.
- Using buzz words that are outdated or have been banned.
- Telling off-color, racist, sexist, or other offensive jokes.
- Wearing clothes that aren't appropriate to the setting.
- Referring to stars, bosses, or local icons in a derogatory way.
- Making assumptions and stereotyping.
- Describing people by their age, color, race, or ethnicity.
- Using strong definitive statements like forever, everybody, nobody, all, always, and never.
- Disagreeing with your audience, but if you have to, at least disagree without being disagreeable.

Changing Shoes and Perspectives

To get your foot in the door with a resistant audience, begin by putting yourself in their shoes. Why might the audience be skeptical? Why should they listen to you? What would compel them to follow your suggestions? Why should they share your passion? And, perhaps, most importantly, what's in it for them? Answer these questions and you'll be on the way to less resistant audiences.

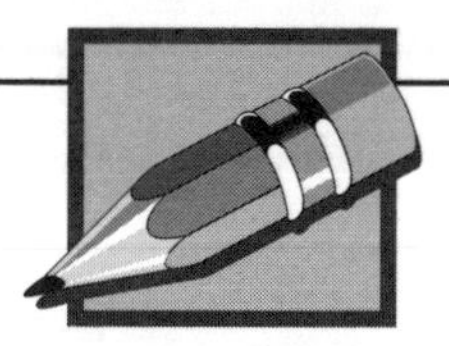

Engage Your Brain:
Offsetting Audience Resistance

What are the top three reasons I'm giving this presentation?

What top three benefits will the audience get from this presentation? Why are they likely to attend?

What do you want the audience to do as a result of your presentation? Why should they make any changes?

What obstacles might they encounter (or resistance might they have) in implementing the changes you suggest?

What are the top three reasons they may want to make changes immediately (or in the next 30 days)? What will happen if they don't?

When you answer the previous questions, you'll gain insights into what you're up against. It's humbling to realize that, perhaps, you have not made the reasons participants ought to listen to obvious enough. The next step is to begin building into your presentation some specific reasons why the audience will want to pay attention and take your suggestions seriously. Simple, right!

Offer Extra Value

Chances are your participants were mandated to attend your training; but in spite of that, they still have basic human needs and expectations and if you fail to meet them, they'll probably want to crucify you. The rougher the audience, the more you *have* to deliver. Delivering the goods includes the following:

All behavior is state-related involving the body, mind, and emotions. In a really good presentation, it's not uncommon to see five or ten state-changers per hour. Monitor the states of your participants throughout your entire presentation. If their state is not appropriate for the moment, change it!

- Finishing on time or a few minutes early, but never late, without the group's approval.
- Engaging the audience in a non-threatening way and listening to their concerns.
- Spelling out the direct benefits of your presentation consistently and clearly.
- Remaining flexible; responding to a spontaneous audience request affirmatively.
- Being funny.
- Maintaining credibility.

All behavior is state-related. As presented in previous chapters, the process for involving your audience can include physical and/or mental involvement. Start with some simple state-changers. These involve the body, mind, and emotions. In a really good presentation, it's not uncommon to see five or ten state-changers per hour. Monitor the states of your participants throughout your entire presentation. If their state is not appropriate for the moment, change it! For a quick review, here are four time-tested suggestions:

1 Involve your audience first thing—before they have a chance to settle in. Start with an icebreaker, a paired activity, or with a small group problem-solving exercise that is relevant to your topic.

2 Present a compelling reason for your audience to get involved. It might be (1) we can't do this without you, (2) it's tradition, (3) it'll be a time-saver or money-maker, or (4) or it's good for the brain.

3 Give your audience some say in the type or level of involvement. Ask them for suggestions or to decide from a few options. This process, itself, encourages involvement.

4 Proceed slowly in incremental steps to minimize the perceived risk. Try one thing; if it works, try another. Use state changers. Use energizers, but respect the advancing gradient of change.

Let Your Modest Side Shine

Even if you are a Nobel Prize winner (If you are by the way, congratulations!), there's no reason to boast about it. Instead build your credibility slowly, artfully, and purposely. Use examples in your presentation that include credibility "plugs." For instance, "I was so embarrassed. I was flying into Minneapolis and realized I had left some key papers behind for a client of mine at 3M. It was so frustrating; I had to recreate them the night before my presentation. It turned out that they liked them enough to contract me for additional work, but was I scared that first day." Note how the emphasis was on the mistake made, not the name of the client or your success with them.

Experiment Often

Sometimes when we feel stressed or pressured as a presenter, we fall back on the tried and true and forget the value of risk and experimentation. Some of the most effective strategies I have developed have been in response to working with resistant audiences. The core of your content doesn't have to change, but the process holds a world of wiggle room. After all, if you're struggling with an audience, or if you know in advance that it will be a challenge, you suddenly have little to lose. No one really expects you to work miracles; suddenly you have more permission to experiment. The following strategies are ones I originally experimented with; yet now, it's hard to believe that I ever thought of them as an experiment:

Sometimes when we feel stressed or pressured as a presenter, we fall back on the tried and true and forget the value of risk and experimentation. The core of your content doesn't have to change, but the process holds a world of wiggle room.

Seat Changes

Ask your audience to stand up and take a deep breath. Then ask them to pick up their belongings and change seats. Say to the group, "You must sit at least three seats away from whomever you're sitting next to now. Plus, if you're on the left side of the room, go to the right side. If you're in the back, go to the front. If you're in the front, go to the back. If you're in the middle, go to the outside and vice versa. Change groupings, too. If you're sitting by yourself, pair up. If you're in one group, change groups." If done strategically and not too frequently, this strategy will work wonders for getting participants more actively involved.

Standing Up

Ask your audience to stand up for a moment. Continue to give your presentation while they are standing up. This can be useful for about a minute, depending on the age of your audience. While standing up, participants will see and hear things a bit differently; but most of all, it is a simple way to get them out of a stuck condition. Just before they sit down, have them give themselves a hand. Clapping stimulates further circulation.

Stretching

An especially useful stretching technique for a training environment is cross-laterals. Cross-laterals use both sides of the body, thus, both sides of the brain. Two examples are "apple-picking" where you reach with alternating arms one at a time and bicycling where you lay on your back and alternate legs in a pedaling motion. Physical movement increases breathing rate and circulation which provides the brain with more oxygen and creates a physiological state change breaking up stuck patterns.

In some form or another, nearly every presenter has experienced the dual evils of the totally non-participatory participant and the overly-participatory individual. The best presenters have learned to offset these difficult states by learning effective ways to react to them.

Talking Time

Provide the audience with time to talk about what they are learning (or not learning!). They need a "reality feedback" not an "authority feedback." This means that they need to integrate and use the material they are learning in their own way. Stop your group (at an appropriate moment) and provide your participants with two or three minutes of time to talk about what they're learning in any way they choose. For example, you might say, "Turn to your partner and talk for two minutes about the key points we've been discussing."

Humor

If you are "a natural" at this, take advantage of it (but avoid overdoing it). Remember the audience may not have your same interest or tolerance level. What audiences dislike the most are jokes that are too long or that poke fun at people. When working with groups or cultures that are generally conservative or reserved, I find that if I smile and use polite humor, I can often "tease" such audiences into more participation.

Breathing

The better the flow of oxygen to your participant's brain, the better the ability to perform. Remind your participants to take in a slow deep breath and exhale even slower, many times an hour. Simply ask the whole group to do it together and you'll not only have a state-changer, but your audience will begin breathing in rapport. The best times to do this are just after a main point or in-between two key ideas.

The Power of Suggestion

Our brain is an associative mechanism which is constantly making connections. Think of hot, you might associate cold, for instance; think of black and your brain probably associates white; think up and your brain associates down, in and out, old and new, fresh and stale, small and big and so on. The point is this: Affirm what you want to have happen. Suggest to your audience that they might want to participate more as the day goes on. Tell them that research suggests those who participate more, learn more. Tell them that others have found that as they get more involved, the day moves faster.

Low-key Games

Sometimes people who may not want to get involved in an activity of a personal or serious nature may enjoy involvement in a simple paper or board game. Make up a bingo game for your group. Use it as an opening icebreaker so the audience can either get interested in the topic or find out how much there is to learn.

Resistance Breakers

In some form or another, nearly every presenter has experienced the dual evils of the totally non-participatory participant and the overly-participatory individual. The best presenters have learned to offset these difficult states by structuring their sessions in a way that is most aligned with how the brain naturally learns best. Consider the following prevention tips when planning each presentation:

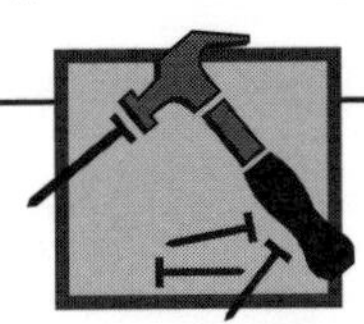

Prevention Tips & Tools

- Create more "W-I-I-F-M" (What's in it for me?) for the participants.
- Make rapport-building a priority.
- Limit the amount of focused learner attention time.
- Use environmental or baroque music in the background (low volume) to soothe and inspire.
- Read and respond swiftly to changing states. Know that frustration often leads to apathy or anger and even revenge.
- Organize audience into cooperative groups or teams (with accountability).

Continued...

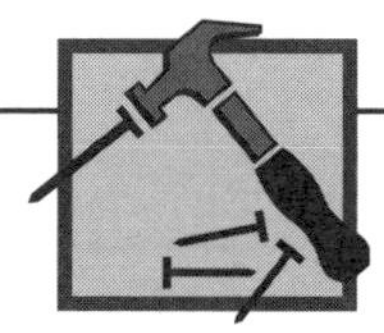

Prevention Tips & Tools

Continued...

- Make a positive contact with several participants within the first few minutes.
- Increase audience input; use a suggestion box. Read all suggestions, respond to them immediately.
- Provide more outlets for participant expression. Assign small group presentations, provide general catch-up "buzz time," utilize partner-partner affirmations, group or team time, discussion, cheers, or sharing.
- Respect the tendencies of auditory learners who tend to talk a lot, and mis-matchers who accidentally disrupt the group in an attempt to learn. They're often pointing out what's off, different, missing, or wrong.
- Facilitate physical movement at least twice per hour. Use partner or group work, hands-on activities, stretch breaks, or simply change activities.
- Make sure you keep your own stress levels low. "Download" each work day. Enjoy de-stressing "mindless" relaxing play.
- Be sure to give clear, short directions. Use the guidelines in Chapter 12 for managing states. Make them consistent, re-check for understanding, then use the same congruent call to action.
- Provide learners far more control over their learning. Offer choice in methods, topics, rules, time frames, partners, scoring, music, etc.
- Have lunch with a participant or spend breaks with them to build relationships.
- Incorporate activities that use the multiple intelligences. For example, have participants work in pairs, doing a large mind-map preview or review on butcher paper. This activity uses interpersonal, spatial, verbal-linguistic, and bodily kinesthetic intelligences.
- Incorporate discussion time, sharing circles, or partner/buddy time.

Only after you have demonstrated consistently that your participants can trust your responses will they feel safe and willing to take risks in the group setting. To increase group trust among participants, always respond with respect. Never, ever put a participant down, *even as a joke*. Never be sarcastic to a participant or make a belittling remark. You must set the tone of love, safety, and respect in the room if you want a productive and participatory audience.

The truth is, we never know, as presenters, who we really affect and how much, on any given day. Getting high marks on evaluations does not necessarily mean we provided real value. Time is the true test. Long-term value ought to be our goal. If the group doesn't seem to warm up during your presentation, that doesn't necessarily mean you weren't successful. Time and again, I've heard stories about how much a presentation I gave years ago positively influenced somebody that I had no idea I touched.

On the other hand, I also know there are plenty of people who aren't implementing much of anything they learned from my trainings. This always provides a reality check for me. It may be temporarily discouraging but it motivates me to improve every time I present. I continue to learn more about learning theory, the brain, and transference to do a better job. To obtain long-term feedback, I pass out a postcard at the end of my presentations addressed to myself. On the back side, I ask participants to send me feedback regarding the training's impact of one month later. This technique provides the presenter with a little different perspective than the immediate feedback gathered the day of the training. It can really help in the humility department, as well.

Only after you have demonstrated consistently that your participants can trust your responses will they feel safe and willing to take risks in the group setting. To increase group trust among participants, always respond with respect.

First Aid for the Heckled Presenter

Your potential solutions for dealing with hecklers will depend on a host of variables. First, discover if the heckler is expressing, primarily, an emotion. If "yes", then make sure you listen to the participant and hear them out. If "no" simply answer the comment. If the heckling continues, discover if the heckler is alone in the way they feel or if others concur? If they are the exception, deal with them quickly or at the first break. If others concur, address the feelings with the whole group as soon as possible.

Take appropriate action, like the following steps, if you continue to meet resistance: Put the group between you and speaker. Take in a slow deep breath. Think of "being of service." Listen for the emotions first (if present). Listen for the participant's real issue to surface. Check the rest of the audience's reaction. Validate their responses. Provide short specific answers. Avoid asking, "What's wrong?" Rather, ask, "What would make it right?"

Keep your interaction short. Avoid "crazy-making" confrontations. Make your response a public promise if need be. If you need more time, set it up for later. Always make a final check to ensure that the participant is satisfied. Re-elicit a positive learning state with the rest of the group.

Your first concern need be understanding and dealing with the emotions of the problem. Is the heckler curious or frustrated, obnoxious or angry? The emotion needs to be heard and acknowledged before the content of the question can even be considered. Most of the time the heckler disguises the problem. They may be frustrated because they were forced to attend, so their real agenda is to make it miserable for others. Instead of creating a "me" versus "them" situation, consider it a customer service opportunity. This disarms the heckler and makes it easy to make the right decision. Never lose your temper with a heckler; rise above the situation and focus on your real priorities.

Priorities for Handling Hecklers

- To restore a positive learning environment
- To elicit a state of satisfaction with the heckler
- To provide specific answers
- To prevent reoccurrence
- To reestablish your credibility

Open your response with one of the following three rapport-builders: "I appreciate..." Or, "I agree..." Or, "I respect..." Complete the sentence as you and the participant move towards co-creating a mutually satisfying solution. The following dialogue, for example, moves the participant towards this end:

Participant:
"You don't know what you are talking about. This is really stupid!"

Presenter:
"Maybe you could help me out a little. What doesn't make any sense to you and what are some things we can do about it?"

Listen, empathize, and respect the heckler's point of view. Repeat back to them what you think their point is, so that they know they've been understood. Always handle an irritated participant completely so that the rest of the group can relax and move on. Ask for an appointment with the upset person from the front of the room so they know you care and are willing to work things out. Never leave someone upset, hurt, or brooding in your audience. Never, ever make fun of anyone except yourself from the front of the room. Never embarrass others or you risk shutting down the rest of the group and reducing their likely contributions. Ask "cut-to-the-chase" questions. The best way to find out if your heckler has a legitimate agenda is to ask the question, "What would make it right?" One with a legitimate concern will respond positively to this question. A "professional heckler" will be trapped and have to "put up or shut up." Make your response a public promise if need be. You might have to say, "Thanks for asking that. I'll check with the staff and get back to you about it at the next break." If you need more time, set a meeting for later. You might say, "I want to help. Can we get together for lunch where I might have more time to do a better job?" Then go back to your group and re-elicit a positive learning state with them. You might say to the group, "Let's all take in a big deep breath... now exhale. If you're ready to move on, raise your hand please." This will transition you and the group into something else.

The suggestions above work universally—in corporate and academic environments, formal or informal, from elementary school-age children to adults, in America and around the world. In spite of this, there are and will continue to be, exceptions to the rule. But the presenters who are best at dealing with the inevitable show stopper have simply learned, over time, how to gracefully move the group along while satisfying the needs of the random element. As with most things, experience and practice is the best first aid.

Listen, empathize, and respect the heckler's point of view. Repeat back to them what you think their point is, so that they know they've been understood. Always handle an irritated participant completely so that the rest of the group can relax and move on.

SECTION FOUR:
Fires That Inspire the Mind

CHAPTER 15

Facilitating Effective Audience Interactions

In general, if you want to boost audience participation, you've got to encourage interactions and make them rewarding and fun. If participants feel stressed, threatened, or frustrated, they will close up. Generally, I ask very few "content" questions because they put people on the spot. Rather, I like to ask whole-group questions which help focus participants on common experiences. For example, "How many of you have had this happen...?" A question such as this creates a bridge between you and the participants, embarrasses no one, and, if timed right, can be a good segue into your next activity or subject area.

- *Setting the Stage*
- *Understanding Follows the Brain's Quest for Meaning*
- *Creating an Ask-Friendly Climate*
- *Preventing Inappropriate Questions*
- *Purposeful Questioning Techniques*
- *Responding to Audience Answers*
- *Handling Off Answers*
- *Sharpen Your Tools*
- *The Real Show*

Setting the Stage

Generally, presenters ask questions in a way that are perceived by the audience as an expedition or "witch hunt" for a specific answer. Be sure your purpose for questioning is not to please the presenter. It makes more sense to acknowledge *all* of the responses you get, instead of seeking the *right* one. After you've collected as many responses as possible, facilitate a discussion that will incorporate all of the interactions. The more participants have invested in the topic (was *my* answer right or wrong?), the more attention they will direct towards *your* answer.

At the start of your presentation, let the group know what your expectations are regarding questions. If you prefer that they wait for a designated question time, let them know this. If you expect participants to raise their hand when you ask them a question, let them know this. When you field a question, really listen. Acknowledge the asker, paraphrase their question, and then answer it concisely. "Thanks for asking. Let me repeat the question. She asked if... For the sake of time, let me give you the short answer..."

Brain Connection

Understanding Follows the Brain's Quest for Meaning

Learning is a process whereby the brain begins to recognize useful associations and connections with previously stored data. Our brain hungers for such "meaning." Each pattern that is discovered adds to the learner's perceptual map at which time the brain finds relief from the state of confusion, anxiety, or stress that accompanies raw data. A participant's question, if answered well, may supply the missing link to strengthen their chain of understanding. Left unanswered, however, their anxiety will remain intact and their understanding incomplete.

Creating an Ask-Friendly Climate

There are various reasons to ask questions of your audience, so check your motivation. An optimal intention is that your questions empower participants. There must be no intention to "win" or make another wrong. Eliminate trick questions unless used in a separate context as a learning tool. Each question, in an emotionally safe climate, will be guided with the intent to stimulate thinking and engage the group.

Each question, in an emotionally safe climate, will be guided with the intent to stimulate thinking and engage the group.

Who should you call on when you ask a question and a sea of hands go up? This depends on the outcome you want? Do you want to keep everyone on their toes? Do you want to work with a few participants who need extra help? There's no pat right answer. However, one technique that is *not* learning-friendly is to draw a name out of a hat, unless it's for a team response. Creating a random "death by embarrassment" drawing can be emotionally threatening and will certainly not encourage interaction and trust. The following alternatives, however, will instill a climate of compassion:

Call on a Volunteer

As you build a safe and open atmosphere, you will find more volunteers anxious to respond to your questions. Be aware, however, of the possible tendency to call on the same people.

Boost a Participant's Confidence

Call on participants who you feel could use the biggest boost in self-confidence, then guarantee their success.

Select a Consultant for the Day

Call on a pre-selected participant or the person who has volunteered to be the group consultant for the day. Every participant has some special talent or experience. Make it your job to bring out that quality.

Provide a "Mistakes Okay" Climate

Downplay right answer searches, and role-model how to deal with mistakes as a natural part of the learning process.

Multiple Answers

Assert that many questions have multiple answers and perspectives, and incorporate open-ended questions. For example, "Customer service is always important. What are some of the ways companies are improving it?"

Ensure Readiness

Before asking audience questions, check in with them to ensure readiness. Provide a time for sharing and getting clarification in small groups. This will make the large-group question time more focused and will elicit higher-order thinking.

Small Group Question Time

Pose questions to teams, small groups, or dyads to work on collaboratively. This keeps the pressure off one person and encourages cooperation.

Boxes of Understanding

Before asking a question, utilize the three boxes of understanding approach. Ask who has either, 1) vague, 2) average, or 3) expert knowledge on the subject.

Make Questions Explicit

Pass out the questions you'll be asking on a handout, or post them for all to see. Give participants time to prepare their responses.

Before asking audience questions, check in with them to ensure readiness. Provide a time for sharing and getting clarification in small groups.

Preventing Inappropriate Questions

Many inappropriate questions can be prevented. Let the audience know exactly *what* your specialty is and what it is *not*. I heard a scientist start his talk recently by saying, "Here's what we'll be discussing this afternoon," as he presented an overview of his topic. "I am *not* an expert on...," as he explained where his expertise ended. "And so, unfortunately, I can't address this area. But I'm happy to focus on..." This simple parameter-setting strategy was really effective and kept participants focused on his area of expertise.

Purposeful Questioning Techniques

Among the many kinds of audience questions that are useful, content-recall questions, process questions, and application questions are the most valuable. *Content Recall Questions* can be asked in various ways for various purposes. The following content-recall questions exemplify some of the most common approaches:

Content Recall Questions

Identifying: What is the name of your favorite book on presenting?
Completing: This chapter is on successful _______.
Matching: What other books are similar to this one?
Listing: Name your favorite chapters in this book.
Observing: What subtitles do you see on this page?
Reciting: Earlier I said we'll be focusing on what types of questions?
Describing: Describe the cover of this book?
Defining: What's the definition of a successful interaction?

The content-recall questions above operate on the principal of a stimulus response mechanism intended to elicit stored data from prior knowledge or experience. The recall question draws from participants the kind of information that a card file or computer might.

The second type, the *Process Question*, is designed to uncover the process acquired or used. It requires different skills than the content-recall question. Some examples follow:

Process Questions

Comparing: What do you and your participants have in common?
Sequencing: In what order would questioning strategies best be learned?
Inferring: What can you infer from the first sentence on this page?
Grouping: How would you rate this book so far?
Contrasting: In what ways is this book different from the last one you read?
Analyzing: What might you say about your answer to the preceding question?
Organizing: How could you better arrange this information?

Questions that require distinguishing, grouping, explaining, and experimenting are also considered process related.

The third type, the *Application Question*, moves the participant into a creative state of make believe, construction, fantasy, and/or invention. In the process, the participant must set aside the immediate content to come up with new or hypothetical information. Some examples follow:

Application Questions

Applying: What would happen if you learned all the tools in this book?
Concluding: Now that you're a better presenter, what can you say about your self-esteem?
Speculating: What would happen if every presenter knew what you now know?
Modifying: How quickly can you adapt this book to your own library?
Forecasting: Based on last year's growth, how good will you be next year?
Distorting: After you succeed with one group, are you the best presenter ever?
Deleting: What is it you want to ignore about this book?
Inventing: I wonder how many ways you could tell others about this book?"

Questions that require theorizing, examples, judging, imagining, and extrapolating are also considered application questions.

Responding to Audience Answers

When you get a favorable answer to an audience question, it's obvious how to respond. But, what do you do if you get an answer that does not represent an understanding of the material? In any answer attempt, whether you like the response or not, the essential first step is to acknowledge the participant's effort and contribution. Thank them and then use the opportunity to follow up. You might say, for instance, "Can you tie your answer into what others have already said?" Or, "Do you know how you came to this way of thinking?" Another option is to just expand on their answer incorporating the important points you want to reiterate along the way. It's never necessary to say, "No, that's not correct."

Handling Off Answers

Many presenters and educators become dogmatic about the importance of the right answer; they reward the participants who know it and penalize those who don't. This viewpoint reflects the philosophy that "either you know it or you don't—there's no in-between ground." In this age of computers and easily accessible mass storage, ask yourself, "What's more useful in today's world—the correct recitation of facts or the ability to think through a situation?" In other words, how your participants arrive at an answer or learning about the process may provide the information necessary to be successful in modern life.

It is natural for your participants to fail momentarily with a wrong answer as long as they are using or learning a process that will eventually allow them to succeed. Failure is encouraged in the larger context of being successful; and in fact, failure is the information needed to become successful. Successful failure means that you discovered the content was not correct and you had an opportunity to discover the process which would lead to the correct answer. Was your strategy useful? Would you use it again? If not, what's an alternative strategy? In this framework, you can't call a wrong answer a failure!

Some professionals believe that handling wrong answers in this way can lead to an artificially low ceiling on performance. However, upon closer scrutiny, in a direct single-answer recall situation, the participant who offers the wrong answer may actually be exhibiting higher-order thinking and a more successful strategy for learning than the participant who delivers the correct answer. Evidence has actually shown that the brightest individuals read more ambiguity into a question than the average learner does leading to more wrong answers.

It is a natural part of the process for your participants to fail momentarily with a wrong answer as long as they are using or learning a process that will eventually allow them to succeed. Failure is encouraged in the larger context of being successful; and in fact, failure is the information needed to become successful.

Yet the strategy for most presenters is to encourage the simplest or most efficient path to the answer, rather than stressing that there are many paths. The real problem with this method is that you end up with inflexible learners. Presenters often listen for the expected answer rather than the answer they get; and the participant who cannot frame their ideas the way the presenter does feels like a failure. As your awareness of multiple learning strategies increases, and as you share this awareness with your participants, you will likely see dramatic gains in test scores, enthusiasm, and even IQ!

Sharpen Your Tools

If you aren't communicating what you intend, your tools probably need sharpening. "Stand and deliver" is dead. Communication is no longer like the proverbial arrow aimed into the air, but more accurately, the quality of understanding between two people. The definition of communication is really quite simple—the transfer of meaning. In other words, the meaning of your communication is the response you get! For example, if the room is burning down and you yell "fire" but nobody responds because they think you're kidding, you better change your communication strategy. It's not enough to do what works for the majority of people most of the time. What's "enough" is determined by your resources and commitment to the outcome. If 90 percent of participants get your message about the fire and leave, are you committed enough to insure the safety of the other 10 percent? Is it enough to present to a group where 90 percent of the participants get the message, and the other 10 percent are getting "burned?"

The Real Show

As a presenter, even a great presenter, you are never the main event. The real show is in your participant's mind. If you think about it, this is a drastically different message than what you likely grew up with. All of our lives we are taught that if someone else doesn't get the meaning of what we have said, it's their fault. However, a more effective way of communicating is to take responsibility for the response you get.

Your message can be broken into three parts: content, delivery, and context. *All* three are part of the process of communication. The effects of any of the three can be destroyed or magnified by the other two. Any time the result of your communications is below expectations, ask yourself the following questions:

Your message can be broken into three parts: content, delivery, and context. All three are part of the process of communication. The effects of any of the three can be destroyed or magnified by the other two.

- Is it *what* I am saying?... I can change this!
- Is it *how* I am saying it?... I can change this, too!
- Is it the circumstances?... I can change these!

The focus of communication needs to be the other party. Focus on what's going on for the learner. Ask questions such as, "Could you rephrase what I just said?" "What's not clear to you?" "How do you know you don't understand?" "What would it take for you to really understand this topic?" "When you say you're not sure, what parts are you sure about already?" Just by asking useful questions, you'll begin to understand how your participants think, learn, and draw conclusions. Top presenters are curious learners, too. They are curious about what helps their participants learn, the process by which they learn, and how they can help them learn better. Here are three areas of influence you have:

1 **Your content...** *What* you are saying.
This, obviously, includes your subject matter. More importantly, it includes your ability to build relationships, add value, create motivation, elicit promises, and prompt requests.

2 **Your delivery...** *How* you are saying it.
This includes your posture, eye contact, positioning, expressions, and gestures. It also includes the workplace's dress code, grooming, and your voice quality including tonality, volume, pitch, tempo, and rhythm.

3 **The context...** The *conditions* and *circumstances* involved.
This area includes the group mood, the rules in effect, what's happened previously, etc. You have within you, at any time and in any place, both the ability and the responsibility to create the conditions and circumstances favorable to the learning process.

One last thought, which is perhaps the most important one: When you present with an emphasis on people, rather than on curriculum, your communications are all participant-based. This means that the focus is on the effects of the communication on your participants, not the generation or creation of the communication. Communication is a two-way conversation with your participants. Your communication is not what you intend, but rather the response you get. A game plan for communication success follows:

- Expect well-defined and positive results in all of your interactions.
- Use well-developed perception and sensory acuity skills to interpret the responses you get.
- Maintain enormous flexibility so that you can use various angles, if necessary, to make your point.
- Maintain a personal commitment to the listener and keep trying until you are successful.

Maybe the most important thing to remember in facilitating effective audience interactions is to bring what is known as "purposeful presence" to your work. For the sake of your participants be mindful of your intention, be caring, and hold a positive vision.

Maybe the most important thing to remember in facilitating effective audience interactions is to bring what is known as "purposeful presence" to your work. For the sake of your participants be mindful of your intention, be caring, and hold a positive vision. This means that for every presentation you make, you are totally committed and fully present. It means that you are doing what you are supposed to be doing—listening, speaking, being in the moment. Most of all, it means integrity, truthfulness, and commitment to your values. When approached this way, your audience interactions can't help but be truly effective.

Engage Your Brain:
Planning for Effective Audience Interactions

What expectations do you have for participant questions in your presentation? How about participant answers? How will you make participants aware of these expectations?

What will you do to make your seminar a safe and mistakes-okay environment for participants?

Write some examples of questions you want to ask in your next presentation; then categorize them as content, process, or application questions. Do you have a good balance of each type of question?

How will you go about selecting participants to answer questions? How will you handle answers that are off?

Give to the world the best you have and the best will come back to you.

–Madeline Bridges

CHAPTER 16

Activities That Fan the Flames

Your presentation and the total learning process can be fired up with active learning. Not only have active learning strategies been shown to accelerate understanding, recall, and meaning, but they add enjoyment. Most learners these days prefer active over passive learning approaches. Perhaps, this has to do with our action-oriented lifestyles and fast pace of today's world. It also matches the current brain research which suggests that new learning and physical learning may be linked. PET scans, which have provided scientists with valuable information about glucose consumption in the brain, reveal that activity in the cerebellum is increased during both physical movement and/or novelty or new learning. This chapter provides a wealth of ideas to activate your presentations.

Hot Tips for Active Learning

- Keep the learning activity short and purposeful.
- Share with your audience the meaning of it—why you're doing it.
- Provide some room for participants to influence the process—present options.
- Give clear directions and time limits—rehearse directions in your mind in advance.
- Change the type of activities you do to keep them fresh.
- Present the activity enthusiastically.
- Always facilitate a debriefing after the activity is conducted.

Brain Connection

Movement Accelerates Learning

Though some may label learning as being more cognitive (mental) or more visceral (physical), to the brain, there is no mind-body dichotomy. There's no "rest of the body"; it's all one entity. The concept of learning activities makes good sense if you realize that "body learning" can be as good as "head learning," and in some cases, better. Learning that is embedded at the cellular level can trigger attention states, evoke emotions for long-term memory, and engage a procedural retrieval for lasting application. In short, learning with the brain-body makes good sense.

Hot Tips for Saving Time

- Use a special sound to get attention (whistle, horn, gong, bell, etc.).
- Make sure that you always know what the next step is.
- Prepare all overheads and flip charts in advance.
- Give crisp, clear, easy-to-understand directions.
- Establish a system for creating teams and selecting volunteers.
- Establish deadlines and time limits and stick to them.
- Incorporate music as a backdrop to an activity. Turn it off when time's up.
- Avoid conversations that endlessly drag on—exit gracefully.

Thinking is the best activity of all. Once a particular topic has been introduced, invite participants to explore it further in pairs or small groups.

Hot Tips for Individual Activities

- Compare and contrast what has been learned with what was already known.
- Mind-map the material, then re-do the original mind-map from memory.
- Visualize the material and make picture links.
- Draw a visual of what's been learned—use a diagram, fishbone or flow chart.
- Write in a journal or learning log. Suggest that participants write about the things they agree with, disagree with, what they have personalized, what they've learned, concluded, or plan to do to incorporate the learning.
- Analyze a problem or do a case study.
- Match up the learning with a set of criteria, possibly a check list or rubric.
- Generate ideas about it or new possible applications of the material.
- Read a short segment of material and locate key ideas.
- Create test questions or questions for the speaker.

Hot Tips for Pairs and Small Groups

Thinking is the best activity of all. Once a particular topic has been introduced, invite participants to explore it further using strategies such as the ones below:

- Make links to other related ideas and topics.
- Predict possible short and long-term consequences.
- Re-state the material in their own way.

- Make guesses about how the material would be understood by another person in another location or circumstance.
- Provide counter arguments to the material.
- Generate examples of the learning.
- Apply the material to the real world.
- Hold a discussion of the topic with no boundaries (open session).
- Compare your own interpretations and notes with another participant.
- Edit or critique someone else's work.
- Create questions for the facilitator or for a test.
- Review a topic or preview the next one.
- Build an abstract or working model of the topic or solution.
- Piece together a jigsaw puzzle related to the material.
- Work together on a joint mind-map.
- Create a one minute TV commercial on the subject just learned.

Though an energizer is considered a learning activity, it is usually used for a different purpose. While learning activities are meant to embed the learning kinesthetically and to master a certain skill or content area, energizers are used to initiate a state change.

Hot Tips for Whole Group Activities

The following activities work well with groups of three or more. They can be adapted to whatever your topic area is, particular group size, and circumstance.

- Provide the group with a survey on the topic you're presenting and have them compile the results.
- Give the first half of your group an article or handout and instruct them to take 15 minutes to read it outside or in another room and discuss it with each other when they finish reading it. The second half of the group remains with you while you provide the same information in lecture format as the other group received in a written format. When the time is up, the readers return to the room where the listeners present what they learned and the readers present what they learned to the whole group.
- Do a choral review where you state a prompt and the whole group finishes the sentence.
- Provide each participant with an index card listing a topic and two related questions for them to research and present back to the group.

Instant Energizers That Brighten the Brain and Body

Though an energizer is considered a learning activity, it is usually used for a different purpose. While learning activities are meant to embed the learning kinesthetically and to master a certain skill or content area, energizers are used to initiate a state change. They are effective at waking up an audience and increasing the involvement and energy level of a group. Yet, as you'll find out, energizers can also be modified to include content as well. The following planning tips may help the process run smoothly. Unfortunately, there's no substitute for experience. The closest thing to experience, however, is detailed planning.

Establish a non-threatening environment. Inform participants that if, at anytime, they don't feel comfortable with an activity, the option to "pass" always exists.

Hot Tips for Energizing With Activities

1 Remind the audience that the mind and body work together: If the body's tired and lifeless, the mind needs a wake-up, too. Make sure the activity is relevant and draws direct links between the activity and learning. People will do all kinds of fun, silly, or even bizarre activities if they understand the reason for them.

2 Think through each step of every activity that you facilitate. The following are some questions to ask yourself before presenting these activities to a group:

- How much room will we need?
- How will I divide the group into teams?
- What can be done with the tables and chairs?
- What music selections shall we use?
- What props, supplies, and materials will we need?
- How will directions be given (posted, verbalized, handouts)?
- How can I maximize participant involvement?
- What possible barriers or setbacks might I experience?
- How can I maximize the relevance of the activity?
- How much time will we need?
- What needs to be covered in the debriefing or closing of the activity?

3 Establish a non-threatening environment. Inform participants that if, at anytime, they don't feel comfortable with an activity, the option to "pass" always exists. *Before* beginning a new activity, give them an opportunity to ask questions or brainstorm possible responses if content is involved. Low to moderate stress is entirely appropriate to the brain in learning; threat, however, is not.

4 Keep activities short. In general, it's better to have an activity run too short than too long. Be certain, however, that the important points have been developed sufficiently before moving on.

5 Novelty is powerful. If you're going to use a game over again, give it a twist. If a game is going to go on for a while, have participants get involved in forming or modifying the rules. Be sure to change the props, the groupings, and the content to prevent the activity from getting stale.

6 Keep the activity fun. If it becomes too content focused, the activity can bog down. Participants ought to be able to be engaged, relaxed, and enjoy themselves in the process.

7 Fun and content *can* go together. Musical chairs, for example, can become a review game if the person left standing shares one or two ideas learned the previous day.

Remember, every energizer can be modified to give it a content twist.

Low to moderate stress is entirely appropriate to the brain in learning; threat, however, is not.

Hot Tips for Timing and Attention

The timing or pace of an activity can be the difference between its success or failure. Like a well-told joke, the well-organized activity will flow along quickly without being choppy. Once the activity is in progress, it's helpful to have a strategy for regaining your audience's attention when you need it. The following quick attention-getters may help:

- Use a consistent verbal message that is inviting. Instead of the phrase, "Stop and listen up," I like to use, "Pause please..."
- Use a clapping signal. A triple clap or a clap-respond ritual both work well.
- Turn lights on and off quickly.
- Play a tape recording of a police emergency siren or other distinct sound (i.e., church bells).
- Use a whistle (i.e., the small plastic tooter whistles or wooden train whistles are preferable over the coach type).
- Use a gong or bell (i.e., a shaker jingle bell or a toning bell work nicely).
- Establish a silent sign. It might be simply a hand raised or the music turned off—anything that your group has learned to recognize as the signal to stop talking.

Energizers and Activators

Ad-Ons

Invite one person to come up to the front of the room and pose in a posture or movement that reminds them of something they've learned in your session. Then ask another volunteer to join the impromptu living sculpture. Keep adding on until everyone who wants to participate is part of the giant human scenario that represents their learning. The final product might be a machine, a model of change, an example of superior customer service, or a human brain.

Bingo

The timing or pace of an activity can be the difference between its success or failure. Like a well-told joke, the well-organized activity will flow along quickly without being choppy.

Ask the entire group or teams to brainstorm key words from the topic learned. Supply a nine-box grid with the center box marked *free*. From the brainstormed list of words, create questions or have participants create them. Have participants write the one-word answers randomly in the spaces of their grids. Then bingo cards are marked according to the questions selected from a hat or fishbowl and read by the caller. A twist on traditional bingo is to make everyone's cards the same so that everyone wins at the same time. Effective as a pre-quiz, icebreaker, pre-exposure, or review.

Body/Brain Gym and Cross Laterals

Touch hands to opposite knees, give yourself a pat on the back on opposite sides, touch opposite heels, do air swimming or ladder climbing, touch nose and hold opposite ear then switch, do figure eights in front of you by tracing the pattern of the number eight with a thumbs-up sign (start your figure eight at the center, arms length, going up and to the right, do big loops on both sides, then switch sides).

Brain Transplants

Participants receive a set of Post-It Notes and are asked to write a talent, experience, or belief that is true about themselves on each piece. A response, for example, might be "surfing," "traveled to Africa," or "UFOs have already landed." Have participants attach Post-Its to their clothing (up high) and let them mingle for a few minutes while they make, at least, one trade (and up to three) with others. After the mingling time is over, ask the group to share what and why they made the trades that they did.

Clapping Games

Incorporate this energizer to align the group. Start a clap rhythm that is repeated by each participant until it goes around the room. When the clap pattern reaches the last person, somebody starts a new one to pass around. Also good for memory and music skills.

Frisbee Review

Content can be added to this energizer to make it a review game. Toss the Frisbee out into the group. The person who catches it states one thing that they've learned in the last couple of minutes or hours then throws it to someone else who does the same. This activity is more fun with several Frisbees going at once. Other objects can be used too, like Koosh or Wiffle Balls.

Holding the Bag

This activity uses the same concept as musical chairs except without chairs. Start by playing some fun music. Give a beanbag to a participant and ask the audience to mill around and give positive affirmations to each other. During the milling, the beanbag is passed among participants. The person who passes the bag on says, "You're now holding the bag, and you're a genius." The receiver has to say, "I know I'm a genius, but now I'm stuck holding this bag." When the music stops, the one holding the bag (or ball or whatever) shares with the group one thing they learned during the day.

Ask participants to raise their hand and ask for a joke-break anytime they feel the group needs one. Funny or not, it's a good break.

Humor

Ask for volunteers to share a joke with the rest of the group, then write their names on the board or flip chart. Be sure to guarantee them a round of applause. Ask participants to raise their hand and ask for a joke-break anytime they feel the group needs one. They get to select a joke-teller from the list. Funny or not, it's a good break.

Lap Sit

Have participants stand in a circle, facing the back of the person in front of them. Each person holds on to the waist of the person before them. On cue the group simultaneously sits down supported by the lap of the person behind them. This energizer is also a good icebreaker.

Matching Faces/Matching Sounds

Have participants stand or sit in a circle facing the center. Choose a volunteer to get the activity started. This person turns to the person on their left and makes a facial expression. The person on their left then passes the same expression on to the person on their left. Like the childhood game "telephone," it is fun to watch how the interpretation changes from person-to-person. Variations include passing a face in one direction, a sound in the other, or starting a motion around the circle from another starting position.

Musical Chairs

Ask everyone to form a circle with their chairs. Begin playing the music and have participants mill around giving positive affirmations to one another while you take a chair away. When the music stops, everyone grabs a chair; one person will be left standing. The person standing shares with the group one thing they learned during the session. Resume the game for about 5 to 8 selections.

New Seats

Have everybody stand up and take 10 large steps towards a new seat. Put on music during the transition and do this whenever things get stale or the audience needs a stretch break.

Before beginning a new activity, give participants an opportunity to ask questions or brainstorm possible responses if content is involved.

Simon Sez

Have everyone stand and do only what Simon (you) says to do. Give instructions, some of them prefaced with "Simon says," and others simply given alone. Go at a moderate pace. If mistakes are made, keep playing. Always make it a win for all, so no one's ever out of the game.

Touch and Go

Have the group stand up. Give them directions: Touch 5 pieces of gold, 4 pieces of silver, 3 pieces of leather, 2 pieces of glass, and 1 clothing label on someone else. All items must be at least 10 feet apart. A content-centered variation on this energizer is to touch the answers posted around the room to a series of questions on the board. This activity is good for pairs to do together.

Toybox

Keep a box of toys in your training room for breaktime. They might include a paddleball, tennis balls, a Frisbee, a Koosh ball, inflatables, Hula Hoops, hats, stress-reducers, models, Playdough, noisemakers, puppets, a football, and other kids toys. This is a great way to relieve stress and make for a more playful training.

Triangle Tag

This energizer requires four people in each group; three to form a triangle by holding hands, and the fourth to stand outside the group. Someone in the triangle is "it" and the person outside has to try and tag "it" while the triangle team tries to keep "it" from being tagged! This activity makes for a spinning good time.

Tug of War

Everyone picks a partner and a topic from a list of information covered. After topics have been chosen, the goal is to convince partners that their topic is more important. After the verbal discussion, settle it "physically" with a giant tug of war. Take the group outside. All partners should be on opposite sides. Settle the "dispute."

Writing Your Name

Participants stand up and write their first name with their elbow, their middle name with their other elbow, their last name with their hip, their best friend's name with their other hip and their mom or dad's name with their head. You can easily add course content. Using your head, write the most important key concept from the last hour. Using your leg, write out the most important key concept from yesterday. Get partners to form a chorus line and do several words from last week.

Red-Hot Ways to Fire Up Pairs

Have individuals or dyads brainstorm a subject, then share their ideas with a partner or another team.

Creative Handshakes

Participants are asked to shake the hands of 5 different people using 5 different handshakes. This activity builds creativity. Variations include 3 ways to say hello, 3 ways to say good-bye, etc.

Expert Interviews

Divide the group in half. One half of the audience becomes the experts on the topic you're presenting and the other half is famed reporters covering the topic. The reporters are given a period of time to get the story from one of the experts, then the roles are reversed.

Get to Know Me Charades

In dyads, partners tell 3 things about themselves using only charades, then the roles are reversed. Variations include demonstrating 3 things about their workplace, their profession, or an idea in charades.

My Friend

Ask participants to introduce themselves to as many people as they can in 60 seconds. Or, to find someone with a birthday in their same month or year. Or, to find three people taller, three people shorter, or the person closest to their height. Or, have ask them to interview each other for 5 minutes, then introduce their partner to the rest of the group.

Pair and Share

Have individuals or dyads brainstorm a subject, then share their ideas with a partner or another team. Some possible topics follow: 1) something you are afraid of in learning; 2) something you are unsure about; 3) something that you found interesting; or, 4) the main idea of a lesson translated into the vocabulary of a five- or ten-year old.

Poster Parade

Ask participants to pair up and pick out a couple of posters they like from the ones hanging around the room. Each partner then describes what they like and what is meaningful to them about the posters they chose.

Red-Hot Ways to Fire Up Teams

Adult Song Redo

This activity, like the Childhood Song Redo, takes about 25 to 60 minutes. Have teams brainstorm key words related to a topic they're learning. Then, ask them to pick a song from a list of five. The songs should be appropriate to the age and culture of the group as a whole. The best songs are those which were popular during the period of adolescence. Suggestions for a baby-boomer audience would be *Great Balls of Fire*, *Rock Around the Clock*, *Splish Splash*, *Ring of Fire*, and *Locomotion*. Once a tune is chosen, have teams then replace key words from the songs with the key words they brainstormed making them content-specific.

Celebrate the progress that has been made so far with high-fives, a party, dance, etc.

Ball Toss

Ball toss works well for forming teams. It can be used to introduce participants, or for review. Five to seven participants stand in a circle about 10 feet apart, facing each other. One has a ball or bean bag, which they toss to another person to start the game. Incorporate content from the presentation. For example, you can structure it as a word association game, or a question and answer format.

Ball Toss Variations

Use a Koosh, a soft Frisbee, a water balloon, or other novel item. Use it as a review or self-disclosure tool. Take one or two balls of yarn. Have the group stand in a big circle. The starter holds on to the end of the yarn and tosses the ball to someone across from them. That person holds onto the yarn and tosses the ball to another across from them. When the ball is unwound, the group has to untangle it all, in the order it became tangled. Celebrate something great about the progress that has been made so far with high-fives, a party, dance, etc.

Barnyard

This game is a good icebreaker or a fun way to form groups. Assign a number to everyone, up to the number of groups you want (i.e., groups, everyone gets a number from 1-5). Or, if you want six groups, simply go by birthday months. (i.e., everyone with birthdays in January and February are one group, etc.) Assign a noisy animal from the barnyard to all groups. For example the ones are dogs, the twos are cats, threes are sheep, fours are goats, fives are chickens, and sixes are horses. Everyone stands up, and mills around for 30 seconds. Next, they all close their eyes and make the appropriate sounds. Groups are formed by individuals locating similar animal sounds. This can be a riot of fun! With more conservative groups, allow them to keep their eyes open.

Case Studies

Each team is either given a written history of an actual event or they are asked to watch a video of it. The team's job is to study the events, understand what happened, how it happened, and second guess the outcome. What occurred? What could have been done differently? Would they have acted differently? If so, why? Ask them to make a presentation on it for the whole group. This is a great way for teams to review or learn new material together.

Childhood Song Redo

This activity takes about 25 to 60 minutes. Ask teams to brainstorm key words of a topic they've been learning. Then, ask them to pick five songs they remember from their childhood. Have the group vote on one favorite song. Suggestions include: *She'll Be Coming Around the Mountain*; *Rover, Red Rover*; *Row, Row, Row Your Boat*; *Happy Birthday*; *Old MacDonald*, etc. Ask teams to replace key words from the song they select with key words they have brainstormed. The new song will be a great way to review and remember what they've learned.

Skits (or charades) provide a quick and fun way to review content and activate the body at the same time.

Run-Ons

Give the audience a topic for review. The group leader starts a sentence on the topic and leaves it hanging, such as, "Energizers are best for..." The person to the leader's left (or right, or whomever's chosen), continues the "run-on" sentence, but again, leaves it hanging for the next person to add to. The goal is to keep the sentence going for as long as possible. This activity is best used as a review.

Commercial Break

Have teams of three to five participants each produce a quick commercial or skit (using content from training) to be performed for the whole group. Give teams a range of topics, a deadline, some paper and felt pens for visuals or slogans, and some possible props. Usually 15 to 30 minutes of planning and rehearsal time is sufficient. Skits (or charades) provide a quick and fun way to review content and activate the body at the same time.

Follow the Leader

In a small group, the leader acts out or says something while the others follow along and repeat what the leader does. Best used as a review, memory game, perception practice, or skills practice.

Gordian Knot

Have teams of six to eight stand in a circle about 2 feet apart facing the center. Each person reaches across with one hand and clasps the hand of another. Eventually both hands are clasped with someone's hands across the circle. The challenge is to get untied from this giant knot while not unclasping hands. This is a great team-building activity.

Hot Seat

Each team sits in a circle and one person is named "it." Everyone else gets 60 seconds to positively acknowledge the person in the hot seat. The listener has to remain silent or say only, "Thank you." Rotate through the circle so that everyone has the chance to be in the hot seat. This is best used as a closure activity.

Though there are many different types of simulations, they have some common threads. Each simulation asks individuals or groups to read about a situation and make decisions about it. While it's rarely able to match the real thing, it does provide some terrific opportunities for problem-solving, creativity, collaboration, and planning.

Laughter Is Good

Each team or group gets a few minutes to share among themselves their favorite jokes. Then at your request, they point to the person whose joke they want shared with the whole group. By the end of the day, each group has had a chance to tell their favorite joke. Always provide the joke-teller with a round of applause.

Team Massage

This activity is best for adult groups. Play some relaxing music. Have everyone stand up and form a circle with their left shoulder towards the center. Participants reach out and gently massage the shoulders of the person in front of them. Now, everyone turns 180 degrees and massages the person who just finished massaging them.

Simulations

Though there are many different types of simulations, they have some common threads. Each simulation asks individuals (but more often groups) to read about a situation and make decisions about it. While it's rarely able to match the real thing, it does provide some terrific opportunities for problem-solving, creativity, collaboration, and planning. My favorites are the survival games like simulated arctic survival, jungle survival, desert survival, and mountain survival.

Team Affirmations

Team leaders read aloud a list of team-building, psyched-up affirmations that you have printed and distributed (or team-brainstormed). Or, rotate the list around and have each person read one and pass it on. At the end, the group does a cheer and takes a seat. Some sample affirmations follow:

Team-Building Affirmations

- I'm glad you're on my team.
- Learning is easy on this team.
- You make it all happen!
- Anything is possible on our team.
- Terrific teamwork!
- This team is getting better everyday.
- Number one and getting higher!
- Together, we achieve more.
- This is what I call amazing!
- Perfect—ten out of ten!
- Each of us is unique and valuable.
- I'm impressed!
- Our team spirit is sky high.
- Yes-team! Yes-team...Yes!
- We are the team of destiny.
- I know we'll succeed!
- This is the best team ever!

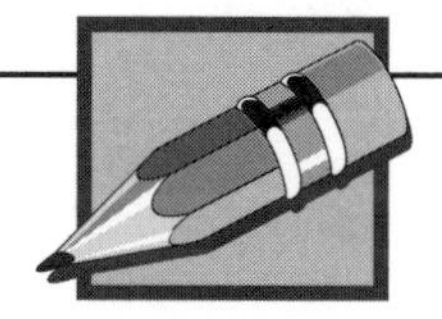

Engage Your Brain:
Planning for Active Learning

How will you incorporate active learning strategies into your next presentation? What activities will you use, combined with what topics?

What steps will you take in the implementation process? What possible contingencies might arise and how might you deal with them?

What activators will you incorporate in your next training? Will you incorporate content, if so, how?

Everything about music carries a message: the beat, the words, the associations, the era in which it was made, and the conditions under which it was recorded.

–Lynn Freeman Dhority
Joyful Fluency

CHAPTER 17

Peppering Presentations With Props and Music

It wasn't long ago that people called props and music "gimmicks." Yet, nowadays, the reality is that if you don't use "gimmicks" in your presentations, you're out of touch. In fact, current research suggests that props and music enhance understanding and recall. This chapter presents some techniques that will optimize your success in this area. The difference between a good presentation and a great one, quite simply, is often related to your "sizzle-factor." A high sizzle-factor means you are effectively stimulating your participants' imaginations and emotions. What better way to accomplish this than with props and music?

- *The Power of Props*
- *Props and Music Enhance Learning*
- *The Three Best Uses for Music*
- *Music for Arousal*
- *Music as a Carrier*
- *Performing a Concert Reading*
- *Mozart Improves Spatial Temporal Reasoning*
- *Music Selections That Prime The Brain for Learning*
- *Hot Tips for Incorporating Music*
- *Hot Tunes*

The Power of Props

About 90 percent of all presentations can benefit from the implementation of some kind of prop. If you think your presentation falls into the rare 10 percent that can't, watch television. This highly visual medium incorporates props in a myriad of ways . You'll see them on the morning talk shows, on *Bill Nye, the Science Guy*, on the late night shows, on the news, and in almost every commercial. As you watch, ask yourself, "What prop would leave a lasting impression and help the presenter explain the concept more effectively?" As you adopt a mindset that thinks of the audience and how they might perceive things, you will realize how props can make abstract concepts more concrete and memorable.

Keep a supply of props in your presenter's toolbox. You might put them in a drawer or trunk near the front of the group and pull them out anytime you need to make a point or change a mood. Props make your presentation more visually interesting and engaging, easier to understand, and hopefully, humorous.

Brain Connection

Props and Music Enhance Learning

What do props and music have to do with the brain? It turns out, a great deal. Props can be used as vehicles to get attention, and boost transference and meaning. The right kind of music can prime the neural pathways, almost like a warm-up for better learning. The combination of props and music can do more than add surface pizzazz. They engage the emotions, and thus, enhance learning.

Simple Props

- Party noisemakers
- Hats (chef's, Sherlock Holmes, hard hat, etc.)
- Oversized glasses (the plastic ones work well)
- Magic show props
- Gardening tools
- Celebrity masks
- Movie director's chair or other Hollywood props
- Charts
- Inflatables
- Hand puppets
- Balls—various sizes
- An empty picture frame
- A rubber chicken
- Models of a concept
- Halloween masks
- Groucho Marx noses
- A squirt gun
- A towel (if need be, you can always "throw in the towel")
- Rubber or plastic brains

The Three Best Uses for Music

Does music belong in a professional presentation? Absolutely yes, and here's why: 1) It can influence states–psych-up or calm down your audience; 2) It can carry words to the unconscious mind; and 3) It can boost thinking and intelligence. Coined "The Mozart effect," (Campbell, 1997) researchers continue to unravel the relationship between listening to particular kinds of music (especially Mozart) and increased spatial reasoning scores. The influence of music in our lives is great. To ignore such a powerful medium in your presentation would be a shame. Consider that music can provide the following benefits:

- Embeds the learning faster and on a deeper level (i.e., the "alphabet song")
- Relieves stress and reduces discouragement
- Unites groups of people
- Motivates people
- Helps build rapport
- Energizes people
- Appeals to the particular cultural values of the group
- Comforts the soul during painful times
- Adds an element of fun and/or novelty
- Activates the thinking portion of the brain
- Harmonizes and calms people
- Arouses the brain and body

Music for Arousal

Music, as a tool to affect the brain and body, is immensely powerful. It can stimulate the brain resulting in better attentiveness, concentration, and creativity. It can also take the pressure off you as the presenter, help create sound curtains to isolate classes or groups, and bring forth qualities of the music that reside in each listener.

The single most important question to ask when introducing music to your presentation environment is, what's the tempo, the pacing, or the beat of the music? Is it slow, medium, or fast? Beats per minute is the standard measurement by which to measure the tempo. The beat of the music affects both heart rate and breathing—the two most important determinants of mood, feelings, and state. So remember, the beat is the first distinction you need to be able to make. In general, your selections ought to be instrumental. Exceptions, however, include some popular music, but only for breaks or special effects outside of lecture time.

Music, as a tool to affect the brain and body, is immensely powerful. It can stimulate the brain resulting in better attentiveness, concentration, and creativity.

Slow: 40 to 60 beats per minute calms your audience down. This music tempo is best for inviting visualization, relaxation, journal writing, or reflection.

Moderate: 60 to 70 beats per minute maintains steady alertness and is good for thinking or working on projects. Also good for problem-solving and creativity.

Faster: 70 to 140 beats per minute energizes your audience. This is best for movement, dance, and working on projects especially those that are more physical rather than mental.

Movie or TV show theme music is exciting, fun, emotionally engaging, and it can be tailored to your audience's age. With teens, check the pop charts and use what's "hot." Watch MTV to find out who's in vogue and who's not. Today's Pearl Jam, Boyz to Men or Hootie and the Blowfish will either become classic bands or forgotten in five years. Don't assume that because a band was popular last year, it is popular this year.

For an audience in the twenty to early-thirty range, try the *Top Gun* anthem, the *Beverly Hills Cop Theme,* the *Miami Vice* theme, the *Love Theme* from *St. Elmo's Fire*, or *Somebody's Watching Me.* For younger participants, ask them what is popular. For Baby Boomers, try themes from *Star Wars*, *Raiders of the Lost Ark* by John Williams, *O-Bla-Di-O-Bla-Da* by the Beatles and *Hooked on Classics*.

Match the music you use to the cultures represented in your audience. You might want to include some of the following diverse artists:

- *The Big Bang, (Drums!)* by Ellipsis Arts 3400
- Chic, *The Best of Chic: Dance, Dance, Dance* (Techno-pop) Atlantic Records
- *Ultimate Dance Party*: Various groups (pop-rock)
- *Steelbands of Trinidad and Tobago: Heart of Steel* by Flying Fish

Other old favorites are theme songs from *The Twilight Zone*, *Mission Impossible*, and *Rocky* by Bill Conti, *Chariots of Fire* by Vangelis, *Eye of the Tiger* by Survivor, *Break on Through* by the Doors, *Mickey's Monkey* by Smokey Robinson and the Miracles, and *The Curly Shuffle* by Jump'n Saddle. Use music to speed up, slow down, have fun, or get confident. Standard special effects, such as trumpet fanfare, applause, and canned laughter, are also effective for engaging emotions.

We learn much of our native language, rituals, rules, and social conditioning through childhood songs and folk songs. Some of these songs carry instructive messages or content to the brain through a catchy or familiar beat and/or melody.

Slower Music

Slow down the group's energy and set the stage for visualization or imagery exercises with music in the 40-60 beats per minute range. Include new-age artists such as Keola Beamer, Kenny G, Steven Halpern, Georgia Kelly, Adam Geiger, Daniel Kobialka, Zamfir, George Winston, and the classic canon in D major by Johann Pachelbel. This category also includes nature music and environmental sounds.

Upbeat Popular Music

These selections are perfect for break time or high-energy activities. Include a variety of upbeat popular music that has both an entertaining beat and positive lyrics. You'll really need to be selective in this category. Many songs have inappropriate lyrics for the group setting.

Background Music

In this category, use primarily baroque (Bach, Corelli, Tartini, Vivaldi, Albinoni, Handel, Fausch and Pachelbel). Use *Four Seasons* by Vivaldi, *Brandenburg Concertos and Water Music* by Handel. When selecting these (often found in the "bargain bins"), make sure most of the compositions are played in the major (upbeat) key and done by a full orchestra (not one or two violins).

Music as a Carrier

We learn much of our native language, rituals, rules, and social conditioning through childhood songs and folk songs. Some of these songs carry instructive messages or content to the brain through a catchy or familiar beat and/or melody. The music is secondary to the content of the words. A good example of carrier music is the *Alphabet Song* which, chances are, helped you learn the letters of the alphabet. As an infant, you heard the common melody, *Twinkle, Twinkle Little Star* enough that it became strongly embedded. When you were ready to learn the alphabet, the letters were simply attached to the melody of *Twinkle, Twinkle Little Star*. This process worked so well that many people today forget that the *Alphabet Song* is the same melody as *Twinkle, Twinkle Little Star*.

Turning content into a rap song (or "opera of the streets") is, perhaps, a more sophisticated example of this same principle at work. The melody or beat carries the content making it easier to remember. The following activities can be easily incorporated into any presentation to provide the Mozart edge:

Another way to incorporate music as a carrier is to add a sort of theatrical music background, known as a concert reading, to your presentation. A concert reading is the purposeful use of music with a planned content interplay creating an effect more like a movie sound track.

Have participants brainstorm key words or ideas from your presentation. Also, have them brainstorm a list of commonly known songs. I don't tell them the purpose of the song at this point. I simply say, "We need some songs for our next project. In your teams, brainstorm a list of at least 10 of the most well known songs in America today. You have 3 minutes. Ready, get set, go!" After they've brainstormed the list (which usually includes *Happy Birthday*, camp songs, nursery rhymes and pop songs), I ask the teams to vote to determine their favorite. Once they have picked it, they can begin the process of dropping their own key words and ideas into the melody of the old song creating a new carrier song. For example, if the topic is learning with music, a song like *Rock Around the Clock* might become *Rock Around the Brain*. I give them about 30 to 45 minutes to do this. Then we write the lyrics on flip chart paper, add some choreography, and practice a performance of it. Though I never make it mandatory to perform the song for the whole group, I make it so fun, there's rarely ever a team that refuses.

A second way to use music as a carrier is to select music that has pertinent lyrics to your presentation. There's a book called *The Green Book of Music* that lists all published songs by topic. Included are songs that highlight topics like respect, loyalty, high expectations, danger zone, working hard, excellence, inspiration, dreaming, change, being the best and more.

Another way to incorporate music as a carrier is to add a sort of theatrical music background, known as a concert reading, to your presentation. A concert reading is the purposeful use of music with a planned content interplay creating an effect more like a movie sound track (or play or opera). Well-delivered concerts can open gateways to learning, reach the subconscious, create better understanding of the subject matter, activate long-term memory, mitigate high stress or anxiety, and reduce overall learning time.

Performing a Concert Reading

A concert reading includes the introductory globalization phase and the active concert phase. The introductory globalization phase incorporates intriguing, attention-getting music; it is meant to be short (3 to 7 minutes), fun, and entertaining. This phase builds confidence and anticipation and provides an overview of the material. Thus, it is usually done at the beginning of a new session when a fresh topic is introduced. The presenter simply provides an overview of the material with the music as a compliment in the background.

Never compete with the music; rather, use a "sound surfing" approach where you take advantage of the musical pauses for impact. Remain silent during the louder, more active parts, then read or present your subject when the music subsides.

The active concert phase integrates more detailed material into in a dramatic presentation. Music selections like Beethoven and Hayden are highly recommended for the backdrop. This phase helps place new material in context using metaphors and suggestion. It is best used in the middle or next to last part of a session for about 5 to 15 minutes. Let the music play for 10 to 30 seconds before you begin to speak. Never compete with the music; rather, use a "sound surfing" approach where you take advantage of the musical pauses for impact. Remain silent during the louder, more active parts, then read or present your subject when the music subsides. The following suggestions help maximize the effect of this powerful presentation technique:

Content

Make sure that you know your content well and are comfortable with the meaning of it. Tell participants what you'll be covering. Give them a short preview of the material verbally, even when you'll also be providing handouts.

Music

Make sure that you have listened to your music many times so that you know it well. How long does the introductory movement last? When does it go up and back down again in volume? How about the pacing and tempo?

Create a Comfortable Environment

You may want to dim the lighting, provide stand and stretch time, do some deep breathing, encourage participants to sit comfortably, and state some positive suggestions of expectancy.

Credibility

Announce the name of the musical selection you're using, the composer, and the title of the piece. Otherwise, some listeners may be distracted by the desire to know more about it.

Volume

Make the volume loud enough to fill in the non-speaking parts of your presentation but soft enough so that your presentation can be heard when the music subsides.

Pause

Get the attention of your audience and create anticipation. Wait until the introductory movement of the selection is over which is usually about 5 to 35 seconds into the piece, then begin speaking.

Dramatic

Make large movements and dramatic gestures to emphasize key points. Think of yourself as a Shakespearean performer and enjoy making a show. Finish with a dramatic closing remark.

Experiment!

Doing concert readings is a great way to have fun, be creative, and embed learning. Use music from the classical era—the years of 1750 to 1820. Composers of this era created music that is full of energy, surprise, and contrast. They include, Mozart, Hayden, Rossini, and Beethoven. Classical music hatched the modern orchestra, the symphony, themes and motives, the sonata, the concerto, and the overture. It's great for creativity, storytelling, and lectures. Repetition is the secret to comfort. With comfort, comes confidence and competency.

Doing concert readings is a great way to have fun, be creative, and embed learning.

Brain Connection

Mozart Improves Spatial Reasoning

Former University of California at Irvine researcher Francis Rauscher said, "We know the neural firing patterns are basically the same for music appreciation and abstract reasoning." In the well-publicized *Mozart Effect* study, researchers (Rauscher, Shaw, Levine, Ky, and Wright, 1993), found that after just 10 minutes of headset listening, the Mozart selection improved spatial temporal reasoning. It should be noted that this study suggests a causal relationship, not a correlation. Another researcher, Larry Parsons of the University of Texas at San Antonio, found other sources, such as tones, rhythms, and like tasks, also prime the brain for learning.

Music Sources That Prime the Brain for Learning

- *Sonatas for Two Pianos in D Major* by Mozart
- Melody of 5 Diatonic Tones
- One-tone Rhythms
- Monotones

Listening to Mozart before specific tasks that require spatial reasoning (assembling objects, mind-mapping, jigsaw puzzles, flow charts, etc.) is valuable; however, during the task involvement itself, music listening causes neural competition and interferes with the neural firing pattern.

Hot Tips for Incorporating Music

Plan to invest some time and money to produce a quality presentation package. Expect to pay from $100 to $1,200 for a new, low-cost portable music system. Get a quality CD player with separate detachable speakers. The new compact speakers are well worth the price. They also make more sense if you travel and need to keep the shipping weight down. Bose makes a high-quality system.

Use music as a partner—an aid in the learning process.

Before your presentation, make sure you have tested the music CDs and tapes and labeled them according to the situation in which they might be most useful. Try color-coding them with multi-colored peel-off dots so that you can quickly identify them at a glance. The dots might signify classical, popular, new age, or special effects categories. Set up your tape player in the front of the room and lay out all of your cued tapes.

Think about what's coming up and decide what type of specific music you will use and when. Prepare ahead of time with several tape options available to you. Use music as a partner, an aid in the learning process. I've labeled my presentation music by the following categories:

- Break Selections
- Background Music
- Movement Music
- Relaxation Selections
- Special Effects
- Start-up Music
- Closing Selections

In general, turn the volume up and down gradually. Just like your eyes are sensitive to lighting, ears are sensitive to sound. The exception is after a final good-bye or closing when you might want to start on high volume to match the group's vocal completion crescendo.

When used sparingly, your audience will love music. Try recording your own. Use music with purpose. Allow quiet times for your audience to breath. Avoid saturation—the effects of music are far more powerful when the freshness is retained. Avoid rigidity. Listen to your audience and try to accommodate their specific needs and desires. Music is a real joy; make sure this is what comes across when you play it.

Hot Tunes

I like music particularly to open my presentation and to close it. But there are many other times when it's perfect, too. Consider using the following situation-specific recommendations:

Background Music During Presentation (low volume):

Four Seasons by Vivaldi, *Water Music* by Handel, *Brandenberg Concertos* by Bach.

Brainstorming/Creative Problem-solving Mindset Music:

Piano Concerto #5 by Beethoven, *Etudes* by Chopin, *Claire de Lune* by Debussy, *Piano Concerto #26 & 27* by Mozart, *Swan Lake* by Tchaikovsky.

When used sparingly, your audience will love music. Listen to your audience and try to accommodate their specific needs and desires. Music is a real joy; make sure this is what comes across when you play it.

Calming Music (see also relaxation music):

Amazing Grace (traditional spiritual song) Classical guitar composers, piano music, *Claire de Lune* by Debussy, *Trois Gymnopedies* by Eric Satie.

Celebration of Something Positive, Successes, Wins:

Ninth Choral Symphony by Beethoven, *Celebrate* by Three Dog Night, *Celebrate* by Madonna, *Grand March* from *Aida* by Verdi, *The Creation & The Seasons* by Haydn, *Celebration* by Kool & the Gang, *Hallelujah Chorus* from *Messiah* by Handel.

Closing Ritual Song (for a positive ending each day):

Hi-Ho, from songs *Snow White*, *Tomorrow*, theme song from *Annie Musical*, *What A Wonderful World* by Louis Armstrong, *Happy Days* theme on *Vol. #3 of TV Themes* by Steven Gottleib, *Happy Trails* by Roy Rogers on *Vol. #1 of TV Themes* by Steven Gottleib.

Special Introduction of Participant or Guest Speaker:

Fanfare for the Common Man by Aaron Copland, *Rocky Theme* by Bill Conti, *Olympics Theme-1984 Summer Games*, *Star Wars & Raiders of Lost Ark* on *Best of John Williams*, *We Will Rock You ("We are the Champions")* by Queen.

Mindset for Thinking of New Ideas, Units, and Subjects:

Thus Sprake Zarathrustra (2001 Theme), *Blue Danube* by Strauss, *Fantasia* by Disney, *Suites for Orchestra* by Bach, *Toy Symphonies* by Haydn, *Musical Joke* by Mozart, *Desert Vision* and *Natural States* by Lanz and Speer, *Silk Road* by Kitaro.

Group Singing, Games, Pop Songs, and Traditionals:
Snow White, *Songs of the South, Bambi*, *Dumbo*, *Winnie the Pooh*, *Mary Poppins* on *Disney Soundtracks (Vol. 1,2, & 3)*, and Hap Palmer songs.

Beginnings, Openings, Everyday Psych-up Music:
Epic Movie Soundtracks: *Chariots of Fire*, *Superman*, *E.T.*, *Rocky*, *Lawrence of Arabia*, *Born Free, Dr. Zhivago. Oh! What a Beautiful Morning* from *Oklahoma*. All of the *James Bond 007* soundtracks, the theme from *The Mission*, *Ravel's Bolero*, *Well-Tempered Clavier*, *Prelude in D Major* by Bach, *Amanda Panda* song from *Saving the Wildlife* by Mannheim Steamroller or the *Hungarian Dances* by Brahms. Many tracks by Yanni. Most of David Arkenstone's works (particularly *Olympia* and *Wake of the Wind*) have terrific selections on them.

When using music, start slow and build your way up as your skills and confidence increase. Most of all, enjoy the process.

Storytelling, Concert Readings, and Metaphors:
Classical artists: Beethoven, Mozart, Haydn, *Neverland* by Suzanne Cianni, Romantic music: Wagner, Dvorak, Rimsky-Korsakov.

Slow Stretching, Deep Breathing, and Relaxation:
Summer, Autumn, Spring, and *Winter* by George Winston, *Silk Road* by Kitaro, *Barefoot Ballet* by John Klemmer, Michael Jones on Piano.

Transition Time or "Mass Movement":
(activities like stretch breaks, cross-laterals, energy-builders, switch seats, etc.) *Hooked on Classics* by Philadelphia Harmonics, *1812 Overture* by Tchaikovsky, *William Tell Overture* by Rossini, *Theme from Rawhide*, or *Peanuts Theme* by Giraldi or Benoit.

Visualization, Relaxation, and Imagery:
All recordings by Daniel Kobialka, *SeaPeace* by Georgia Kelly, most selections by Kitaro. *Summer, Autumn, Spring,* and *Winter* by George Winston, Steven Halpern's music. *Theme from Exodus* by Handel, *Nocturnes* by Chopin, *Peter and the Wolf* by Prokofiev, *The Egmont Overture* by Beethoven, Environmental Music: birds, flute, waterfalls.

One last tip: when you're getting started, keep it simple. When I first began using music in my presentations, I used one selection only—a baroque composition by Beethoven. Within a month, I was comfortable bringing several tapes. Now, I bring a stack of CDs, dozens of custom tapes, and I regularly use all of them in a training. Start slow, build your way up as your skills and confidence increase, and most of all, enjoy the process.

Engage Your Brain:
Incorporating Props and Music into Your Next Presentation

What props do you currently use in your presentations? What props might you incorporate in your next presentation? How and for what purpose?

Do you currently use music in your presentations? How might you further incorporate music in your next presentation? How will you do this?

Have you ever done a concert reading before? Do you think your presentation would benefit from this technique? If so, how? If not, why not?

Man [humankind] is a knot, a web, a mesh into which relationships are tied. Only those relationships matter.

–Antoine de Saint-Exupery

CHAPTER 18

Igniting Social Learning

A great deal of learning takes place by talking to one another—exchanging emotions and feelings, discussion, brainstorming, and problem-solving. In fact, the natural tendency for both adults and children in a learning environment free of threat is to talk in class. Participants can be valuable resources for each other—generating ideas, offering assistance or encouragement, and providing feedback. Some presenters demand that participants "pay attention" to the person at the front of the room at all times; however, today we realize that learning takes many shapes. Sometimes it's quiet, other times noisy; sometimes participants learn best by themselves, other times with a group. The most important thing is this: Do not discourage participants from asking each other for help. This chapter focuses on strategies for creating a presentation environment that encourages interaction among participants and downplays the old fashion value of always listening attentively to the platform speaker.

Key Topics

- *Creating Teams of Two*
- *The Human Brain Is a Social Brain*
- *The 5-Step, 15-Minute Teambuilder*
- *Quick Picks and Instant Groups*
- *The Role of Feedback*

Creating Teams of Two

One way to encourage participant interaction and group cooperation is to incorporate team activities and assignments into your presentation. Generally, a good guideline is that social learning is worth at least 25 percent of your total training time. A variety of ways exist to establish quick pairings that mix up partners.

Brain Connection

The Human Brain Is a Social Brain

The brain develops better in concert with others. Our brain cannot be good at everything; therefore, it selects over time that which will ensure its survival. The human brain has evolved to use language as our primary means for communication. This may partly explain why groups, teams, and cooperative learning benefit our understanding and application of new concepts—they require us to communicate with each other. Through this process, learning seems to be enhanced. We can certainly learn without others around, but in this situation we'd never learn to be part of a family or community.

Pairing Participants

The following approaches for pairing participants can be adapted and built upon to create hundreds more.

Start by saying, "Please stand up and take seven steps (at least 5, less than 25) in any direction and pause."

- "Now, find the person closest to your own height."
- "Find a person wearing the same color shoes as you."
- "Find the first person who has a birthday in your same month."
- "Let's be psychic—close your eyes, spin around once and point to another person. Did that same person point to you? If yes, they're your partner. If not, do it again (or raise your hand and find someone else with their hand raised.")
- "Make the sound of a pet you have. Pair up with the first person you find making that same sound."
- "Find the person nearest you who has your same hair color."
- "Find the person nearest you who you don't know."

After the teams have completed their task, which is commonly a pair and share, remind them to thank each other (or celebrate) before having a seat. This keeps the atmosphere light and polite.

The 5-Step, 15-Minute Teambuilder

The old way of presenting—stand and deliver—was simple. Obedient participants sat quietly in their lined up rows of seats while the presenter stood in front of the room and lectured. Today's presentation environment is very different. It is busy, interactive, and flexible. And participants may be "in front" as much as the presenter. Why the change? Two reasons: We now realize the brain's need for social learning; and we understand more about learning styles and multiple intelligences which are maximized in interactive environments. The following steps break down the essential building blocks and time involvement (based on a group of 3 to 4) for creating cooperative teams:

1 ***Orchestrate Composition of Teams (approx. 4 minutes)***
In composing teams, consider what criteria you want to include (i.e., group size, cultural diversity, experience, age, gender, recreational interests, horoscope signs, etc.) You may want your teams to be homogenous or diverse, novel or serious, or departmental or general

depending on the purpose of the activity. If the training is restricted to a single organization, your criteria may include department, skill area, years on the job, classification, etc. You might have participants classify themselves and label their nametags (i.e., CS=Customer Service, HR= Human Resources, T=Technical, P=Production, etc.) If it is appropriate to the purpose of the activity, explain to the group what your criteria is. Have everyone stand and mix with others as they look for a group based on the criteria you've presented. Once basic teams have been formed, ask if everyone has a team and if any team needs to make a trade to get the criteria met. When a team's composition is set, have them sit down.

If you wish to create random teams, you can adapt the pairing approaches at the beginning of this chapter. (i.e., "Find three others who are your same height.") Another approach is to put the names of nursery rhymes, music groups, or movie titles, etc. in a hat. If you want five teams of four, then you'll need five titles listed four times each on a scrap of paper to be stirred up in the hat. Each participant draws out a title to determine their group. (i.e., All *Itsy-Bitsy Spider* members begin singing the song to find each other.) Or, if teams are movie titles, you might have all *Titanic* members stand by the door. The variations on this approach are as varied as your imagination.

We now realize the brain's need for social learning; and we understand more about learning styles and multiple intelligences which are maximized in interactive environments.

2 ***Facilitate a Get-To-Know-You Time (approx. 3 minutes)***

Until the magic and bonding of synergy occurs, a group of people is simply a group of people. Getting to know each other is critical to the development of teams. To accomplish this, have each group determine a timekeeper and establish the signals they will use to keep the group within their time limits; then, instruct the timekeepers to give each person 30 seconds of uninterrupted time to share something about themselves that is not work-related (i.e., family, school, hobbies, sports, etc.) For example, someone might say, "I was born in Prague, I have a dog named Sofia, and my passion is gardening." After a person speaks, everyone claps, but no questions are asked until everyone has completed their introduction. The remaining time can be used for participants to ask follow-up questions or to chat among themselves.

3 ***Identify Team Leaders (approx. 2 minutes)***

Never appoint team leaders; rather, have team leaders self select. To facilitate this process, instruct groups to go around the circle and have each participant share why they do, or don't, want to be the team leader. If two people want to lead, have them share the leadership responsibilities.

4 *Develop Team Spirit (approx. 3 minutes)*
Team spirit can be generated from a name, a challenge, a cheer, or a ritual. Give each group 60 seconds to pick a team name. Then, give them 90 seconds to create a wild cheer that lasts 5 seconds or less. Use your imagination for even more spirit-building ideas. It's critical to allow and encourage rituals and noise. If you suppress this energy, it'll disappear fast, and it's essential for teambuilding. Keep the energy high, use sound effects, and enlist the support of other teams to celebrate another team's success.

5 *Identify Team Goals (approx. 3 minutes)*
If groups are going to be working together on a long-term project or for more than a brief activity together, they will benefit from having a common purpose or team goals. Give them a framework for goal-setting. For example, their goals need to be positive, specific, measurable, and agreed upon by the whole group. Have teams record and post their two to four top goals on a flip-chart pad. Ask team leaders to announce the goals to the larger group.

Once you've established a foundation, many activities can help groups to become a team. The key elements are common purpose, clear pathways, sufficient resources, and a realistic time-frame.

Once you've established the foundation described above, many activities can help groups become a team. The key elements are common purpose, clear pathways, sufficient resources, and a realistic time-frame.

Quick Picks and Instant Groups

In a brief presentation, you don't have time for extended democratic processes. In this instance, you'll need to assign tasks and roles quickly. To keep the group moving at a good clip, simply announce your decision to the group in a matter-of-fact and fun way: "The person who will (do the task, start up, etc.) will be the one who..."

- Is wearing the most (or least) amount of jewelry
- Has the longest (or shortest) hair
- Is sitting closest to the door (or window, etc.)
- Has the curliest hair
- Is the team leader for the day
- Has the most (or least amount of buttons)
- Has the shiniest shoes
- Is wearing the most white (or blue, black, etc.)

Of course, there are many permutations this strategy can take. For example, you can say to your group, "Please indicate the person in your group with the curliest hair." Once the audience has picked that person (and has had a good laugh), simply say, "Now, the person to their left is the one who will begin." This adds a bit of surprise element and removes the stigma of being selected. This strategy is best for selecting roles to be played by individuals within small groups; the larger the group, the more potential there is for threat or embarrassment of individuals. Other possible quickie approaches to forming groups include the following:

Numbering

Have everyone number off. Use whatever sequence of numbers you want to achieve your desired group size. For example, if you have 50 participants and you want groups of 5, have participants number off from one to ten. Then ask all ones to group up, all twos, etc. An easy way to accomplish this is to have participants hold their hands up signifying their number and to put their hands down once they've found everyone in their group.

The larger the group, the more potential there is for threat or embarrassment of individuals.

Pets

Break into groups based on the type of pets participants have. If the group size is too large, for example, in the case of dogs or cats, break the categories down further (i.e., dogs over 25 lbs. and dogs under 25 lbs. or solid color cats or tabby cats).

Birthday

Break groups up by birth months. This will generally give you 12 groups, although the sizes may vary quite a bit.

House Numbers

Have participants hold up the number on their fingers of the first digit of their house number (or last digit of their phone number) and find others who are holding up the same number.

Name

Have participants find others whose first or last name starts with the same letter as theirs (name tags suggested).

Clothing

Have participants find others who are wearing the same primary color they are.

Top presenters help foster strong collaboration skills and group trust in many ways. Beyond facilitating a variety of team activities, keep your promises, be consistent, respect differences, self-disclose, remain non-judgmental, and create a climate for cooperation instead of competition. Offer choice and variety and time to develop appropriate relationships among participants. And most of all, role-model cooperative instead of adversarial relationships.

The Role of Feedback

Top presenters help foster strong collaboration skills and group trust in many ways. Beyond facilitating a variety of team activities, keep your promises, be consistent, respect differences, self-disclose, remain nonjudgmental, and create a climate for cooperation instead of competition.

Minimal or delayed feedback are deadly to participant motivation. To optimize learning, make it a rule that your participants get feedback at least every 30 minutes. The secret for being able to accomplish this task, when there's only one of you and many of them, is to remove yourself as the primary source of feedback. Whether the ratio of audience members to presenter is 10 to 1 or 50 to 1, there's too few of you and too many of them for you to provide quality feedback to everyone. So, how then do you do it? The key is to utilize both self-assessment strategies and group assessment strategies or peer review for the purpose. Incorporating these feedback functions into the group process can be as simple as the following activities:

- Utilize pre-established criteria from which learners can self-assess or assess each other.
- Hold small-group discussions.
- Have participants pair up and present to each other what they have learned.
- Set up simple systems for group self-assessment, scoring, and analysis.
- Incorporate debates or mock quiz shows.
- Have groups generate mind-maps.
- Within the small group, have individuals share their projects, mind-maps, or ideas.
- Assign major group projects that are challenging; the project, itself, will provide valuable feedback.
- Participants keep score charts for their team and post the results.
- Groups work together to create a performance review or test.
- Groups correct their own work.
- Participants present to the group and get oral or written feedback.

Feedback comes in many forms. It may be the single, most powerful motivator there is. The research, however, suggests that when it is learner-controlled, feedback is far more effective. If you're giving a presentation and a participant shouts out what you're doing wrong, this is immediate feedback; however, this does not mean it's good for you.

You need to have some control of the feedback: In this case, you need appropriate timing. A more effective feedback method for you might be for participants to complete an evaluation at the end of the training. Using such, you can key into the feedback when you're most open to hearing it.

To apply the principle of choice, have participants tell group members how and when they want to receive feedback. Small group work allows participants to interact in a casual way where their ideas can be discussed, encouraged, critiqued, and molded. Feedback is critical and it works wonders for inspiring learning; just be sure to include the element of learner choice and set ground rules for the feedback process.

Some ground rules for feedback: the more often, the more immediate, the more specific, the more appropriately presented, the better.

Engage Your Brain:
Planning Social Learning

What group activities do you currently conduct in your trainings? What is the purpose of each?

What other group activities would you like to incorporate? How will you select the make-up of the groups?

How do you plan on ensuring sufficient participant feedback?

SECTION FIVE:
Captivating Closings, Carrying the Torch

Chapter

CHAPTER 19

Kindling Audience Recall

How far should presenters go in helping their audience remember what they learn? My feeling is that we go as far as we can. We know that recall improves when content is embedded on a physical and emotional level. Material that is manipulated and talked about rather than strictly lectured or read about will be retrieved more quickly. A new computer program will be remembered longer by participants who actually manipulate the keys versus the participants who passively observe the presenter manipulating the keys. Children know this instinctively: You've probably observed a child pulling a toy away from someone who's demonstrating how it works. They crave first-hand experience. Your audience is no different. To enhance their memory, engage them fully in the learning. This chapter presents some techniques that engage learners through multiple memory pathways, thereby enhancing memory.

Key Topics

- *Multiple-Memory Pathways*
- *The Memory Process*
- *Strategies for Tapping Into Multiple-Memory Pathways*
- *Strategies for Reinforcing Learning and Recall*
- *Strategies for Making Your Presentation Memorable*
- *Visualization Techniques for Enhancing Memory*

Multiple-Memory Pathways

Neuroscientists generally agree that we have two separate memory and retrieval processes: the *declarative*–an explicit system, and the *non-declarative*–an implicit system. The declarative system has two pathways: semantic, which is word-related, triggered by word associations, mnemonics, and active processing; and episodic, which is spatially or contextually-based, triggered by location and circumstances.

The non-declarative system also has two separate pathways: *procedural*, which is motor-related, triggered by movement, activity, postures, aroma, states, and action; and *reflexive*, which is the automatic, stimulus-response system that comes from either a "knee-jerk" type response or "flash-card" learning. Each type of memory has advantages and disadvantages. They can overlap and also work independently.

Brain Connection

Memory Is Not Fixed; It Is a Process

Three concepts are impacting today's scientific dialogue on memory. First, our memory is often referred to as being "good" or "bad." But many neuroscientists assert that memory is only a process, not a fixed thing like a memory bank. Second, we do not store complete experiences; rather, they are broken down and become highly fragmented for storage. In fact, only the salient and discriminating features of our lives are usually stored. Finally, many speculate that memory is rarely the problem; it's retrieval that generally presents a problem. Most of our frustration over being unable to remember something may simply be a temporary performance deficit.

By presenting in a way that taps into multiple-memory pathways, your audience will consistently experience better recall. Memory can be activated by odors, tastes, sights, sounds, locations, music, body movements, rhymes, stories, emotions, colors, mnemonics, and dozens of other triggers. In one study, learners were asked to use either rote or multiple-memory strategies to memorize words. The learners who used the rote method had higher forgetfulness ratios and lower recall performances. The rote method, also called "taxon" memory or "list-related" memorization, involves simple repetition. The learners who used multiple-memory strategies had dramatically superior recall. We can all improve our recall and the quality of our memory by utilizing our multiple-memory pathways. The following strategies are highly effective for this purpose:

Material that is manipulated and talked about rather than strictly lectured or read about will be retrieved more quickly. To enhance your audience's memory, engage them fully in the learning.

Strategies for Tapping Into Multiple-Memory Pathways

- Have teams list key ideas from the learning on index cards and then re-sequence the course material by manipulating the index cards.
- Combine intense visual images (use pictures, posters, video) with spoken and printed words.
- Go multi-media: Enhance your presentation with visual, auditory, and kinesthetic elements.
- Learn through a rap song. The best one is the one that the audience makes up.
- Pre-expose participants to material in advance; then review or post-expose participants to the material again after the learning.
- Have teams list key ideas on poster-board or flip-chart paper; then have them share their work with the whole group.
- Have participants play the role of presenter; then have them share what they've learned in small groups.
- Use flash cards for review.
- Use role play to engage the learning. The planning/rehearsal time is actually more important to the learning than the performance itself.
- Ask the audience to prepare a list of the 10 most important questions that ought to be asked of anyone in this program/course for the first time.
- Have teams generate 2-minute commercials and present them to the whole group.
- Ask audience members to pair up with a study partner and work together in their off time.
- Create a chant or military-type march (i.e., "1, 2, 3, 4... we learn fast, so give us more.")
- Have teams create a color-coded system with highlighter pens to prioritize key information in their handouts or workbooks.

- Determine key concepts from the material and print each one on colored paper. Have teams put concepts into categories like "Wow" for good ideas, "Humm" for uncertainties and "Oops" for boring or useless ideas. Also take note of what worked for the group and what didn't to improve future trainings.
- Present seven or fewer chunks of information at a time. No matter how much you have to say, break it up into chunks of seven or less for ease of recall.

Any system utilizing two or more of the brain's natural memory processes is considered a complex strategy. Complex strategies enhance memory. For example, learners tend to remember more when they go on a field trip, or when watching a musical, or during a disaster, or in a novel study location—situations where multiple-memory systems have been activated. A complex strategy may involve the use of music, mnemonics, location triggers, intense sensory experiences, theater, motor manipulation, or humor.

Strategies for Reinforcing Learning and Recall

- Have learning partners re-present the material to each other.
- Have participants mind-map the material.
- Have teams do a collage, mural, or graffiti depicting the key concepts.
- Have teams create a physical model of the learning.
- Use recency/primacy—the more you review and the more recently you review, the better.
- Use the BEM principle (beginning, end and middle): Emphasize beginnings and endings.
- Be sure to review after 10 minutes, 48 hours, and 7 days.
- Use future pacing—phrases like "*when* you remember this...."
- Unfinished tasks are recalled better than completed ones; purposely leave some incomplete.
- Use mnemonics–each letter stands for an idea.
- Have learners tell an embellished story or tall-tale about the material.
- Hold an unguided group discussion on the material, it's value, and implications.

How does the brain know whether something is important or not? The answer lies in the body's total physiological response to the event. This means that the physical, psychological, and emotional responses are, at least, as important as the intellectual aspect. In fact, emotional stimulation seems to be one of the strongest influencers for recalling information. The stronger the body's response, the stronger the likelihood of the memory.

Many people believe themselves to be slow learners, or they believe they have a poor memory when they really don't. Often times, just one memory system is being relied on, which results in less than total memory capacity. The brain works best with multiple systems engaged. When the learning is memorable, it *will* be remembered.

Research has verified a tried-and-true way to remember something: Make it new and different. This is because our brains have a high attentional bias towards things that do not fit a pattern (novelty). Some researchers think that novelty creates stress (depending on the level of stress, this can be good or bad) which releases hormones. Too much novelty creates chaos; however, a moderate amount increases attention.

Strategies for Making Your Presentation Memorable

- Relate the material to something similar through metaphor or story-telling.
- Give the material an unusual, bizarre, humorous, sexy twist.
- Give the material a personal or real-life twist (i.e., field trips).
- Use an unusual voice to signal the material's importance.
- Attach a strong positive or negative feeling to the material.
- Provide a concrete reminder like a token, trophy, certificate, toy, or artifact.
- Create a silly story to recall the information.
- Use an interesting, funny, or novel prop.
- Incorporate catchy, energetic, or surprising music.

Demonstrate first, then ask them to do it. Instead of just telling your audience to review the material, show them some strategies that will engage their multiple-memory pathways.

Visualization Techniques for Enhancing Memory

Another tool that can intensify an experience, hence, strengthen the memory is guided visualization. This simple, relaxing, and enjoyable memory technique can be used to review material, to extract meaning, or to prepare for the future. Leading a guided visualization requires a little practical experience, the ability to speak with a relaxing voice, some smooth-paced background music (like George Winston) and a script if you prefer. The following is an example of a script that has worked well for me:

Sample Guided Visualization Script

Find a comfortable position—one where your hands and feet are uncrossed and your body is loose and limp. Allow your eyes to close. Take in a big breath and hold it in for the count of 3...then exhale slowly and fully. Take in another deep breath; inhale even more this time and hold it in for the count of 5...then exhale slowly as if you are blowing up the largest balloon in the world. As you continue to relax, you may be feeling more loose and open to learning. Take in another deep breath from the center of your body, and this time inhale as much air as you possibly can...hold it for the count of 1-2-3-4-5-6-7-8, then exhale slowly, fully, and completely. Now, totally relaxed and loose, you may notice that your breathing continues to be smooth, deep, and easy.

And as you continue to enjoy the relaxation, you find yourself on the seventh floor of a building in a garden lobby. You walk towards a glass elevator, step in, and prepare for an exciting journey through the building. Notice your favorite color on the walls as the elevator begins to descend easily and quietly downward. As you pass the sixth floor, you feel yourself becoming more and more confident, knowing that you fully understand the concept of (______) that we began the group with. Your feelings of certainty and confidence are growing and, with another deep breath, you notice how relaxed you feel as the elevator arrives on the fifth floor. Here we have a chance to recall the concept of (______) which we studied so successfully earlier. You continue your confident descent as you near the fourth floor and the concept of (______).

Often times, just one memory system is being relied on, which results in less than total memory capacity. The brain works best with multiple systems engaged. When the learning is memorable, it will be remembered.

On this floor, thoughts and images of (______) surround you. With another deep breath, you comfortably and gently continue your descent to the third floor where you easily and quickly review the concepts of (______) and (______). You know you understand them well and have total recall when necessary. Now descend to the second floor—a calm and comfortable place of learning—a place where you recall that you learned about (______) and (______,) as well as (______) so confidently.

Like a feather, you float gently down to the first floor. You step out of the elevator and into the future. Notice how confident you feel at this time. Tell yourself how glad you are that you know this material. Congratulate yourself on how well you remember it. Take a moment to glance back at the elevator and remember how far you've come. Feel good knowing that knowledge stays with you. Take another deep breath, feeling confident and prepared for your next step... and when you are ready, let your eyes open... feeling relaxed, complete, and wonderful.

Notice the sample script first puts the participant into a very relaxed state, then consistently uses suggestions of things being easy, smooth, and simple with multiple references made to confidence. By filling in the blank spaces with your content, you personalize the visualization for your group. Speak slowly, pause frequently, and use a relaxing (deeper than average) tone of voice.

Success breeds success. The more participants can remember and recall, the more confident they'll feel. Actually present to your audience the various strategies for remembering. Indicate to them that there are many ways to develop their memory. Incorporate strategies, such as mnemonics, peg words, and review time. Learn some of the methods yourself from books such as *Bs and As in 30 Days*, also by Eric Jensen, which presents varied memory systems such as chunking, location, mnemonics, peg words, linking, key words, imagery, association, and synesthesia. Using these multiple-memory systems not only ensures greater memory, they increase the fun.

Another tool that can intensify an experience, hence, strengthen the memory is guided visualization. This simple, relaxing, and enjoyable memory technique can be used to review material, to extract meaning, or to prepare for the future.

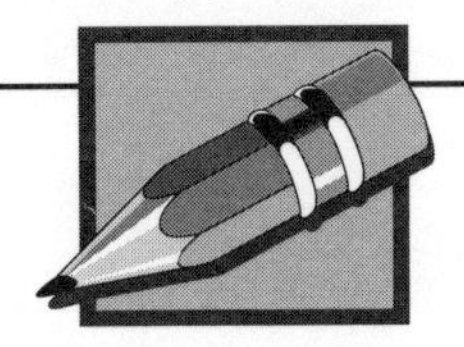

Engage Your Brain:
Enhancing Your Memory

Close your eyes and take a deep breath...hold it for a count of 3. Now, exhale... and feel your lungs relax. Inhale again, this time even deeper, and exhale on the count of 5. As you begin to relax, imagine yourself closing a presentation. The audience is clapping and celebrating; then they begin standing up. You know your presentation has had a memorable effect on them. You begin reviewing the techniques you incorporated. They were meant to engage multiple-memory pathways, and they have proven successful. Now, in this relaxed and confident state, begin writing down the techniques you used.

No one succeeds without effort. Those who succeed owe their success to their perseverance.

–Ramana Maharshi

CHAPTER 20

Ensuring the Learning for Later

Some presenters are happy just to get a contract, do the presentation, and get out as "unscathed" as possible. Presenters with short-term thinking like this rarely last. The best presenters care about the long-term effects of their presentation. They want their participants to not only learn, but to transfer the learning to their lives and apply it in the real world. Unless you purposefully and strategically plan for the transfer of the learning, it probably won't happen. If what you present is valuable and meaningful, the application of it is the next step. This chapter focuses on the essential process, therefore, of learning transfer.

- *Transfer of Learning*
- *Routine Patterns Drive the Brain*
- *Make the Learning Valuable*
- *Create Better Buy-In*
- *Use Multiple Approaches*
- *Use a Condition-Action Framework*
- *Use Retrieval Strategies*
- *Present Operating Schemas*
- *Link With Prior Learning*
- *Use Mind-Mapping Techniques*
- *Influence Audience Motivation*
- *Increase Audience Accountability*
- *Match Contexts*
- *Consider Potential Barriers*
- *Apply Structural Analogies*
- *Make Solutions the Audience's Idea*
- *Utilize the Nonconscious*
- *Future Pace the Learning*
- *Support In a Real-Life Context*

Transfer of Learning

The transfer of learning or the stimulus to recall and use a particular skill or knowledge base is triggered outside the learner—by the learner's environment and usually nonconsciously. This underscores the difficulty, therefore, of facilitating the application of learning. Because people and circumstances are so different, no one single strategy will succeed with everyone. But collectively, the strategies presented in this chapter will provide a foundation for the steady transfer of learning and its applications to your participants' lives.

Brain Connection

Routine Patterns Drive the Brain

The human brain controls our behaviors through programs, routines, patterns, and rituals which shape our lives. Making changes to them can be difficult. There are many pieces of the puzzle that hold the familiar structure in place. Primarily, they are emotions—fears, hopes, past traumas, hardships, and stress—which are generated from our beliefs and experiences. Under conditions of stress, humans tend to rely on known patterns of behavior, rather than risking new ones in which the outcome is unknown. Since most of us lead stressful lives, change is often difficult. Therefore, learning isn't always transferred to the level of routine practice. This explains the phenomenon of knowing something intellectually, but not using it. As professional presenters, our role is to understand the factors that hold people back from adopting more productive behaviors and provide solutions that encourage the application of the learning.

Make the Learning Valuable

In planning your next presentation, ask yourself, "Have I satisfied the needs of this particular audience?" If the answer is not an unfailing "yes," then the audience will likely be less than optimally interested in the training. If your role is to train customer service agents, what you teach better be useful, relevant, and valuable, or chances are, it won't get used. Such things as how to deal with a disgruntled customer, for example, or how to deal with a brand new customer, or how to deal with threats will be the kind of topics that will be perceived as valuable by this audience. The more value your participants recognize in your presentation, the more likely they will be to implement the learning. In general, audiences want to learn things, like the following, that will directly impact their lives:

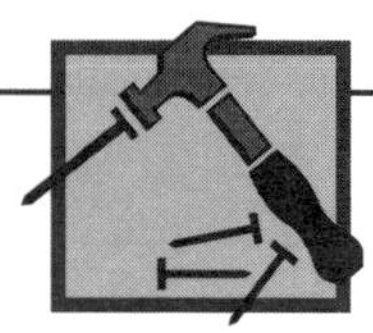

Learning Value Tips & Tools

- Skills that will help participants stay up to speed in the industry
- Knowledge that makes participants' jobs easier or less stressful
- Ways to increase their income or save money
- Strategies for dealing with annoyances and frustrations
- What the trends and forecasts are, and how to prepare for them
- Frameworks for improving chances of promotion
- Tools that boost their self-confidence and competency
- Resources that allow them to do a better job or better serve their clients

Create Better Buy-In

Does your audience agree with the ideas you are suggesting? Do they think they are valid, informative, and valuable? If so, chances of transfer are greater. How can you increase the likelihood of agreement? Present more background and angles on the subject so that your audience has a better understanding of it. Provide all of the necessary pieces of the cognitive puzzle. Make the benefits of the learning explicit. Present reasons why something is a good idea. Present counter-arguments and explain why they are no longer valid. Invite discussion. Encourage questions and debate. Let the audience generate their own ideas so they have more energy and thinking invested. Provide a comfortable environment that encourages enjoyment and cooperative group structures. Give the audience options and choice.

Use Multiple Approaches

Transfer is aided by stronger initial learning. Present the material or skills in multiple contexts. Present it both personally and professionally, if possible. Repeat it in alternative forms. As an example, after a brief lecture, have participants review it with a skit, a ball toss game, role play, quiz show or hands-on learning. Then, activate it with a simulation or with discussion time.

Use a Condition-Action Framework

Putting a situation in a condition-action framework ("if this, then that") means stating a specific occurrence and possible actions. This simple technique links declarative learning to procedural memory and, thus, encourages the transfer of learning. For example, if a participant says, "I don't understand," the condition-action response would be, "Would you like more information on A, B, C, or D?" Your response, A=B, demonstrates a productive thinking strategy that clarifies and simplifies the problem.

In planning your next presentation, ask yourself, "Have I satisfied the needs of this particular audience?" If the answer is not an unquestionable "yes," than the audience may be less interested in, and certainly less likely to incorporate, the learning from your training.

Use Retrieval Strategies

To apply learning, we need to be able to retrieve it from memory. There are many ways to increase the likelihood of retrieval: review it, mindmap it, create an acronym or mnemonic, make it emotional, turn it into a story, draw it, sing it, act it out, make a quiz on it, associate it with a location, or provide a concrete reminder of the learning—a novelty item, certificate, or memento.

We tend to make distinctions about information by both how it is different than, and the same as, other information we have already encountered and stored in our memory pathways. For example, when you meet someone new, you might say to yourself, she's a lot like..." Yet, we also retrieve our memories through differences. If you are asked to describe who you met yesterday, you have to differentiate that person from others, store the similarities, and retrieve the unique factors. This underscores the importance of recognizing both the qualities that are similar *and* different from prior learning when introducing new material in your presentation.

Present Operating Schemas

Schemas are the deep, functional relationships embedded in any context that illuminate rules, problems, and potential solutions. These are the pieces of the puzzle that experts identify, sort, and map when attempting to solve complex problems. Experts in a subject are usually able to identify operating schemas while novices looked for superficial characteristics that do not represent the guts of the matter. When presenters identify relevant features of a context and make them explicit, participants' ability to apply what they've learned in problem-solving situations and real life increases.

Schemas are the deep, functional relationships embedded in any context that illuminate rules, problems, and potential solutions. These are the pieces of the puzzle that experts identify, sort, and map when attempting to solve complex problems.

Link With Prior Learning

Another strategy for increasing transfer of learning is to link up what participants already know with what is new. The links might be in the areas of content, rules, or process, participant's personal history, or from other learning contexts. Here are some examples: "Remember in yesterday's conversation we talked about the purpose of learning new writing skills?..." Or, "Do you remember what it was like learning to ride a bicycle? Your parents may have helped you or maybe you used training wheels for awhile; and then at some magical point, you were ready to go it alone."

Use Mind-Mapping Techniques

The use of graphic organizers, clusters, or mind-mapping techniques are also important devices for transferring learning. Mind-maps allow the learner to sort a great deal of information, even if it is seemingly unrelated. Making a visual representation of the material helps participants understand the topic's breadth and scope, which can bring clarity and understanding to a situation.

Influence Audience Motivation

Another consideration in the transfer of learning is audience motivation. Motivation strategies are discussed extensively in Chapter 10; however, for review, some common motivating factors for applying learning are the possibility of promotion, a raise, or even the ability to keep a current job. Popularity, fun, sense of belonging, self-esteem, confidence, feeling of success, competence, or acceptance may be other factors. In an academic setting, motivation may also be impacted by grades or graduation. It is very useful to set up activities where the audience can brainstorm these factors, discuss them, or simply list them for themselves.

Increase Audience Accountability

Participants may learn new material, but if no follow-up is made, they may forget to apply it. So, how can presenters build more accountability into the training process? The following strategies help to focus more responsibility on participants: 1) Use teams—the group acts as positive peer influence; 2) Use team charts—results are posted for public display; 3) Use reporting systems—team leaders or individuals give oral or written reports; 4) Assign projects—the results are obvious; it either works or doesn't work; 5) Facilitate performances role plays, or on-the-job learning; or 6) Utilize a quiz or test.

Match Contexts

Our memory retrieval systems are strongly triggered by context. If participants learn how to deal with conflict resolution in an accurate simulation environment, the learning is more likely to be applied. But if, on the other hand, they role play how to deal with an angry customer in person, when most of their customers communicate via telephone, the unmatched contexts may result in low transfer of learning.

Our memory retrieval systems are strongly triggered by context. If participants learn how to deal with conflict resolution in an accurate simulation environment, the learning is more likely to be applied.

Consider Potential Barriers

Before you can attempt to mitigate the potential barriers to implementation of new learning, you have to recognize them. Thus, the framework described on the following page provides a look at the most common barriers participants face.

Potential Barriers

1. ***Intuitive-Emotional***
   Participants have fears, concerns, and resistance to learning, which might sound like, "Will I be the only one who uses it? Will I fail? What will others think if I fail?"

2. ***Critical-Logical***
   The implication by sound or unsound reasoning, facts, or authority figures—hinted at or stated overtly—that failure is inevitable.

3. ***Ethical-Moral***
   Conflict with personal values, religious or political beliefs, or parental influence.

4. ***Biological-Medical***
   Inadequate nutrition, abuse of drugs/alcohol, poor sleep habits, illness, etc.

5. ***Cultural-Social***
   Barriers include the potentially negative influence of peers, ethnic biases, and learning styles, which may be mismatched for the person or environment.

6. ***Institutional-Physical***
   Limited or inadequate physical, economic, institutional, or social access—discrimination on any basis (i.e., "I can't do my job right because if I do, I'll make my boss look bad.")

Have participants brainstorm the most likely barriers they will face in implementing what they have learned; then have them brainstorm some potential solutions. Discuss and refine the ideas.

Apply Structural Analogies

Provide the audience with an analogy of how the new learning might be implemented. The following example uses analogy in a product sales pitch: "This new learning aroma will trigger attention and memory. Plus, it's simple to use. Have you ever used a spray paint or a perfume atomizer? It's that simple. You just fill the container, aim, and spray." Make sure to point out the matching qualities (i.e., absorb the information, aim or practice, and apply the learning).

Make Solutions the Audience's Idea

Most participants want to succeed, but competing agendas interfere. One solution is to encourage your audience to brainstorm potential obstacles to applying what they're learning, then let them generate the solutions. If it's their idea, they're more likely going to use it. A twist on this idea is to have the group brainstorm a list of key concepts learned. Then type up the list, copy, and mail it to the participants with a "reconnect" letter a month after the course.

Most participants want to succeed, but competing agendas interfere. One solution is to encourage your audience to brainstorm potential obstacles to applying what they're learning, then let them generate the solutions.

Utilize the Nonconscious

Even the way a presenter describes the material and its applications can influence its transfer. The incidentals that are not processed on the conscious level, but are absorbed in the unconscious, are important. Like a magician who gets you to look at the wrong hand, or hat, or rabbit, the skilled presenter "slips in" key words that seem unimportant. Here are some examples:

"After you use this skill, you'll feel a real sense of pride" (note the presupposition and positive suggestion). Or, "After you've successfully and easily installed the new software, you'll be able to produce projects immediately." (note the presupposition and suggestion that they'll do it successfully and easily).

Future Pace the Learning

Future pacing is a tool that allows the participant to imagine a situation in the future where their new learning will be useful. There are a of couple ways to empower participants for future experiences. One is to lead a visualization, taking the participants into the future where they can experience success and, as a result, increased confidence. The other is to use the tool of future pacing. Future pacing is a language pattern that embeds positive suggestion. For example, saying, "*when* you do this," or "*when* you implement this skill," or, "*as* you use more and more of your new knowledge," rather than *if* assumes right action. Your assumption that they'll use what they learn and that it'll help them do their job better is a step towards the desired result.

The way a presenter describes the material and its applications can influence its transfer. The incidentals that are not processed on the conscious level, but are absorbed in the unconscious, are important.

Support In a Real-Life Context

Consider, for a moment, the actual context in which you expect the learning to be applied. What forms of long-term support exist? Are participants aware of these? If there's not sufficient support, devote a few minutes to a brainstorm session and encourage participants to consider what forms of support they might need. They may suggest things like systems or organizational support, additional trainings, workshops, guest speakers, monthly meetings, hats, booklets, administrative support, conferences, video follow-up, internal or external consulting, computer programs, or discussion and debriefing time. Perhaps, the group will find a solution they can enact themselves, like a monthly support group, a phone-tree, or visits to each others places of work.

One of the activities I like to conduct is what I call a "How Do You Think This Idea Might 'Fly'"? This is where participants are asked to write their name and phone number on a piece of paper before folding it into a paper airplane. After a quick, plane-throwing madhouse, everyone ends up with somebody else's plane. This is the person who they are assigned to follow-up with one week or one month after the training.

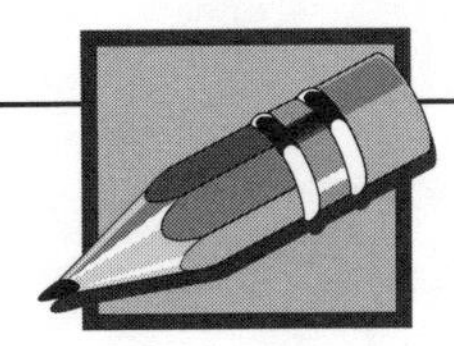

Engage Your Brain:
Planning for Learning Transfer

What are the key concepts from your next presentation that you hope participants will most apply?

What strategies will you apply from your learning in this chapter to help them apply what they learn?

How will you know whether or not your strategies were successful?

Will you be conducting a follow-up activity? If so, how will it be implemented? If not, have you built in some accountability procedures or group support structures for participants?

Our business in life is not to get ahead of others but to get ahead of ourselves, to break our own records, to do our work with more force than ever before.

–Stewart B. Johnson

CHAPTER 21

Closings With Flare

How you close your presentation is just as important as the other aspects of a training, if not more. After all, one of the best opportunities for cementing learning is during the last few minutes of a session. It's not what participants come with, but what they leave with, that really counts. So, what's the best way to end a presentation? It's not when you've run out of material or time. A good closing will be orchestrated methodically and with purpose. This chapter focuses on ways to create closings that facilitate a feeling of wholeness about the subject and, ideally, an inner sense of accomplishment.

Key Topics

- *Closing Essentials*
- *Embedding Learning*
- *Five Elements of Memorable Closings*
- *Eliciting a Feeling of Movement*
- *Ensuring Meaning*
- *Establishing Value*
- *Eliciting a Feeling of Wholeness*
- *Eliciting Audience Feedback*
- *Next Step Activities*
- *Eliminating Barriers to Action*

Closing Essentials

A well-planned closing will satisfy multiple objectives: It will tie various learning segments together; handle participant questions and/or concerns; acknowledge participants; and celebrate the learning experience. The simple act of closure, itself, adds value to the session by evoking positive emotions and enhancing recall. Even if you're short on time, cut from the middle of your presentation rather than the end. A good rule of thumb is to plan about 10 percent of your total presentation time for the closing. If your session is only 10 minutes long, do a 1- or 2-minute closing. In a 1-hour presentation, set aside approximately 5 or 6 minutes. Include in your notes the exact time to start the closing and stick to it.

We most often recall first and last impressions. It is of great value, therefore, to create a closure that captures the attention and imagination of your participants. This can be complicated by the fact that as the session winds down audience members begin, mentally (if not physically), preparing to leave. To ensure your message has impact, engage participants' emotions. Not everything about the closing can be emotionally engaging, but at least one aspect of it should have the kick of a wild horse. After all, this is what the learner will be left with when all is said and done.

Brain Connection

Embedding Learning

The term "closing" means a couple of things. First, it's a content-related term which indicates that the content for that session or day is complete. How do we know it's complete? When it feels done! We all want that feeling of achievement when we finish something. The best closings elicit an emotional state that celebrates this feeling—the internal reward of accomplishment. When this happens, the learning is embedded. The chemical states you induce, as a presenter, will determine the final (and lasting) feelings of your group.

As your session nears completion, also keep in mind that participants will likely be asking themselves concluding questions like, What was the point of this session? Did I learn anything? How do I feel? How can I grow from this experience? Does anyone else feel the same way I do? What can I do with what I've learned? And, how can I continue to learn more on this subject? Be prepared to help participants make the most of this critical time of introspection. They need to feel that their internal, as well as external, needs have been satisfied—their questions answered, their upsets handled, and their excitement shared.

Participants want to feel they've made progress as a result of your session. The affirmation of such can come from many sources including a review or test, group discussions, acknowledgments, or self-discovery. It usually takes the form of generalizing the experience to other areas of the participant's life. Completion also means that you have led participants into the future or future-paced them with the information. This includes how they can expect to use the learning and when. Additionally, make sure that you acknowledge participants for their attention and presence. And finally, include housekeeping information like announcements, evaluations, and additional resources. Ideally, participants will leave your group with a feeling of excitement and curiosity to learn more.

To ensure your message has impact, engage participants' emotions. Not everything about the closing can be emotionally engaging, but at least one aspect of it should have the kick of a wild horse. After all, this is what the learner will be left with when all is said and done.

Five Elements of Memorable Closings

While it is not necessary to include all five elements in every closing, the more emotions that are evoked, the more memorable the learning will be. Put yourself in the participant's shoes for a moment and consider what activities would give you a sense of the following essential elements:

1. Movement: a feeling that something was accomplished ("ta-da!").

2. Meaning: a feeling that the learning made sense, was well understood, believed, and meaningful.

3. Value: a feeling that your time was well invested, the experience was worthwhile, and your efforts and learning were validated.

4. Completeness: a feeling that nothing important was missing, that the learning was complete (at least for now).

5. Next Step: a feeling that you have additional resources for further learning on the subject if desired.

Eliciting a Feeling of Movement

The actual strategies for closure are straightforward and simple. Use your experience and sensory acuity to determine the closure activities most appropriate for your group. Try all of them (though not at once!), and decide which of the following are your favorites:

- Participants brainstorm the key points of the learning in a small group or with a partner.
- Participants reflect on learning for 2 to 10 minutes, then share insights with the group or a partner.
- Presenter reviews key points while participants close their eyes and listen to music playing in the background.
- Teams make and maintain charts to track and discuss their progress. (i.e., Use evaluative criteria like having fun, meeting goals, new and useful ideas, and participation levels).
- Presenter hands out a thermometer graph at the beginning of the session labeled "least confident" at the bottom and "most confident" at the tip of the thermometer. Participants color in their feelings as the course progresses, and then discuss the process in the closing.
- Each team thinks of two or three pertinent questions with one-word answers related to the training. Combine questions with those from other teams to form a giant crossword puzzle.
- Play Musical Chairs—the participant left standing shares one key concept learned from the session.
- Participants review notes together in small groups or with partners.
- Play a word association game—participants get a list of 10 wild words to link up with 10 key concepts from the presentation.
- Incorporate a quiz, test, or other form of assessment.
- Participants write in a learning log or diary, then share it with a partner.
- Participants evaluate learning against a list of goals.
- Teams are asked to come up with a catchy bumper sticker slogan that reflects something important they learned in the course.
- Participants summarize a key idea from the course with a slogan written on a small piece of paper. Slogans are then rolled up and placed inside a blown up balloon. All the balloons are thrown up into the air and batted around. After a few minutes, everyone picks a "fortune balloon" to take home.
- Teams create posters that reflect the "gems" discovered in the course. They are posted around the room, whereby individuals can view and mark the posters with their initials if they also learned the same thing.

Participants want to feel they've made progress as a result of your session. The affirmation of such can come from many sources including a review or test, group discussions, acknowledgments, or self-discovery. It usually takes the form of generalizing the experience to other areas of the participant's life.

- Each group reviews the session using a different learning style: auditory, visual, and kinesthetic. Then, while reflecting that particular learning style, each group shares their process with the rest of the group. (i.e., auditory = lecture format or talking book; visual = mind-map or collage; kinesthetic = theater or role play.
- Each participant receives two index cards, one on which to write a question and one on which to write the answer. Collect all the cards, mix them up, and redistribute them to everyone. The goal is for participants to locate the two people who hold the corresponding cards.
- Participants respond in oral unison to presenter's strategic questions (i.e., "Today we started with the concept of ________ and how it affects the ________. Then we learned about __________.") The oral response (fill-in-the-blanks) drill requires mostly simple recall skills. This exercise is meant to reinforce participants' confidence in themselves; thus, it is important to ask questions that have a singular unambiguous answer and that have been emphasized in the session.

Closing Activities That Ensure Meaning

- Participants do individual or team mind-maps.
- Invite participants to talk about what the learning means to them in small groups.
- Teams are invited to make a list of top-10 concepts to remember from the presentation, then record them on an audiotape for later review.
- Elicit participant's conclusions drawn from the day's learning.
- Ask participants to share something with the group that symbolizes their learning in the session: It might be a personal story or experience, a piece of music, a natural object, an art piece, a case study, a journal article, or a poem, for example.
- Facilitate a discussion on the relevancy of the learning to participant's lives.

If a participant comes to a potentially damaging conclusion about an activity, you'll want to lead them to a more resourceful one. For example, if a participant draws a conclusion like, "What I learned about myself is that I don't work well with others," ask some clarifying questions. If ignored, such a conclusion could negatively impact the progress of the group, or worse, the rest of the participant's life. Some examples of clarifying questions follow:

- "I appreciate you sharing that. What do you think, specifically, causes you not to work well with others?"
- "Thanks for letting me know. When you say others, I wondered if anyone specific comes to mind?"

- “Thanks for sharing this with us. I was thinking, if you could solve this, how would you go about it?”

With each question you ask, you are politely and respectfully helping participants reach inside themselves to discover resources they didn’t know they had. You also have an obligation, as a learning coach, to make sure that any conclusions drawn are useful for the participant’s life. This intervention is not only preferred, it’s the reason that you are in the business–to shape participant’s beliefs, attitudes, and values.

Establishing Value

- Participants explain to a partner or team how they can use what they’ve learned.
- Participants get confirmation or congratulations from an outside source.
- Have participants do a rating or rubric with each other.
- List what has been learned; ask participants to select what will be implemented.
- Have individuals or groups demonstrate a skill.
- Listen to others share about how they’ve used the learning.
- A completed project is shared with the group, demonstrated, or talked about.
- In teams, participants compare what was learned with a pre-existing list of criteria.
- One month after the presentation, ask everyone for a letter or note sharing how they’ve used the material from the course. Then, publish the letters in an inspiring newsletter for all to read.

Facilitating a group discussion is a common and useful way to establish value. If the relationships you've cultivated are moderate to strong, a large group discussion will probably work. Otherwise, break the group into smaller groups and have them each open a discussion.

Facilitating a group discussion is a common and useful way to establish value. If the relationships you’ve cultivated are moderate to strong, a large group discussion will probably work. Otherwise, break the group into smaller groups and have them each open a discussion with questions such as:

- “What was interesting?”
- “What was valuable?”
- “What did you agree with or disagree with the most?”
- “What did you learn about yourself today?”
- “How might you use what you have learned?
- “How does the learning affect your life?”

Reconnecting is also important. Make sure that you have reconnected what you are doing with what the audience wished to get out of the training. The following activities can help accomplish this task:

- Checking in with an oral contract you made.
- Verifying results from a checklist.
- Posting a list and having participants check off completed items.
- Having participants do a self-assessment with team or individual checklists.
- Having participants share about connections made or value received.
- Giving individual participants and groups an evaluation form to complete.
- Scheduling a reunion with the group a week, month, or year later.

Mind-mapping is an excellent method for reviewing the learning and eliciting a feeling of wholeness. The process taps into the conscious and unconscious mind.

Eliciting a Feeling of Wholeness

- Use a closing ritual (i.e., a song, clap, prop, role play, sharing, activity, etc.).
- Facilitate a group or partner discussion around the question, "How do I feel about what I've learned?"
- Ask participants to trace their steps for the day with a partner.
- Use celebration, certificates, and handshakes.
- Participants or teams complete a mind-map.
- Tell a story of the group's journey for the course.
- Provide question and answer time.
- Pass out ballots for the group to nominate roles for participants like best laugh, wildest dresser, most fun, biggest volunteer, most likely to use the materials, etc. Then hold an awards ceremony.
- In pairs, one participant interviews the other about the topic; then reverse roles.
- Solicit presenter evaluations from participants.

Have teams create a group mind-map. Mind-mapping is an excellent method for reviewing the learning and eliciting a feeling of wholeness. The process taps into the conscious and unconscious mind. It calls for participants to use their recall, organization, and planning skills. In addition, the process itself improves recall as participants arrange the material visually (right brain) and sequentially (left brain). Usually a group can put together a quality mind-map in 10 to 20 minutes. Make sure they have the time and the resources (big paper, space to lay it out, and colored markers) to do it well. Put completed mind-maps on display around the room.

Eliciting Audience Feedback

One of the most useful things a presenter can do before dismissing a group is to get feedback. Though not all of the feedback you get will have the potential to positively impact your future efforts, some of it will. It is critical, however, that you keep negative (and positive) feedback in perspective. Much like a movie review, one person will love you and one will not. This is the nature of the business and of human beings. What is useful is to look for patterns that emerge and reemerge, specific and well-intentioned suggestions, and answers to questions you may have been asking yourself. There are many ways to elicit audience feedback. To get the most complete picture of the situation, use multiple methods. Some examples follow:

- Ask participants to write a one-page process review of the presentation (open-ended).
- Facilitate an open discussion with the audience.
- Ask teams to hold a discussion and provide you with an evaluation of the training created among themselves.
- Post a flip-chart page filled with descriptive words. Ask participants to circle or mark the words they feel most appropriately describe their experience. Include words like, enjoyable, too easy, too hard, boring, needs more movement, too slow, too fast, needs more content, I disagree with content, etc.

Though not all of the feedback you get will have the potential to positively impact your future efforts, some of it will. It is critical, however, that you keep negative (and positive) feedback in perspective.

Even if you only have a few minutes at the end of the session, at least, take the time to give your participants a simple feedback form. Experiment with questions until you get the information you need. A sample feedback survey is included on page 48.

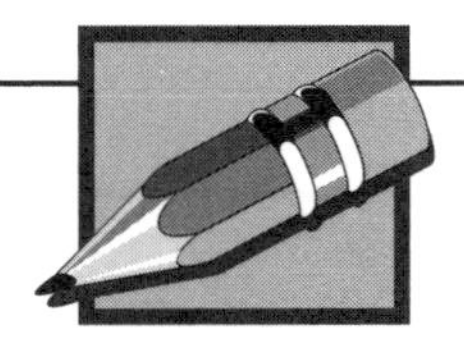

Engage Your Brain:
Closing Reactions

What are your feelings about the topics presented in this book thus far?

What are some practical applications for what you have learned?

What do you want to remember from this book? How will you ensure your own recall?

Next Step Activities

- Clean up learning area and return things to their proper place.
- Participants brainstorm what to do next (including how to deal with obstacles).
- Assign or discuss follow-up work and activities.
- Handle participant needs (i.e., lost items, transportation, messages, phone numbers, etc.).
- Help participants set up a network among themselves for further study.
- Provide participants with a list of suggested resources.
- Put on celebration music, use streamers, and party poppers.
- Use future-pacing and positive suggestions to affirm learning.
- Provide participants with information about additional trainings you offer.
- Throw a party or have a celebration: If it's worth learning, it's worth celebrating!

Tantalize participants with interesting tidbits of information that might represent their next step. Use suggestions that emphasize an immediate, concrete benefit to the participant.

Tantalize participants with interesting tidbits of information that might represent their next step. This might take the form of a question, challenge, or muse. For example, you might say, "Next group we'll be learning how to add 10 percent to the bottom line with one simple question. Anyone interested? Great! See you next time!" Or, perhaps, "Next session we'll learn the 10 words that can turn any upset customer into a happy one in just 30 seconds." Or, "At our next meeting, we'll learn to use a special planning format that can save you dozens of hours of valuable time." Or, "Next time, we'll discover the best ways to increase productivity on little or no budget." All of these suggestions emphasize an immediate, concrete benefit to the participant.

Eliminating Barriers to Action

Addressing the potential barriers that may inhibit participants from taking action on the learning is also an important aspect of the closing. It is best to have participants brainstorm (either individually or in teams) the barriers as they perceive them. This exercise requires pencils and paper and can be used with any age participants. The process takes from 10 to 60 minutes depending on the presenter's experience, the group size, depth of analysis, and course content. The steps are outlined on the following page.

Steps to Brainstorming Potential Barriers

1. On the first piece of paper, write down all of the useful tools or ideas you learned in this session.
2. Next, start a second sheet titled "Barriers to Action." List all of the potential barriers to using the skills you learned or recalling the information later.
3. Now, cross out any of the barriers which can easily be dealt with and eliminated.
4. Brainstorm solutions to the remaining barriers. The goal is to find a possible solution for each barrier.
5. Conclude with each participant creating a personal action plan to initiate the solutions most workable for them. Ask for volunteers to share their action plan with the rest of the group. Affirm the success of everyone in the session.
6. Have the entire group affirm their individual and mutual success by shouting, "We can do it!" in unison.

If you observe body language and facial expressions closely, you may determine there are some participants who don't feel complete or positively affirmed. Near the end of the session, inconspicuously invite them to talk to you.

Many variations to this activity exist, so improvise as needed. At this stage, also handle participants' emotional and physical concerns so that a sense of completion is accomplished. Some typical concerns include the following:

Weather: Has it created any special circumstances? Do any of your participants have transportation problems?

Upcoming Events: What other opportunities exist to further the learning? Provide logistics.

Projects or Deadlines: Is there a deadline coming up? Remind participants of it at this time.

Confusion or Depression: Do any participants need ongoing support or special attention following the session? If you observe body language and facial expressions closely, you may determine there are some participants who don't feel complete or positively affirmed. Near the end of the session, inconspicuously invite them to talk to you. You might say to them, "You seem a bit troubled. Is it anything you can talk to me about?"

Organization: Enlist the support of others to return any equipment or furniture used back to its proper place.

Transportation: Make sure everyone has a ride, that carpools have been arranged if appropriate, etc. Simply ask participants if they have any unmet travel needs.

Handouts: Remind participants to take their handouts and other belongings with them when they leave.

Future Meetings: If the session is just temporarily ending, remind participants what they need to bring, know, or do for the next session.

Close With a Final Ritual: This can be a visualization, a big symbolic clap, a dance, a gesture, a rap, or a high-five. Introduce the ritual with energy and enthusiasm. Be consistent and have fun with it. Some participants may be slow to join in. Be patient, they'll learn to enjoy the routine. The closing ritual is the final experience participants have in your group so make it fun and upbeat!

Close with a final ritual: this can be a visualization, a big symbolic clap, a dance, a gesture, a rap, or a high-five. Introduce the ritual with energy and enthusiasm. Be consistent and have fun with it.

The following sample guided visualization suggested by communication specialist and NLP co-founder Richard Bandler, provides an example of this powerful medium for final closure:

> Allow your eyes to close for just a moment. Take in a slow deep breath and let it out slowly...good...now relax and let your shoulders drop. You've learned a lot in this workshop. Now it's time to go out and use what you've learned.
>
> If at any moment you find yourself not using the learning or hesitating with it, or you find yourself putting off some new behavior you could have tried today, stop. Look over your left shoulder. There will be a shadow there. This shadow represents the uncertainty of life...the dark side...the unknown...all that which we would rather not think about, but which is ever present, since, after all, at any moment, this time called life could end.
>
> The way you act today, the risks you take, and the love you give could be construed as your final statement on this planet–a bit heavy, but true nonetheless. And one of the ways you can use this thought in a positive way is to realize that it is foolish and arrogant to hesitate. When you hesitate, you are acting as if you are immortal. And that, you are not. And when you need a reminder of the importance of this, glance over your left shoulder. You'll remember that something powerful is waiting for you. Don't hesitate to act.
>
> Rather, make your shadow a positive reminder of your mortality—a lurking force that will always encourage you to live up to your potential. You can afford nothing less. Now, take in a deep breath...and nod your head yes as you slowly exhale. Open your eyes when you're ready. And as you bring yourself back to this room, if you're committed to using what you consider to be the most powerful and valuable ideas from this workshop, raise your hand and say, "yes!"

The closing is also the perfect time to acknowledge and appreciate your participants for their participation. For every single group, regardless of what was taught or how well the participants learned, find something that you can appreciate or acknowledge. Make sure that your participant congratulations are sincere and that you demonstrate this with congruent posture, voice, words, tonality, and gestures. Learners especially remember the openings and closings. Thus, make your last word–your final thought, your ribbon around the package–a memorable one!

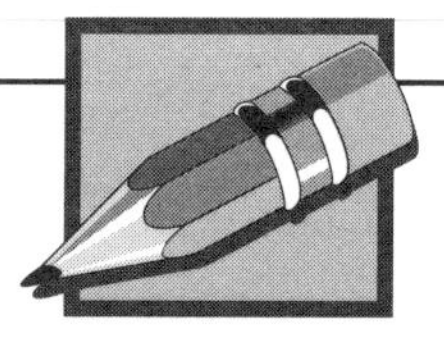

Engage Your Brain:
Closing Mind-Map

Depict with colored markers the ideal presentation environment based on what you have learned thus far.

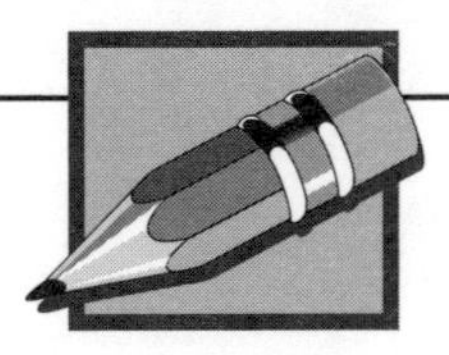

Engage Your Brain:
Planning to Close With Flair

How have you closed your presentations in the past? What strategies from this chapter do you currently use?

Have your past closings been successful? Did you learn anything in this chapter that might enhance them further?

Does the plan you have for your next closing include the five essential elements for a memorable closing? Which ones are included? Which ones are not?

Under the appropriate category, list the activities you'll be including in your next closing:

1. Movement 2. Meaning 3. Value 4. Wholeness 5. Next Step

When we accept tough jobs as a challenge and wade into them with enthusiasm, miracles can happen.

–Arland Gilbert

CHAPTER 22

Light the Sky With Your Fire

The starting point for becoming a great presenter is introspection. Choosing such a profession is a big decision. Being a trainer or presenter is full of joys and frustrations. If you know what you're getting into ahead of time and are willing to pay the price for success, you can and will succeed. Before you carry the torch forward, however, it is best to consider (or reconsider) your plan.

- *The Value of Your Message*
- *The Brain Is Easily Distracted*
- *Marketing Yourself*
- *Handling the Lows*
- *Putting a Price on Your Services*
- *Turning Down Work*
- *Defining Success*
- *Paying the Price for Success*
- *The Feedback Formula*
- *Presenting With Passion*

The Value of Your Message

The value of your message in the marketplace was one of the first subjects in this book, now it's one of the last. To carry the torch forward successfully, you must have a compelling message that you are passionate about, that you can articulate well, and that is perceived as valuable by the marketplace. If any one of these three essentials is missing, go back to square one. Determine your message, then put it together in a thoughtful, entertaining, and persuasive way. Be an original. Even if the content of your message is similar to others, present it uniquely. If you can't bring something of yourself to the party, stay home. If you can, get out there and sizzle with the best of them.

Once you've determined that your message is compelling, discover how the marketplace relates to your niche. For example, my particular niche–applications of brain research to training–is a relatively new field and a difficult one. Keeping up with the latest knowledge is nearly a full-time job in itself. The positive angle, however, is that there is a rapidly increasing interest in the brain—both in the scientific and lay community. My message is that you'll get better training results when you use applications from recent brain research. These applications are clearly spelled out and people want to learn them. The marketplace foundation is, thus, clearly intact.

Brain Connection

The Brain Is Easily Distracted

The brain is very good at adapting, and changing, and acquiring both simple and complex programs. Unfortunately, our brain is also very easily distracted by novelty and emotions, so we get sidetracked. As a result, we often learn something new, but may not practice it enough to actually transfer the learning. To master a skill or subject, we must get our brain to stay focused on the learning long enough to make sure that the next step is implemented.

If however, there is no apparent market for your message, I strongly suggest you alter it or look for a different market. Let's say, though that you've discovered a hungry audience for your message, now consider what resources you have available to invest. Resources include time, energy, travel capabilities, money, emotional support, and training aids. You'll also need supplies, information, and a professional network to keep you updated. Finally, you'll need office space. If you determine that you have sufficient resources available to you, maximize them.

Marketing Yourself

Discover your message, then put it together in a thoughtful, entertaining, and persuasive way. Be an original. Even if the content of your message is similar to others, present it uniquely.

Some presenters are more natural than others at selling their services. Since, there is no way to avoid this aspect of the profession, it is best to ask yourself some tough questions: Do you have the willingness to follow-up on each lead you get? Do you have the skills to develop a quality package of professional marketing materials? Do you know others who will refer clients to you? Do you have access to mailing lists of potential clients? Do you have the resources to establish a web site? Do you have a product to sell at your presentations (i.e., books, newsletters, or CDs)? Do you have an advanced session or follow-up training to offer clients? Do you have a system for attracting referrals and obtaining testimonials? Do you know how to attract the kinds of customers who can pay higher fees? A full-spectrum of marketing strategies will be needed to market yourself in this competitive world.

Handling the Lows

The "lows" can come in many forms, but most commonly, presenters face financial and/or emotional hardships. Perhaps, you can't find enough work to support yourself, or your work gets criticized. The nature of the profession is such that you have to learn to "suck up" such challenges and turn criticism into something positive. A common denominator of all successful presenters is a strong self-esteem. Those who don't have it end up self-selecting themselves out of the profession. It hurts to have your work criticized. But you either let it stop you or you learn from it and move on.

Putting a Price On Your Services

At some point, as a presenter, you will have to deal with how to price your services. If you charge too little, you may end up with too much work, and your creditability can suffer. However, if your fees are too high, you may not find enough work. The following five ranges of speaker fees are most common in the training and presenting industry:

1 Speaking fees for someone who is not a veteran presenter range from $250 to $1,000 per day; or $150 to $750 per half day. This "starter" range is appropriate for someone who has good information and solid presentation skills, but their overall package is still a bit raw.

2 Speaking fees for someone who has a strong message, good presentation skills, excellent materials, and a name in the community or area of their specialty range from $1,000 to $2,000 per day. It is in this "shirt-sleeves" range that most presenters fall.

3 The next range is known as the "top-dog" range. These are the career freelance trainers and presenters who have all the work they want. Fees range from $2,000 to $7,500 per day. They demand these high honorariums because they can get them. They represent the best in their field. They are household names to their peers.

4 Speaking fees for presenters who have a rare specialty niche command between $5,000 and $25,000 per day. These presenters, referred to as "specialists," don't necessarily have the best presenting skills, but people want to hear them. They include celebrities, authors, professional athletes, top scientists, Nobel Prize laureates, media personalities, Olympians, and business CEOs.

5 The "skybox" range is for the superstars who command from $20,000 to $100,000 per presentation. They are known, not just to the training industry, but to the general public. They include household names like Colin Powell, Pat Riley, Bill Gates, Lee Iococca, Zig Ziglar, Anthony Robbins, and Norman Schwartzcof.

A common denominator of all successful presenters is a strong self-esteem. Those who don't have it end up self-selecting themselves out of the profession. It hurts to have your work criticized. But you either let it stop you or you learn from it and move on.

To determine what category you fit into, start a bit lower than you think you can command. If you are getting too much work, your fees might be too low. If you're not getting enough work, consider the following possibilities: 1) your marketing may not be strong enough; 2) your reputation may not be strong enough; 3) the competition may be too strong; 4) your fees may be too high; or 5) the quality of your work may not match your fees. To make it to the "top-dog" range or above in this competitive and dynamic industry, you'll need a strong desire to succeed and a great deal of experience.

Turning Down Work

If you want to be the best at what you do (or even pretty good), you've got to know your limitations. A deluded self-concept or over-hyped ego ("I can do anything!") will do much more harm than good. Consider your situation carefully, and don't accept the work if any of the following issues exist:

- You lack the time to prepare.
- You lack the expertise to do a good job.
- The sponsors are flaky or unethical.
- You are unhappy with the fee.
- The work conditions will prevent you from doing a good job.
- It's not the right audience for your message.
- It will take you away from something else more important.

Early in your career, it's tempting to take any work you can get, especially when it comes to paying the bills. Make sure, however, that once you've positioned yourself, you accept only the work that is right for you. Some of the worst presentations are given by presenters who are actually very good at their craft, but they've accepted contracts that should have been turned down.

Set monthly, annual, and five-year goals. Set goals related to the types of presentations you want to do, the number of clients you want, and the amount of gross income you want to generate. Consider the values you hold and the lifestyle you want; then, set your long-range goals accordingly.

Defining Success

Set monthly, annual, and five-year goals. Set goals related to the types of presentations you want to do, the number of clients you want, and the amount of gross income you want to generate. To follow-up, determine at the end of each month how you did compared to your goals and then take steps to correct the gaps. Your success is relative only to what you want, not to what others are earning or achieving. For many people, earning $50,000 a year would be fabulous. For some, earning this much per month is realistic. Consider the values you hold and the lifestyle you want; then, set your long-range goals accordingly.

Although initially I was happy to get any presentation work, now when deciding which jobs to take, I ask three questions: Can I have fun doing it? Is it the right amount of money? And, will it make a difference in people's lives? I have a rule–I don't lower my fees; therefore, if an organization can't afford me, I either turn down the offer or I volunteer my time as a charity. This is how I avoid discounting my reputation. If I allow only 25 possible work dates per year, each one must count. I ask myself, "Is this a good group that really wants to hear my message and that will take action on it?" If so, the work becomes much more attractive to me.

Paying the Price for Success

To achieve success in this industry you may have to work 50 to 60 hours a week and be out of town and away from your family for 3 to 6 months a year. You may miss out on weekends or holidays. You may have to pay for your own IRA, SEP, or other retirement plan. You may have to undergo a dramatic change in lifestyle, an inconsistent income, or face mean comments from insensitive people. You'll probably have to slay the dragons of doubt that come up as you wonder if you've chosen the right career path. However, if you can effectively deal with all of these considerations, this profession may be right for you. In short, once you've dealt with the big questions addressed in this chapter, the next step is to transfer the learning from *Sizzle & Substance* to real-life. If you are ready to carry the presenter's torch, step forth.

How do you make the ideas in this book work for you? There's no doubt that to use them all would be major overkill! Each idea has a particular function. Try out those that sound good and seem appropriate for your group. Information is only of value if it's used and managed. The way that you extract value from this book depends upon your learning style and personality. You'll have to choose the methods that fit you best. The following are some possible suggestions:

Learning Reinforces

- Highlight the key ideas in the book with Post-It Notes or highlighter pens. Then when you go back to review something, you can find it quickly and easily.
- On a large sheet of paper, mind-map the ideas you want to remember and use. Start with the main topic in the center and add branches like a tree to represent secondary information and relationships. Color in key ideas, and personalize it with simple illustrations.
- Record one strategy per index card and label it "today's idea." On the flip side of the card, write out when you used the idea, the group, the course content, the results, and any thoughts or suggestions for the next time. Many office supply stores offer index cards in a variety of colors. This allows you to color-code your ideas and group them accordingly.
- Write out three ideas on flip-chart paper using large colorful markers. Post them at the back of the room to use as your "cheat sheet."
- Talk to a friend or partner about a new idea you want to try, both before and after you try it. Troubleshoot the idea, brainstorm improvements, and debrief it afterwards.
- Copy all of the "Engage Your Brain" exercises throughout this book and insert them into a 3-ring binder for your convenient completion and review.

The Feedback Formula

As you know, there is no magic pill for becoming a great presenter. The willingness to learn from feedback, however, is the closest thing I've found to a secret formula. Quite simply, feedback is information about your past performance. It's *not* about how good or bad you are, but rather, how fast you learn. Good presenters make it a point to learn and improve their presentations each time no matter how experienced they are. Inexperienced presenters can become quality presenters if they are willing to learn quickly. The following are some suggestions for obtaining helpful feedback:

- Keep a paper and a pen up front and take notes on yourself during your presentation.
- Audiotape your talk and review it later. Take notes on what you learn.
- At break times, lunch time, or before or after your presentation, ask participants how they liked or didn't like something specific. Learn from others.
- Ask your sponsor or a room assistant to provide you with feedback. Be specific. Tell them what to look and listen for so that the feedback will be in the area you need it.
- Ask the audience for written feedback each time and use it!
- Get a colleague to sit in on your presentation and critique it. Again, be specific about what kind of information will be valuable to you.
- Watch the body language and facial expressions of your audience. Take note of what excites them and when they seem to get sluggish.
- Videotape your presentation and debrief it afterwards.

Remember, practice does not make perfect immediately. Practice makes permanent. You have to be willing to be imperfect first. Experiment, learn, debrief, and adjust. These steps are the hallmark of any expert in their field.

Remember, practice does not make perfect immediately. Practice makes permanent. You have to be willing to be imperfect first. Experiment, learn, debrief, and adjust. These steps are the hallmark of any expert in their field.

Anthony Robbins, for instance, is a top-notch speaker. He is entertaining, persuasive, and motivating. Though, he now commands "skybox range" speaking fees, he wasn't born a polished presenter. He, like most of us, began establishing his reputation in the "starter" range. He got where he is today because he is relentlessly committed to learning from feedback. He is still learning today. When people say, "Oh, he's just a natural at it," they're missing the point. He worked harder at it than anybody I know. When he was starting out, he spoke everywhere he was given a chance. Why? Because he knew if he could learn from his mistakes fast enough, he would excel. And that he has done!

Presenting With Passion!

In closing, I want you to think about the passion Anthony Robbins puts into each and every engagement. Your energy must be contagious. This is your challenge. Everyday is a chance to try out something new, to make a difference, to do something better, to take a risk, to grow. Commit to that relentless quest for perfection. And if the "fire in your belly" or the "spark in your soul" ever leaves you, it's time to do something else. Your audience deserves the best you have. You deserve to "sizzle with substance." Shoot for the stars and have a great time as you light the sky with your fire!

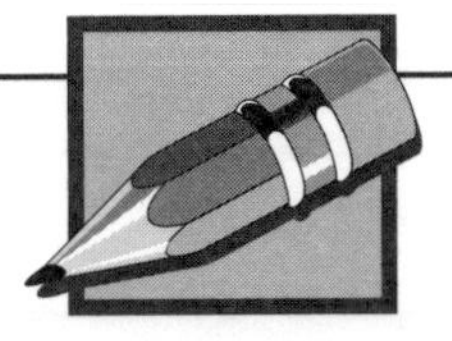

Engage Your Brain:
Planning to Light the Sky

The brain is easily distracted; What techniques do you use to stay focused on your goals and learning? How do you handle the inevitable blues or emotional lows?

What are your monthly, annual, and 5-year goals? How will you follow up with them?

What fee range are you in? How will you know when you're ready to raise your speaking fees? How do you define success?

What strategies will you use to transfer the learning from this book to real life?

What else do you want to learn about the topics presented in this book? How can you accomplish this?

APPENDIX

Trainer Resources

Books to Read:

- *101 Ways to Make Training More Active*
  by Mel Silberman, Pfeiffer & Co., San Fransisco, CA.
- *Trainer's Bonanza: Over 1000 Fabulous Tips & Tools*
  by Eric Jensen, The Brain Store, Inc., San Diego, CA.
- *Money Talks*
  by Dr. Jeffrey Lant, JLA Associates, Boston, MA.
- *Secrets of Successful Speakers*
  by Lilly Walters, McGraw-Hill, NY.
- *The Creative Trainer*
  by Michael Lawlor and Peter Handley, McGraw-Hill, NY.
- *Creating a Climate for Power Learning*
  by Carolyn Chambers Clark, Whole Person Assoc., Duluth, MN.
- *Active Learning*
  by Mel Silberman, Pfeiffer & Co., San Fransisco, CA.
- *Tune Your Brain*
  by Elizabeth Miles, Berkeley Books, NY.
- *Creative Training Techniques Handbook*
  by Bob Pike, Lakewood Books, Minneapolis, MN.
- *Inspire Any Audience*
  by Tony Jeary, High Performance Resources, Dallas, TX.
- *How to Get Your Point Across in 30 Seconds*
  by Milo Frank, Simon & Schuster, New York, NY.
- *Present Yourself*
  by Michael Gelb, Jalmar Press, Los Angeles, CA.
- *Awaken the Giant Within*
  by Anthony Robbins, Summit Books, New York, NY.

Trainings to Attend:

- *Rich Allen's 5-Day Facilitator's Training*
  This is a great program emboding all of the critical principles described in this book. (888) 63-TRAIN or fax (858) 642-0404.

Networks to Join:

- Brain/Mind Forum (ASTD) for Business trainers
  (218) 223-4040.
- Brain-Based Learning & Teaching Network (ASCD)
  Offers membership and an annual conference (816) 501-4651.

Better Ways to Eat:

- Brain-Mind Nutritional Supplements
  Smart products, herbs, vitamins, amino acids, nutritional oils,
  Nutrition Plus (800) 241-9236.
- *Life Enhancement* (Brain nutrients) newsletter
  Offers monthly newsletter and terrific mind-brain products
  (800) 543-3873.

Subscribe to These Newsletters:

- *Sharing Ideas*
  Dottie Walters, Free sample (818) 335-8069.
- *Application News*
  Center for Accelerated Learning (414) 248-7070.

Use the Best Work Tools:

- Tool Thyme for Trainers
  Cool training aids (504) 887-5558.
- The Brain Store Catalog
  Full of resource books, props, tools, and learning aids
  (800) 325-4769, (858) 546-7555, or fax (858) 546-7560.
  Website: http://www.thebrainstore.com
- CTI (Creative Training Institute) Newsletter & Catalog
  (612) 828-1960 or fax (612) 829-0260.

About the Author

Eric Jensen is an international presenter who has taught school at all levels, trained trainers for major corporations, and spoken at countless conferences and training seminars. Jensen's passion is the brain and learning; he remains deeply committed to making a positive, significant, lasting difference in the way the world learns. He has been a key part of brain-compatible training programs around the world. Trainers from AT & T, Disney, Motorola, BMW, Digital, Polaroid, GTE, Hewlett-Packard, CIA, Burroughs, Atlantic Bell, SAS, and three branches of the military have used his methods. A member of the Society of Neuroscience, he has taught as adjunct faculty at the University of California, San Diego, National University, and the University of San Diego. He's listed in "Who's Who," and is a former "Outstanding Young Man of America" selection.

Jensen was the co-founder of SuperCamp, the nation's first and largest brain-compatible learning program for teens. He's authored numerous books on brain-compatible learning, teaching, and training including *Brain-Based Learning*, *Trainer's Bonanza*, *Super Teaching*, *The Learning Brain*, *Completing the Puzzle,* and *Teaching with the Brain in Mind.*

Training Programs: The author and his staff provide 6-Day trainings on "Teaching with the Brain in Mind," 5-Day trainings on "Presenting with the Brain in Mind," and 3-Day trainings on "Learning with a Different Brain in Mind." In addition, customized trainings for groups and corporations can be arranged.

Overseas Inquiries Welcome: If you are a publisher in U.K., France, Germany, Spain, Mexico, Canada, Asia, Australia, or elsewhere, please contact our office.

Distributor Inquiries Welcome: If you operate a mail-order bookstore, a catalog, or do trainings, your audience may be interested in learning more about these skills and strategies. Contact our publishing office for more information on the distributor program including a distributor price list.

The Brain Store Publishing Office
(858) 546-7555 or Fax: (858) 546-7560
4202 Sorrento Valley Blvd., Suite B
San Diego, CA 92121 USA
Email: info@thebrainstore.com
www.thebrainstore.com

Jensen Learning
(Trainings/Speaking Engagements)
(858) 642-0400 or Fax: (858) 642-0404
P.O. Box 2551, Del Mar, CA 92014 USA
Email: info@jlcbrain.com
www.jlcbrain.com

Selected Bibliography

Booher, Dianna (1995). *67 Presentation Secrets to Wow Any Audience*, Minneapolis, MN: Lakewood Books.

Buzan, Tony (1996). *The Mind Map Book*, NY: Penguin Books.

Campbell, Don (1997) *The Mozart Effect*, NY: Avon Books.

Castorri, Alexis and Heller, Jane (1992). *Exercise Your Mind*, Seacaucas, NJ: Carol Publishing Group.

Dennison, Paul and Dennison, Gail (1989). *Brain Gym*, Ventura, CA: Edu-Kinesthetics Inc.

Gelb, Michael (1988). *Present Yourself.* Rolling Hills, CA: Jalmar Press.

Goleman, Daniel (1995). *Emotional Intelligence*, NY: Bantam Books.

Grinder, Michael (1993). *Envoy*. Battle Ground, WA: Grinder & Associates.

Harmin, Merrill (1993). *Strategies To Inspire Active Learning*, Edwardsville, IL: Inspiring Strategy Institute.

Hart, Leslie (1983). *Human Brain and Human Learning*, Kent, WA: Books For Educators.

Hobson, Alan (1994) *Chemistry of Conscious States*. Boston, MA: Little, Brown & Co.

Hoff, Ron (1992) *I Can See You Naked*, Kansas City, MO: Andrews and McMeel.

Hooper, Judith (1986). *The 3-Pound Universe*, NY: Putnam Books.

Jensen, Eric (1997). *Bs & As in 30 Days*, Hauppauge, NY: Barron's Books .

_______. (1996). *Completing the Puzzle: The Brain Compatible Approach to Learning*, San Diego, CA: The Brain Store, Inc.

_______. (1995). *Super Teaching*, San Diego, CA: The Brain Store, Inc.

Lawlor, Michael and Handley, Peter (1996). *The Creative Trainer*, NY: McGraw-Hill Inc.

LeDoux, Joseph (1996). *The Emotional Brain*, NY: Simon & Schuster.

Miles, Elizabeth (1997). *Tune Your Brain: Using Music to Manage Your Mind, Body, and Mood*, NY: Berkley Books.

Nilson, Carolyn (1995). *Games That Drive Change*, NY: McGraw-Hill Inc.

Pike, Bob and Arch, Dave (1997). *Dealing With Difficult Participants*, San Francisco, CA: Jossey-Bass Inc.

Promislow, Sharon (1998). *Making the Brain-Body Connection*, Vancouver, BC: Kinetic Publishing Corp.

Rauscher, F.H., Shaw, G.L., Ky, K.N., and Wright, E.L. (1993). "Music and Spatial Task Performance." *Nature*, 365:611.

Silberman, Mel (1995). *101 Ways to Make Training Active*, San Francisco, CA: Jossey-Bass Inc.

Solem, Lynn and Pike, Bob (1997). *50 Creative Training Closers*, San Francisco, CA: Jossey-Bass Inc.

Walker, Morton (1991). *The Power of Color*, NY: Avery Publishing Group Inc.

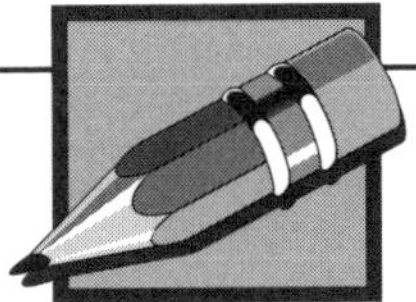

Notes, Thoughts and Author Feedback

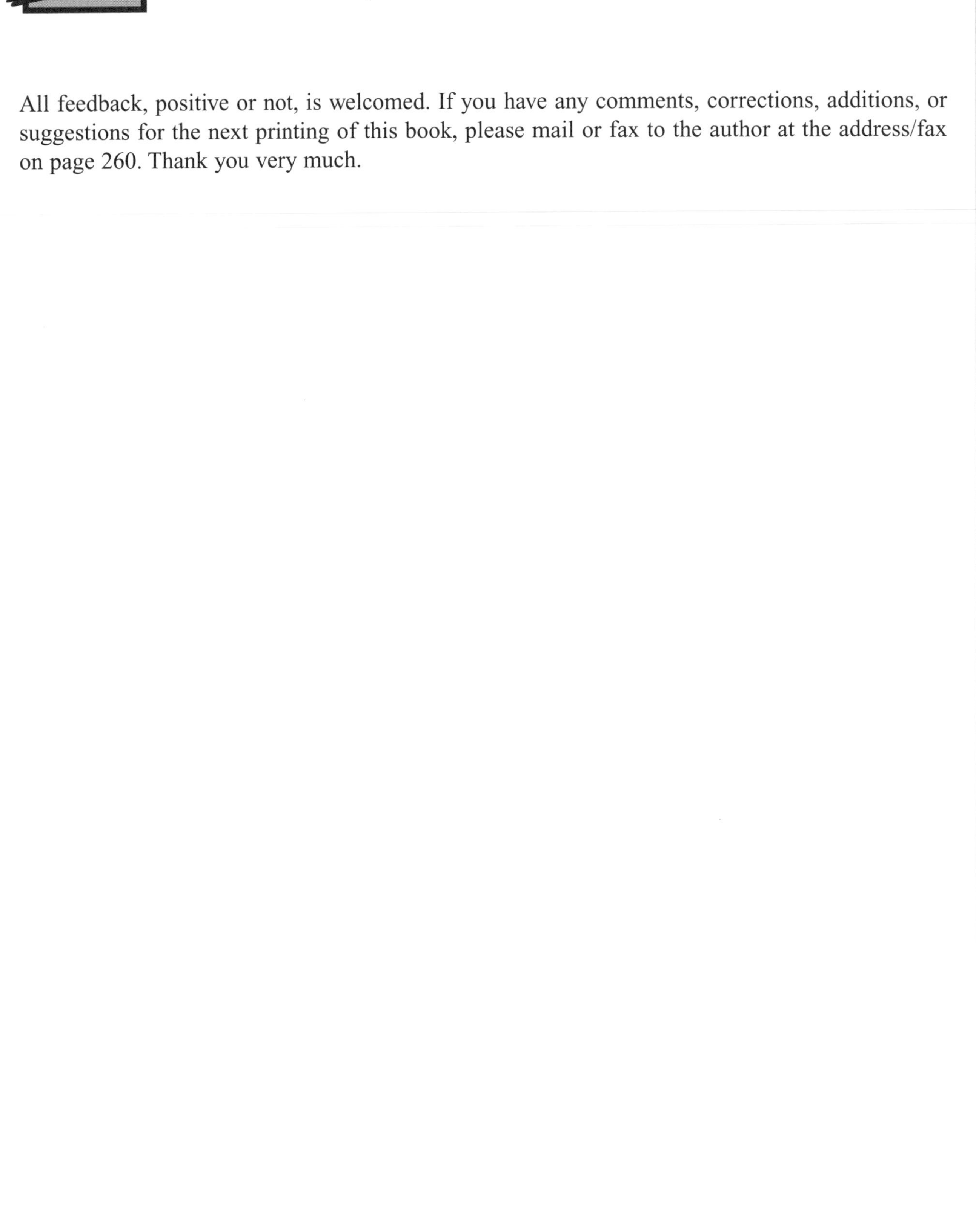

All feedback, positive or not, is welcomed. If you have any comments, corrections, additions, or suggestions for the next printing of this book, please mail or fax to the author at the address/fax on page 260. Thank you very much.

Index